Television and its Viewers
Cultivation Theory and Research

*Television and its Viewers* reviews "cultivation" research, which investigates the relationship between exposure to television and beliefs about the world. James Shanahan and Michael Morgan, both distinguished researchers in this field, scrutinize cultivation through detailed theoretical and historical explication, critical assessments of methodology, and a comprehensive "meta-analysis" of twenty years of empirical results. They present a sweeping historical view of television as a technology and as an institution. Shanahan and Morgan's study looks forward as well as back, to the development of cultivation research in a new media environment. They argue that cultivation theory offers a unique and valuable perspective on the role of television in twentieth-century social life. *Television and its Viewers*, the first book-length study of its type, will be of interest to students and scholars in communication, sociology, political science and psychology and contains an introduction by the seminal figure in this field, George Gerbner.

JAMES SHANAHAN is an Assistant Professor in the Department of Communication at Cornell University. He has published widely on the effects of television. His books include *Democracy Tango* (with Michael Morgan) and *Nature Stories* (with Katherine McComas).

MICHAEL MORGAN is Professor and Chair of the Department of Communication, University of Massachusetts/Amherst. He is the author or editor of numerous books and articles, including *Mainstream(s) and Margins* (with Susan Leggett) and *Cultivation Analysis* (with Nancy Signorielli).

# Television and its Viewers

*Cultivation Theory and Research*

James Shanahan and Michael Morgan

CAMBRIDGE
UNIVERSITY PRESS

PN 1992.6 . S417 1999

PUBLISHED BY THE PRESS SYNDICATE OF THE UNIVERSITY OF CAMBRIDGE
The Pitt Building, Trumpington Street, Cambridge CB2 1RP, United Kingdom

CAMBRIDGE UNIVERSITY PRESS
The Edinburgh Building, Cambridge CB2 2RU, UK  http://www.cup.cam.ac.uk
40 West 20th Street, New York, NY 10011–4211, USA  http://www.cup.org
10 Stamford Road, Oakleigh, Melbourne 3166, Australia

First published 1999

Printed in the United Kingdom at the University Press, Cambridge

Typeset in Plantin 10/12 pt in QuarkXPress™   [SE]

*A catalogue record for this book is available from the British Library*

*Library of Congress cataloguing in publication data*

Shanahan, James.
Television and its viewers: Cultivation theory and research
/ James Shanahan and Michael Morgan.
    p.   cm.
Includes bibliographical references.
ISBN 0 521 58296 2. – ISBN 0 521 58755 7 (pbk.)
1. Television broadcasting – Social aspects.   I. Morgan, Michael.
PN1992.6.S417   1999
302.23′45–dc21   98–48327   CIP

ISBN 0 521 58296 2 hardback
ISBN 0 521 58755 7 paperback

# Contents

# Figures

# Tables

# Foreword by George Gerbner
## What Do We Know?

Most of what we know, or think we know, we have never personally experienced. We live in a world erected by the stories we hear and see and tell. Unlocking incredible riches through imagery and words, conjuring up the unseen through art, creating towering works of imagination and fact through science, poetry, song, tales, reports and laws – that is the magic of human life. Through that magic we live in a world much wider than the threats and gratifications of the immediate physical environment, which is the world of other species.

Stories socialize us into roles of gender, age, class, vocation and life-style, and offer models of conformity or targets for rebellion. They weave the seamless web of the cultural environment that cultivates most of what we think, what we do, and how we conduct our affairs. The story-telling process was once more hand-crafted, home-made, community-inspired. Now it is mostly mass-produced and profit-driven. It is the end result of a complex manufacturing and marketing process. It both defines and then addresses the public interest. This situation calls for a new diagnosis and a new prescription.

The stories that animate our cultural environment have three distinct but related functions. These functions are (1) to reveal how things work; (2) to describe what things are; and (3) to tell us what to do about them. Stories of the first kind, revealing how things work, illuminate the all-important but invisible relationships and hidden dynamics of life. Fairy tales, novels, plays, comics, cartoons, and other forms of creative imagination and imagery are the basic building blocks of human understanding. They demonstrate complex causality by presenting imaginary action in total situations, coming to some conclusion that has a moral purpose and a social function. You do not have to believe the "facts" of Little Red Riding Hood to grasp the notion that big bad "wolves" victimize old women and trick little girls – a lesson in gender roles, fear, and power. Stories of this kind build, from infancy on, the fantasy we call reality. I do not suggest that the revelations are false, which they may or may not be, but that they are synthetic, selective, often mythical, and always socially constructed.

Stories of the second kind depict what things are. They are the presumably factual accounts, the chronicles of the past and the news of today. Stories of what things are may confirm or deny some conception of how things work. Their high "facticity" (i.e. correspondence to actual events presumed to exist independently of the story) gives them special status in political theory and often in law. They give emphasis and credibility to selected parts of each society's fantasies of reality. They convey information about finance, weddings, crime, lotteries, terrorists and so on. They alert us to certain interests, threats, opportunities and challenges.

Stories of the third kind tell us what to do. These are stories of value and choice. They present things, behaviors or styles of life as desirable (or undesirable), propose ways to obtain (or avoid) them, and the price to be paid for attainment (or failure). They are instructions, laws, regulations, cautionary tales, commands, slogans, sermons and exhortations. Today most of them are called commercials; they are the advertising messages and images we see and hear every day. Stories of the third kind clinch the lessons of the first two and turn them into action. They typically present an objective to be sought or to be avoided, and offer a product, service, candidate, institution or action purported to help attain or avoid it.

Ideally, the three kinds of stories check and balance each other. In a commercially driven culture, however, stories of the third kind pay for most of the first two. That creates a coherent cultural environment whose overall function is to provide a hospitable and effective context for stories that sell. With the coming of the electronic age, that cultural environment is increasingly monopolized, homogenized and globalized. We must then look at the historic course of our journey to see what this new age means for us and for the public interest.

For the longest time in human history, stories were told only face to face. A community was defined by the rituals, mythologies and imageries held in common. All useful knowledge was encapsulated in aphorisms and legends, proverbs and tales, incantations and ceremonies. Writing was rare and holy, forbidden for slaves. Laboriously inscribed manuscripts conferred sacred power to their interpreters, the priests and ministers. As a sixteenth-century scribe put it:

Those who observe the codices, those who recite them. Those who noisily turn the pages of illustrated manuscripts. Those who have possession of the black and red ink and that which is pictured; they lead us, they guide us, they tell us the way.

State and church ruled in a symbiotic relationship of mutual dependence and tension. State, composed of feudal nobles, was the economic, military and political order; church its cultural arm. The industrial revolution changed all that. One of the first machines stamping out standardized artifacts was the printing press. Its product, the book, was a prerequisite for all the other upheavals to come. Printing begins the industrialization of story-telling, arguably the most profound transformation in the humanization process. The book could be given to all who could read, requiring education and creating a new literate class of people. Readers could now interpret the book (at first the Bible) for themselves, breaking the monopoly of priestly interpreters and ushering in the Reformation. When the printing press was hooked up to the steam engine the industrialization of story-telling shifted into high gear. Rapid publication and mass transport created a new form of consciousness: modern mass publics. Publics are loose aggregations of people who share some common consciousness of how things work, what things are, and what ought to be done – but never meet face-to-face. That was never before possible.

Stories could now be sent – often smuggled – across hitherto impenetrable or closely guarded boundaries of time, space and status. The book lifts people from their traditional moorings as the industrial revolution uproots them from their local communities and cultures. They can now get off the land and go to work in far-away ports, factories and continents, and have with them a packet of common consciousness – the book or journal, and later the motion picture (silent at first) – wherever they go.

Publics, created by such publication, are necessary for the formation of individual and group identities in the new urban environment, as the different classes and regional, religious and ethnic groups try to maintain some sense of distinct integrity and also to live together with some degree of cooperation with other groups. Publics are the basic units of self-government. They make it possible to elect or select representatives to an assembly trying to reconcile diverse interests. The maintenance and integrity of multiple publics make self-government feasible for large, complex and diverse national communities. People engage in long and costly struggles to be free to create and share stories that fit the reality of competing and often conflicting values and interests. Most of our assumptions about human development and political plurality and choice are rooted in the print era.

The second great transformation, the electronic revolution, ushers in the telecommunications era. Its mainstream, television, is superimposed upon and reorganizes print-based culture. Unlike the industrial revolution, the new upheaval does not uproot people from their homes but transports them in their homes. It re-tribalizes modern society. It challenges and changes the role of both church and education in the new culture. For the first time in human history, children are born into homes where mass-produced stories can reach them on the average more than seven hours a day. Most waking hours, and often dreams, are filled with these stories. The stories do not come from their families, schools, churches, neighborhoods, and often not even from their native countries, or from anyone with anything relevant to tell. They come from small groups of distant conglomerates with something to sell.

The cultural environment in which we live becomes the byproduct of marketing. The new symbiotic relationship of state and television replaces the historic nexus of state and church. The "state" itself is the twin institution of elected public government and selected private corporate government. Media, its cultural arm, is dominated by the private establishment, despite its use of the public airways.

Giant industries discharge their messages into the mainstream of common consciousness. Channels proliferate and new technologies pervade home and office while mergers and bottom-line pressures shrink creative alternatives and reduce diversity of content. These changes may appear to be broadening local, parochial horizons, but they also mean a homogenization of outlooks and limitation of alternatives. For media professionals, the changes mean fewer opportunities and greater compulsions to present life in saleable packages. Creative artists, scientists and humanists can still explore and enlighten and occasionally even challenge, but, increasingly, their stories must fit marketing strategies and priorities.

Viewing commercials is "work" performed by audiences in exchange for "free" news and entertainment. In fact, we pay dearly through a surcharge added to the price of every advertised product that goes to subsidize commercial media, and through allowing advertising expenditures to be a tax-deductible business expense. These give-aways of public moneys for private purposes further erode the diversity of the cultural mainstream. Broadcasting is the most concentrated, homogenized and globalized medium. The top US 100 advertisers pay for two-thirds of all network television. Four networks, allied to giant transnational corporations – our private "Ministry of Culture" – control the bulk of production and distribution, and shape the cultural mainstream. Other interests, diverse ideologies, minority views, and the potential of any challenge to dominant perspectives, lose ground with every merger.

Formula-driven assembly-line produced programs increasingly dominate the airways. The formulas themselves reflect the structure of power that produces them and function to preserve and enhance that structure of power. It is fair to say that such nearly total control of the cultural mainstream and the consequent marginalization of political alternatives to a two-party system consisting of the "ins" and the "outs" who are otherwise more alike than different makes a mockery of any claim of a democracy.

The condition of the physical environment may determine how long our species survives. The cultural environment affects the quality of survival and its governance. We need to begin the long process of diversifying, pacifying, democratizing and humanizing the story-telling process that shapes the mainstream of the cultural environment in which we live and into which our children are born.

Shanahan and Morgan review and analyze research conceived and conducted as a not-too-early warning system of the dangerous condition of the cultural environment. They begin that task by presenting a sweeping historical view of television as a technology and an institution. They make it clear that "The Age of Television" may be remembered in the history books as that one in which we governed ourselves through the medium. It was (and is) an era of governance through distraction.

This is an age when stories of a President's sexual activities preempt information about the greatest (and still growing) inequalities in the Western world; about the polarization of society into the few "haves" and the many "have-nots"; about corporations making record profits while playing the globalization game and firing workers to raise their stock prices. Throwing people and families on the societal scrapheap while corporate profits are out of sight – that should be news to fit the airways, a public resource. But in a consumer-oriented broadcasting system the poor and disenfranchised have no place except when involved with crime, drugs, violence. This provokes a backlash of the good consumer class that sees more jails and executions as the way to address the "urban crisis." So the cycle of repressive governance continues.

It is more than a cultural perversion to license the airways, and to assign all the other channels that cable and the new technologies make possible, to marketers who preempt them for buying audiences for celebrity worship, sex scandals, public show trials and the like. It is one of the greatest give-aways of public resources in history.

Shanahan and Morgan give a thorough and lively explanation of the process that makes all that possible. They relate the history, theory and methodology of the research that reveals the making of our contemporary mythology. They describe the debates surrounding those revelations. And they examine the consequences of living in a cultural environment created by the market-driven mythology.

I am flattered and privileged to have been given the opportunity to write a preface to a work about research with which I have been so closely associated, and rather shamelessly (but proudly) commend it to your attention.

GEORGE GERBNER

Bell Atlantic Professor of Telecommunication Temple University, Philadelphia

# 1    Origins

Supreme among the many available symbols of postmodern progress and alienation – more than political assassinations, microwave ovens, gene splicing, moonwalks, family breakdown, AIDS, ozone depletion, youth culture, suburban sprawl, the Cold War, feminism, the computer explosion, Watergate, ethnic conflicts, fast food, homelessness, minivans and economic globalization – the ultimate icon for the final half of the twentieth century is television. Although television predates the 1950s and will certainly survive the millennium, there is no gainsaying that for roughly fifty years the medium has permeated every corner of public and private space, shaping consciousness, defining our "reality," drawing us together, and pulling us apart, in ways that will uniquely enshrine this historical period as The Age of Television.

Over the past five decades, television has been a perennial and vexing object of passionate debate. Upon it has been heaped immense cultural and intellectual scorn. Feared by the righteous and not-so-righteous, ridiculed by those who never fail to miss their favorite shows, television is continuously lambasted, lampooned and impugned, serving as the culture's straw-man and whipping-boy; yet it is also consumed – assiduously, diligently, almost religiously – by most of us, and in massive doses. There is no better example of a "love-hate relationship" than that between television and contemporary society.

Parents, teachers, academics, politicians, moral guardians, social critics, those who work in the medium, and those who simply watch it without thinking much about it, have all offered a vast array of charges, counter-charges, complaints, defenses, interpretations and opinions about just what this device is and what it may be doing to us and our children. Although other media "panics" may pop up from time to time, such as those surrounding raunchy rock lyrics, horror comics, gory films, violent video games, and pornography on the Internet, television usually remains the most likely suspect, the focus of the most recurring social concern and the medium to which we are most – in the end – devoted.

Television, both as technology and institution, has changed on many levels in the past fifty years, yet the public debates it propels often sound like a broken record – but one that is going faster and faster. Each new crop of parents and teachers sings the same refrain about zombie-eyed, anemic children wasting too much time watching television, imitating the aggressive behavior of whatever super-heroes currently adorn bedsheets and lunchboxes, having no attention span in the classroom, and so on. Political pressure groups of all stripes proliferate, railing against specific portrayals or programs they find objectionable (sometimes for not being politically correct, and sometimes *for* being so), often calling for boycotts or censorship. At the same time, seemingly perennial Congressional hearings have given executives from the industry many opportunities to express their deep, heartfelt concern about the social impacts of television. Meanwhile, academic research, rarely able to influence media policy in any meaningful way, has become more specialized, arcane, complicated and increasingly divorced from the reality of people's everyday media consumption.

Altogether, these debates, too often driven by wishful thinking, economic self-interest and moral posturing, become more disturbing and irrelevant as time passes. To a great extent, it is conveniently easier (especially for politicians) to decry the ills of television than to deal with more serious social problems, but the very real and very important problem of television risks being lost in a shrill muddle of tendentious discourse.

Some years ago, Michael Novak offered a refreshingly simple way to frame the question of how television might affect us.

If you practice the craft of writing sedulously, you begin to think and perceive differently. If you run for twenty minutes a day, your psyche is subtly transformed. If you work in an executive office, you begin to think like an executive. And if you watch six hours of television, on the average, every day . . . ? (Novak, 1986, p. 583)

Novak's idea is that the ways in which we think about ourselves, our lives, our society, and our world should be influenced in some ways by how we occupy our time, by the roles we assume, and by the images and stories we consume. Given that we as a society spend more time watching television than doing anything else except working and sleeping (and many people watch *more* than they work), it should not be surprising if television "shapes the soul," as the title of Novak's article asserts.

If we assume that the messages of television have some commonality and consistency to them – that they are not just a random collection of entertainment "units" in a media universe without purpose – then we might be tempted to conclude that exposure to those messages over time should mean something. So if we spend hours a day watching television, over the weeks, months and years, we might be expected to pick up a thing or two, and to think about life and the world in ways different from people who rarely watch television. Or, to extend this a bit further: a person who has the sort of values, beliefs, mindset, lifestyle and outlooks most congruent with the images, messages and stories of television, and who therefore would be drawn to (or choose to) spend a great deal of time watching the medium, would likely find those beliefs and outlooks to be nourished and sustained over the long run. If not, why do so many continue to watch?

This conceptualization of the role of television in our lives is the essence of George Gerbner's theory of "cultivation." This simple hypothesis – that watching a great deal of television will be associated with a tendency to hold specific and distinct conceptions of reality, conceptions that are congruent with the most consistent and pervasive images and values of the medium – may, at first glance, appear to be so thoroughly reasonable and self-evident that one may be tempted to wonder what all the fuss is about. Who could possibly argue against such a cut-and-dried assertion? Why write a book about something so obvious?

Yet, obviousness notwithstanding, cultivation theory and research have become a major arena in which questions about the "effects" of television have been debated. Indeed, although the elegant simplicity of the idea has both attracted adherents and antagonized opponents, cultivation analysis has also been an extraordinarily controversial approach to media effects and communication research, and not only within the narrow confines of the academic community. After over twenty years of intense theoretical and methodological development, testing, criticism and refinement, it turns out that cultivation is neither so simple nor so obvious. In the time-honored tradition of "good" scientific progress, the more work that is done, the more complex the questions (and the answers) become (see Signorielli and Morgan, 1990; Morgan and Shanahan, 1997).

This book takes stock of these past two decades of cultivation research. Through detailed theoretical and historical explication, critical assessments of methodology, and a comprehensive "meta-analysis" of twenty years of empirical results, we scrutinize cultivation in terms of its assumptions, its methods, its findings, its development, its conflicts, its limitations, its problems, its contributions, and its future. We do not pretend to be disinterested, neutral observers of the debates that have swirled around cultivation analysis; we are teachers and practitioners of the technique, and we embrace it sufficiently to have written this and other books and articles about it. As such, this book is an exposition and defense of the merits of cultivation theory. Nevertheless, we do attempt to be as even-handed and equitable as possible to those who have been critical of cultivation even as we endeavor to provide a thorough conceptual and empirical response to many of those criticisms. Working in this spirit of advancing the scientific debate, we propose to demonstrate that cultivation theory, though by no means flawless, offers a unique and valuable perspective on the role of television in twentieth-century social life.

## Cultivation analysis as a field of research

Cultivation analysis is the study of television's independent contribution to viewers' conceptions of social reality. In practice, cultivation analysis typically uses survey research methods to assess the difference amount of television viewing makes (if any), other things held constant, to a broad variety of opinions, images and attitudes, across a variety of samples, types of measures, topical areas and intervening variables (Gerbner, Gross, Morgan and Signorielli, 1994). Stated most simply, as hinted above, the central hypothesis guiding cultivation research is that those who spend more time watching television are more likely to perceive the real world in ways that reflect the most common and recurrent messages of the television world, compared to people who watch less television but are otherwise comparable in terms of important demographic characteristics.

Since the first results of cultivation analysis were published over twenty years ago (Gerbner and Gross, 1976), literally hundreds of studies have explored, enhanced, questioned, critiqued, dismissed or defended the conceptual assumptions and methodological procedures of cultivation analysis (see Hawkins and Pingree, 1982; Potter, 1993; Signorielli and Morgan, 1990). Although cultivation analysis may once have been closely identified with the issue of violence, over the years researchers have looked at a broad range of topics, including sex roles, aging, political orientations, the family, environmental attitudes, science, health, religion, minorities, occupations and others. As its topical concerns have expanded, so have its international extensions: replications have been carried out in Argentina, Australia, Brazil, Canada, China, England, Hungary, Israel, the Netherlands, Russia, South Korea, Sweden, Taiwan, Trinidad and elsewhere.

In 1986, Jennings Bryant noted that cultivation was one of only three topics covered in over half of "mass media and society" courses offered at US colleges and universities. He also reported that cultivation research is one of the few contributions by mass communication scholars to appear with any regularity in basic textbooks in social psychology, sociology and related disciplines. He even quipped that studies of cultivation seem "almost as ubiquitous as television itself" (1986, p. 231). The status of cultivation as a "core" theory of media effects has probably only increased since Bryant made his observations. As Newhagen and Lewenstein (1992) put it, "Despite criticism, the theory persists, perhaps because the social implications of the idea that a mass medium can define our culture [are] too important to dismiss" (p. 49).

The findings of cultivation research have been many, varied and sometimes counter-intuitive. Cultivation has generated a great deal of theoretical colloquy, and methodological debate. Though not everyone in the field of communication agrees on the validity of cultivation findings, cultivation is arguably among the most important contributions yet made to scientific and public understanding of media effects. Nevertheless, the assumptions and procedures of cultivation analysis are sometimes misunderstood or misrepresented by other researchers and critics; one goal of this book is to set the theoretical and methodological record straight.

Much of the social debate about television focuses on specific issues, problems, controversies or programs which are current at any given time. Many of these interesting and important questions about media effects are largely irrelevant to cultivation analysis. Cultivation is *not* about how voters' feelings about a political candidate might be affected by some newscast or ad campaign. Cultivation is *not* about whether a new commercial can make people buy a new toothpaste. It is *not* about whether children (or others) become more aggressive, or have nightmares, or experience catharsis, after watching a violent program. It is *not* about how different viewers might develop conflicting interpretations of the motivation of a character on a soap opera to leave her lover, or disagree on the ultimate resolution of a complex murder mystery. It is *not* about teenagers being corrupted by sleazy talk shows or leering sex-obsessed sitcoms. It is *not* about how this season's (or this week's) new smash hit or hot star is changing the public's hair styles or career plans. It is not, really, about many of the more dramatic alleged effects of television that figure so frequently in public debate. All of these are fascinating and important questions, but they are tangential to the issues addressed by cultivation.

Cultivation *is* about the implications of stable, repetitive, pervasive and virtually inescapable patterns of images and ideologies that television (especially dramatic, fictional entertainment) provides. As we will argue more fully below, cultivation research approaches television as a *system* of messages – a system whose elements are not invariant or uniform, but complementary, organic and coherent – and inquires into the functions and consequences of those messages *as a system*, overall, *in toto* for its audiences. The focus of cultivation analysis is on the correlates and consequences of cumulative exposure to *television in general* over long periods of time.

Would watching a film of adults batting around clown dolls cause children to imitate that behavior? This is not a question for cultivation analysis, but cultivation could say something about how exposure to many thousands of violent images over time might have something to do with our perception of the likelihood of encountering violence in the world. Did *Kojak* cause Ronald Zamora to murder his elderly neighbor, as his lawyer famously argued in 1977? Again, cultivation research wouldn't tell us, but it might help us understand something about the broader social environment in which such a question could even be asked. Would seeing Jodie Foster gang-raped on a pool table in the film *The Accused* cause some viewers to imitate that crime? Again, cultivation couldn't answer that question, but it could say something about broader patterns of association between television demography, favoring male power and female victimization, and the chances for women to succeed in society. Although the consequences of the cultivation process are related to everyday current events and issues, the research does not study direct effects from messages sent and received in the short term. The point is that cultivation's role is to examine broad patterns of relationships between the social consumption of media messages and stable, aggregate belief structures among large groups of people.

### The Cultural Indicators Project

Cultivation analysis is one component of a long-term, ongoing research program called "Cultural Indicators." The concept of a cultural "indicator" was developed by George Gerbner as a complement to the more common idea of an economic or social indicator, a kind of barometer of important cultural issues (Gerbner, 1969, 1970). Gerbner conceived of Cultural Indicators as a way to add a relatively disinterested "Third Voice" to the ongoing contentious conflicts being waged between political forces and private commercial concerns over cultural policy. With less at stake over the outcomes, he argued, an independent research project could provide a more "objective" accounting of media practices, outputs and impacts, and therefore a better basis for judgment and policy (Gerbner, 1973). In the USA, Cultural Indicators research has focused mostly on the implications of growing up and living with television, since it is the country's most widely shared cultural agency and most visible disseminator of cultural symbols.

The project was developed as a three-part research framework for investigating the structure, contours, and consequences of pervasive symbol systems, premised on three global, interrelated questions:

1 What are the processes, pressures, and constraints that influence and underlie the production of mass media content?
2 What are the dominant, aggregate patterns of images, messages, facts, values and lessons expressed in media messages? and

3 What is the relationship between attention to these messages and audiences' conceptions of social reality?

Perhaps the most innovative and intriguing aspect of the Cultural Indicators paradigm is that the answer to any one of these questions is seen as having significant implications for the other two. Early on, Gerbner maintained that the "effects" of communication are not to be found in short-term attitude or behavior change, but in the history and dynamics of the reciprocal relationships between the structure of the institutions which produce media messages, the message systems themselves, and the image structures which are embedded within a culture.

Each of these three research questions involves a distinct conceptual framework and set of methodological procedures (Gerbner, 1973). "Institutional process analysis," the first prong, is used to investigate how media messages are selected, produced and distributed. "Message system analysis" quantifies and tracks patterns of demography, action structures, relationships, aspects of life and recurrent images in media content, in terms of the portrayal of violence, minorities, gender-roles, occupations and so on. The study of how exposure to the world of television contributes to viewers' conceptions about the real world is cultivation analysis, the third prong (and the primary focus of this book). Altogether, Cultural Indicators research sees media institutions, messages and audiences as intertwined in a complex, dynamic multi-hued tapestry.

Like many landmark efforts in the history of communication research, the Cultural Indicators project was launched as an independently funded enterprise in an applied context (Gerbner, 1969). The research began during the late 1960s, a time of national turmoil, violence and social unrest. In 1968, the National Commission on the Causes and Prevention of Violence was formed to probe the problem of violence in society, including a review of existing research on violence on television (Baker and Ball, 1969). The commission also funded one new study: a content analysis of violence in prime-time programming in the 1967–68 television season, under the direction of Gerbner at the Annenberg School for Communication, who earlier had conducted other large-scale content analyses and institutional analyses of media policies. This first step into what was to become the Cultural Indicators Project documented the frequency and nature of television violence and established a baseline for long-term monitoring of the world of television (Gerbner, 1969).

In 1969, even before the report of the Commission was released, Congress appropriated $1 million and set up the Surgeon General's Scientific Advisory Committee on Television and Social Behavior to implement new, primary research on television and violence. Altogether, twenty-three projects, including Cultural Indicators, were funded.

Cultural Indicators research focused primarily upon the content of prime-time and weekend-daytime network dramatic programming (Gerbner, 1972). Message system analysis has continued annually since 1967; week-long samples of US network television drama (and samples in other cooperating countries, whenever possible) are recorded and subjected to content analysis in order to delineate selected features and trends in the overall "worldview" television presents to its viewers. In the 1990s, the analysis has been extended to include the Fox network, "reality" programs and various selected cable channels.

The cultivation analysis phase of the Cultural Indicators research paradigm was first implemented with a national probability survey of adults during the early 1970s in a study funded by the National Institute of Mental Health (Gerbner and Gross, 1976). Many other agencies and foundations have supported the project over the years, including the White House Office of Telecommunications Policy, the American Medical Association, the Administration on Aging, the National Science Foundation, the Ad Hoc Committee on Religious Television Research, the W. Alton Jones Foundation, the Screen Actors' Guild, the American Federation of Television and Radio Artists, the National Cable Television Association, the US Commission on Civil Rights, the Turner Broadcasting System, the Institute for Mental Health Initiatives, the American Association for Retired Persons Women's Initiative, the Office of Substance Abuse Prevention and the Center for Substance Abuse Prevention of the US Public Health Service, and others.

As it developed, the project has continued to explore an ever-wider range of topical areas in both message system and cultivation analyses. Cultivation research has expanded its scope in studies directed by the original investigators and in studies undertaken by many other independent investigators in the USA and around the world. In order to better understand the conceptual assumptions and methodological procedures of cultivation analysis, in the next section we step back a bit and look at the world of communication research before the birth of cultivation theory.

### Historical Context

Researchers began inquiring into the "effects" of television almost as soon as these strange and marvelous new devices started to appear in living rooms across the land in the late 1940s and 1950s. An early research strategy, logically enough, was to compare the behaviors and attitudes of people (often, children) who lived in households or communities that received television with people who lived in places that were otherwise relatively similar except for the lack of television reception. These studies were trying to approximate a "before/after" controlled design in the real world, and they produced many valuable insights (see Schramm, Lyle and Parker, 1961; Himmelweit, Oppenheim and Vince, 1958).

Since television was spreading so rapidly, however, these kinds of studies mainly described novelty effects accompanying the adoption of the new medium; they told us little about what television means in a society when most people have grown up living with (and been baby sat by) its stories. Moreover, these studies had only a brief window of opportunity, as it soon became impossible to find households or communities (or societies) that were "relatively similar" but for the presence of television. (For what is probably the final such comparison possible in the industrialized world, see Williams, 1986).

The other major approach used in early television research was the experiment, where (for example) a group might be exposed to some sort of stimulus (say, a scene of violence) and then given some (often deceptive) opportunity to imitate that violence or otherwise behave aggressively; the response of that group would be compared to the subsequent behavior of another, control group, exposed to something innocuous or nothing at all. A vast number of studies of this type were carried out, descendants of attitude change experiments in social psychology and Albert Bandura's early studies with film clips of people attacking Bobo dolls (1965). Ironically, although those kinds of lab studies have become seen as the quintessential studies of television and violence, the original studies had much more to do with theories of observational learning than with violence. Indeed, in most such studies, there is no need to know anything about the institution of television, or its status as a cultural object, or how people typically use it, to be able to interpret the results.

Prior to the development of cultivation analysis, then, most researchers in mass communication were interested in knowing how specific messages, channels and sources could produce *changes* in attitudes or behaviors. This was a natural outgrowth of the way mass communication research had developed from the 1920s (see Katz and Lazarsfeld, 1955), fueled by public fear of the "power" of the media, along with anxious politicians, eager advertisers, crusading social engineers, and others itching to use the massive reach of the media to "get their message across" quickly and efficiently. Government, military and corporate funding sources played an important role in the decision of those working within the field to take this direction (Simpson, 1994). The goal was to determine what kinds of persuasive messages could be used most "effectively" in campaigns of various kinds – political, advertising, public health, educational, military and so on. Therefore, early research on television's impacts had typically focused on the effects of single programs or messages, usually measured immediately after exposure in a relatively artificial context and for "subjects" (such as college sophomores) who are often not particularly representative of the larger population.

A media "effect" was defined entirely in terms of *change* – no change meant no effect. Thus, the before/after community studies, or experimental methodologies, or evaluations of specific persuasive campaigns were thought to be well-suited to detecting any "change" that might occur as a result of watching television. Also, using these methodologies in turn reinforced thinking about effects in terms of changes; as long as these were the dominant designs and models, it was difficult to think of "effects" in any other ways. The classic laboratory experiments on the attitudinal effects of persuasive communications or the ability of messages to evoke behavioral changes tend to promote thinking about communication (and television's messages) as foreign "objects" somehow inserted or injected into us, as discrete, scattered "bullets" which either hit or miss us.

Eventually, when strong experimental results from the artificial isolation of the lab were found to be not so easily replicated in various field studies or in actual campaigns attempting to change attitudes, prominent theorists argued that there was little "effect" of mass communication and it became *de rigueur* to argue that asking how media "affect" people is the wrong kind of question (even though the later violence research began to show that there were some consistent effects, replicated in the field). The failure of social science to isolate a consistent effect of media on attitudes turned researchers back to the social group (the "primary group") and eventually back to the individual as the source of all meaning. Yet, this tendency is also fraught with political implications. Indeed, the "limited effects" school had (and has) a very specific political agenda to defend, and the "bullet" or "hypodermic needle" theory it attacked – the idea that media messages affect beliefs or behaviors in mechanical, automatic, straightforward ways – was always made of straw and never seriously entertained by real live researchers. In the political world of limited effects and individually styled "uses" of mass media, little place was made for thinking about the media as social institutions with their own agendas, and less room for the notion that social control is one important aspect of what the media do. In this world, "ineffective" media prove that democratic media institutions do what they are supposed to do: entertain, inform, amuse, even annoy, but never "influence."

So, with little empirical support in the "real world" outside the lab, no wonder that the very notion of media having effects was under scholarly –

and industry – fire (see Klapper, 1960). Public concern about dramatic, direct effects notwithstanding, cultivation thus emerged from a historical period in which the prevailing intellectual view was that media had at most only minimal effects, that any effects were likely only to echo "pre-existing dispositions," and that they could more profitably be explained by such factors as selective exposure and selective attention.

## The Development of Cultivation Theory

In the course of events, the roots of cultivation theory have at times been obscured by legitimate methodological disagreements as well as by sometimes acrimonious and hyper-technical debates. Within all this, researchers have often lost sight of Gerbner's original theoretical premises. Gerbner's original conception of cultivation was nothing less than an attempt to alter the nature of the conventional academic discourse about the social and cultural implications of mass communication. The goal was to develop an approach to mass communication using terms different from those of the then-dominant paradigm of persuasion and propaganda research and to escape the scientism and positivism of the "effects" tradition. This required dispensing with traditional formal aesthetic categories along with conventional concerns about style, artistic quality, high culture vs. low culture, and selective exposure, as well as idiosyncratic judgments, interpretations and readings. It was not that he denied the existence or importance of these concerns and phenomena, but rather that he sought to go beyond them, to address issues that could not be explained in or limited by such terms. Furthermore, it required a reworking of the traditional tactics that had been used to assess communication "effect."

Gerbner's early writings (1958) attempted to develop models of the communication process that distinguished it from purely persuasive exchanges and from concerns with prediction, control and change. Rather than seeing communication research as a way to achieve a specific practical aim (e.g., selling soap, selling a candidate, improving public health or raising environmental awareness), he saw it as a *basic cultural inquiry*. Above and beyond its communicative "power," he argued that any message is a socially and historically determined expression of concrete physical and social relationships. Messages imply propositions, assumptions and points of view which are understandable only in terms of the social relationships and contexts in which they are produced. Yet, they also reconstitute those relationships and contexts. They thus function recursively, sustaining and giving meaning to the structures and practices that produce them. This is far different from earlier attempts to discover scientific "laws" explaining the persuasive properties of messages, sources, channels or receivers.

Communication to Gerbner is "interaction through messages," a distinctly human (and humanizing) process which both creates and is driven by the symbolic environment which constitutes culture. The symbolic environment reveals social and institutional dynamics, and because it expresses social patterns it also cultivates them. This, then, is the original meaning of "cultivation" – the process within which interaction through messages shapes and sustains the terms on which the messages are premised.

A note here about the use of the term, and the metaphor, of cultivation. The very notion of "cultivation" builds on the assumption that the major impacts of television materialize by means of the way it exposes people to the same images and metaphors over and over again. Moreover, the cultivation metaphor is best understood as providing a way to talk about "influence" without talking about "effects." That is, cultivation means that deeply held cultural perspectives and assumptions will not be efficiently nurtured (or gradually – even glacially – shifted) as a result of a single one-shot message blast, much as an unwatered or unweeded crop will do poorly. Learning from the advertising field, which teaches that repetition sells, the cultivation metaphor was adopted as providing the quickest way to convey how researchers felt about the chicken-egg question of causality. As we will describe more fully below, at some level, the messages were seen as having some causal impacts, but only when seen from the broadest possible macro perspective.

Also, we should note that water metaphors have been common in the cultivation literature. "Mainstreams," "currents," "flows" and other water-terms have been used to suggest the ubiquitous and cumulative influence that cultivation researchers attribute to cultural messages. We will see throughout that cultivation researchers often conceive of television as kind of cultural river, in which everyone to some degree is carried along.

Thus, cultivation is an agro-aquatic metaphor for the function of television in the construction and maintenance of cultural meaning, and for the way culture works generally. Within this metaphor, the *production* of messages then takes on special significance, since the resulting social patterns imply cultural and political power – namely, the right to create the messages which cultivate collective consciousness. But this is a two-part process: *the right to produce messages stems from social power, while social power is accrued through the right to produce messages.* This too confounds simplistic notions of "causality," and is a significant reason why some of the "causal" critiques of cultivation tend to miss the point. With mass communication we have the mass production of messages, the cultural manifestation of the industrial revolution. If not television, another medium could have accomplished this function (although television is perhaps ideally suited to it). Given the social functions of messages, the mass production of messages and of the symbolic environment represents a profound transformation in social relationships, in power, and in the cultural process of story-telling.

If cultivation in form resembles water, its substance is stories. Above all, cultivation is a theory of narrative's role in culture. Humans uniquely live in a world experienced and conducted through story-telling, in its many modes and forms. Much of what we know, or think we know, we have never personally experienced; we "know" about many things based on the stories we hear and the stories we tell. "Story-telling fits human reality to the social order" (Gerbner, 1986).

Whereas most message-effects research had assumed that human communication was composed mostly of exchanges of "information," cultivation preferred to see humans as mostly engaging in story-telling transactions (Fisher, 1984). Gerbner often quotes Scottish patriot Andrew Fletcher's observation that "If a man were permitted to make all the ballads, he need not care who should make the laws of a nation." Such a romantic notion is not easily testable, but that makes it no less compelling. The stories of a culture reflect and cultivate its most basic and fundamental assumptions, ideologies and values. Story-telling occupies a crucial role in human existence; from the start, Gerbner's theory development stemmed from the observation that story-telling is being increasingly monopolized by a small and shrinking group of global conglomerates whose attention does not normally extend beyond the bottom-line and quarterly reports to stockholders. Mass communication institutions have progressed toward greater speed of, control over and profit from the mass reception of cultural stories in the form of entertainment messages.

It is in the context of an unprecedented centralization of message-producing resources that cultivation carries on its work. Disquiet over the commercialization and mass-production of stories sharpens the critical edge to cultivation research. In earlier times, the stories of a culture were told face-to-face by members of a community, parents, teachers or the clergy. Although we do not mean to imply that this was some sort of narrative "golden age" without today's problems of violence, inequality and fear, we do argue that the special characteristics of television, harnessing mass distribution of messages to a commercial purpose, are historically unique. Today, television tells most of the stories to most of the people, most of the time. The cultural process of story-telling is now in the hands of global commercial interests, who are largely unknown, unchosen and unelected, and who have little incentive to be interested in the content of their stories beyond their ability to attract specific, well-defined, profitable audiences, with a minimum of public objections. Thus, the symbolic world we are inhabiting and (re)creating is designed according to the specifications of marketing strategies, as opposed to public service, education, democratic negotiation, or other potential and available driving principles.

Gerbner has noted that in order to fit the marketing and commercial needs of this world, television tells (at least) three different kinds of stories. There are stories about how things *work*, in which the invisible dynamics of human life are illuminated. These stories are called "fiction," and they build a fantasy that informs the story we call reality. There are also stories about how things *are*; today, we mostly call them "news," and they tend to confirm the visions, rules, priorities and goals of a particular society. And finally, there are stories of value and choice, of what to *do*. These have been called sermons, or instruction, or law; today they are called "commercials." Together, all three kinds of stories, organically related, constitute mediated culture; they are expressed and enacted through mythology, religion, legends, education, art, science, laws, fairy tales and politics – and all of these, increasingly, are packaged and disseminated by television.

Thus, cultivation sees television as an increasingly unitizing cultural force, bringing together previously disparate narrative sectors into the same arena, tending to absorb what used to be the "public sphere." But this absorption process is not "persuasion," because it does not occur in a specifiable time interval, nor as a result of exposure to a particular message. The impacts on those who consume messages and stories are not linear, mechanical or hypodermic. Because this is a dialectical process (Gerbner, 1958), the "effects" of messages are relatively indirect.

Uncovering aggregate and implicit patterns in mass-produced messages "will not necessarily tell us what people think or do. But they will tell us what most people think or do something *about* and in *common*" (Gerbner, 1970; emphasis in original). This argument has some affinity to the notion of agenda-setting (McCombs, 1994), but it is cast on a deeper and more fundamental level. It is not so much the specific, day-to-day agenda of public issue salience which culture (and cultural media) sets as it is the more hidden and pervasive boundary conditions for social discourse, wherein the cultural ground-rules for what exists, what is important, what is right and so on, are repeated (and ritualistically consumed) so often that they become invisible.

Therefore, "Cultivation is what a culture does," because "culture is the basic medium in which humans live and learn" (Gerbner, 1990, p. 249). Culture is a "system of stories and other artifacts – increasingly mass-produced – that mediates between existence and consciousness of existence, and thereby contributes to both" (p. 251). Since messages reflect social relationships, mass-produced messages bear the assumptions of the organizations (though not necessarily of the individuals) that produce them. As our most pervasive and widely shared story-teller, television is perfectly poised to play a crucial role in the cultivation of common and specific images, beliefs, values and ideologies.

## Cultivation as a Theory of Social Control

Cultivation research is more than an abstract examination of an interesting question. Rather, we see cultivation as a "critical" theory of communication, insofar as it subjects the institution of television and mass communication to an investigation which can show the dimensions of important problems and even suggest ways to fix them. While cultivation does not look like the average critical theory (at least in communication, most critical studies tend toward interpretive and abstract examinations of social processes), cultivation passes the entrance exam for critical social science research (Lent, 1995; Morgan, 1995).

Above, we suggested that traditional mass communication researchers were often motivated by their unstated political agenda. But of course, we too are motivated by an ideo-political agenda, the nature of which is fundamental to understanding cultivation. In this section, we explore some assumptions that underpin the research, in order to help the reader place our activities in a historical and intellectual context. While the standard view is that ideology "pollutes" social science research, it has never been the purpose of cultivation to provide factually "pure" observations without critical comment (something we assume is impossible anyway). Thus, we examine some propositions which we think undergird the conduct of cultivation as a critical form of research.

If cultivation is a critical theory, it is a theory of media's role in social control. That is, it examines how media are used in social systems to build consensus (if not agreement) on positions through shared terms of discourse and assumptions about priorities and values. We argue that the system works so as to benefit social elites. These elites are not a mysterious cabal enmeshed in pernicious conspiracies; they are simply the "haves" of global, industrialized society who enjoy its benefits disproportionately. In this section we advance some simple propositions that specify how cultivation contributes to processes of social control, through which these elite groups tend to retain their power and privileges.

First (P1), we assume that *institutions of mass communication are owned by social, cultural and primarily economic elites*. Cultivation researchers are most concerned with the aspects of a media system in which ownership and access are limited and tightly controlled. Cultivation researchers have analogized television to institutions such as preindustrial religion. It has not typically been an aim of cultivation researchers to "prove" this assumption with empirical data; this assertion can be taken as true prima facie. Still, many separate types of evidence are relevant here, especially the well-known analyses of economic concentration of the mass media (e.g., Bagdikian, 1997), as well as the mega-mergers of the 1990s, in which a smaller and smaller number of larger and larger media organizations coalesce before our eyes. Also important are analyses that show how government policy has favored commercial interests over public interests (Barnouw, 1978; McChesney, 1993) and analyses of institutional practice that show how those employed within the media are guided by institutional norms (Altheide, 1985).

It is important to note that "elites" are not necessarily individuals, though specific individuals often behave in ways to accomplish the goals of elite institutions. (Many well-intentioned and sincere media professionals find themselves "trapped" in the media system which requires them to behave in certain ways.) For our purposes, "elites" can be seen both as dominant institutions and, in a lesser sense, the individuals who play roles within institutional rule structures. "Institutional process analysis," which is a component of Cultural Indicators, has as its goal the explication of institutional media performance.

Second (P2), *social and economic elites codify messages in their media which serve elite aims*. This proposition is also assumed by cultivation researchers, not generally directly nor empirically tested. Cultural Indicators researchers have not directly attempted to measure whether the messages of television are in agreement with measured ideological positions of message producers. Again, though, critical mass communication research helps out. There is a body of both television criticism and critical media theory that has documented the relationships between messages and ideology (see Stevenson, 1995, for a good review of these critical approaches, also Dahlgren, 1995). The work of those in cultural studies is also very relevant (Lewis, 1991). Congruent with critical research, cultivation tends to assume this link particularly by virtue of the evidence which is gathered with respect to the third proposition (discussed below).

This second proposition can be controversial, particularly for those who see the American media culture moving in a more democratic, diversified and demographically segmented direction. In particular, for those who see the media as controlled by market forces and protected by the First Amendment, it can be maddeningly perverse to suggest that social elites somehow use the media for their own purposes. To be clear: we are not asserting that there is a conspiracy of trilateral-commission one-worlders somehow getting their message through to a duped public. Rather, we would simply suggest that dominant cultural institutions, clearly serving economic elites, are *systemically* structured so as to most often favor the viewpoints and information that would help those economic elites in the long run.

Thus, the fact that television programs sometimes criticize corporations and the business community would not count as a disproof of proposition 2 (though there are many examples of how multinational corporate ownership of key media outlets has stifled debate on any number of issues). Of course, in specific programs there are always opportunities for nonelite and countercultural viewpoints to get through.

(P3) *The tendency for media messages to conform to elite needs and desires can be revealed through empirical study.* Messages, while varying on the surface, tend to reveal patterns and systems when empirically evaluated. Gerbner has noted that analysis of television's message systems (content) provides clues to cultivation. Cultivation analysis must therefore be grounded in real data about over-arching content patterns, shared by large groups over long periods of time.

(P4) *Audience members, whether or not they are seeking to fulfill individual needs, participate in a social process in which they hear and internalize messages of social elites.* This is the key proposition for cultivation as a theory of social control. Note that we do not say that audiences are "persuaded" by social elites. That would imply an active and intentional program of persuasion, along with a passive and defenseless reaction by audiences. What we suggest here is merely that audiences frequently "get" messages from message systems that have been structured to reflect the interests of social elites. Any "absorption" of meaning from that process is different than straight persuasion.

Cultivation assumes that massive attention to television results in a slow, steady and cumulative internalization of aspects of those messages, especially the aspects with ideological import. Why do viewers internalize messages? An economic argument comes first. Viewers participate in "exchange" relationships with their television programs: they accept the terms of an economic system preferred and perpetuated by economic elites, which are the same elites which control media structures (Jhally and Livant, 1986). While this need not prove an ideological effect, we can at least accept that viewers' viewership is on the terms of social elites. The time and attention of viewers is required to make the system work, otherwise advertising becomes ineffective. Thus, viewer attention is a precondition for the overall economic health and purposiveness of the system. This may also have the effect of commoditizing the relationship as some would suggest, but at the very least it guarantees a fair hearing for the viewpoints and aims of social elites.

This proposition does not necessarily imply that aims of social elites will be universally accepted by viewers (see next proposition), but it does suggest that social elites have an excellent resource with which to color public discussion of social, political, and economic issues. Thus, cultivation argues that an important outcome of our media system is that social elites can play a disproportionate role in determining the "boundaries" of social discourse. This tilts the field in favor of social elites, and predisposes toward an eventual outcome of social control.

(P5) *Audience members more "committed" to media will have belief structures more consonant with those desired by social elites.* This proposition is the one most directly tested by cultivation analysis: viewership (i.e., exposure to television) is related to belief structures, under the assumption that more time spent with an elite-dominated media system reflects: (1) a willingness to accept the propositions within those media as useful, and (2) a tendency to accept propositions within those media as, in some sense, factual or credible or normal. This proposition means that the internalization processes hypothesized in proposition 4 will serve social elites. This derives not from changing anyone's mind about anything, but from the cultivation of stable and consistent patterns of meaning and resistance to change.

This, as a kind of final capstone proposition, is directly susceptible to empirical analysis, and so has been the key focus of Cultural Indicators research and especially cultivation. This is what most students of mass communication see as "the" proposition of cultivation. But if we approach this proposition without knowledge of the preceding arguments, it may well seem that cultivation is indeed a rather vacuous social science approach – not very sophisticated at that – for discussing the complex social issue of elite control.

At this point, it is evident that the superstructure of cultivation is built on a foundation of assumptions and beliefs which guide the inquiry. This, of course, is true of all social science, though not all social scientists always make their beliefs explicit in this way. In any case, these considerations and propositions show that cultivation is certainly not a value-free exercise in abstract empiricism. If one denies the validity of any one of our propositions, one opens a route to criticize cultivation theory. And we accept that.

Of course, to be critical of television as an institution does not imply a mysterious conspiracy against social progress (although sometimes one wonders), nor do we see television as the most powerful force for social control that has ever been devised. Our propositions imply systemic forms of control. In some ways, we argue that television creates "propaganda without propagandists," a system wherein no particular individual or entity can be found responsible for the effects of messages. Such a system, ineffable as it may be, is perhaps more effective than the more sinister government-controlled propaganda systems, because audiences are not generally under the impression that control processes are taking place.

Now, in the rest of this book, we will look at the cultivation research process in depth. Chapter 2 provides a detailed description of how the research is done. We detail the assumptions and procedures associated with cultivation research over the years. Then Chapter 3 looks at the early cultivation work based on these methods. We describe the landmark studies, some of which attracted a great deal of attention in the media and political arena.

As the early work drew a great deal of attention, it also drew a great deal of criticism. Chapter 4 looks at these critiques. We go over in detail the debates of the early 1980s and provide responses to most of the issues raised. Chapter 5 looks at later cultivation research, with a particular focus on theoretical developments related to the issue of "mainstreaming." Mainstreaming was one of the main responses to the early criticisms.

Chapter 6 is a meta-analysis of over twenty years of cultivation research, summarizing published cultivation work since 1976. Chapter 7 continues the meta-analysis, and looks at what large data sources such as the General Social Survey have to say about cultivation. The purpose of these two chapters is to assess the consistency of cultivation research over the years and to answer the basic question: "Are people's beliefs related to television viewing?"

In Chapter 8 we look at the issue of "how" cultivation works. This has been a vexing question over the years, dealing with psychological questions related to how people remember and process television messages. We try to provide some answers about interesting new research directions. In Chapter 9 we look at how the new media technologies may influence cultivation. Finally, in Chapter 10 we provide a summary, looking at the overall question, with some answers about the broader social and cultural questions raised throughout the book.

# 2　Methods of Cultivation: Assumptions and Rationale

## Prelude to Cultivation Analysis: a Whole New Medium

As we described in the previous chapter, cultivation emerged in the shadow of two contrary historical trends: while the prevailing intellectual discourse held that media effects were, at most, limited, heightened concern about television and violence dominated public and Congressional discourse. It was in this atmosphere that Gerbner and Gross (1976) built up their case against both the prevailing apologia and the more simplistic "monkey-see, monkey-do" violence hysteria of the day by pointing to some unique and unprecedented characteristics of television. Their initial empirical testing of cultivation in the mid-1970s grew directly out of these arguments about the nature of television and its role in society. Although these assumptions have been questioned by many, and despite some obvious institutional and technological changes in television since then, these "starting points" should nevertheless be reiterated briefly.

First, overall amount of exposure to television dwarfs the use of most other media for most people. People simply do not, on the average, spend as much time with other media or in other leisure pursuits as they spend with television. There are of course voracious readers, movie fanatics, mouse potatoes, web surfers, magazine devotees, and those who never turn off the radio (whether they're wearing it as headgear or not). But for most people, television dominates the media diet.

Second, exposure to television begins before we first use most other media. Most people under fifty have been watching television since before they could read or probably even speak. For almost everyone, television viewing begins before we develop the tastes and selective patterns of consumption that we apply to other media; usage patterns for other media are informed by the fact of being born into households where television is virtually a member of the family. Children enter kindergarten, their first formal exposure to the official public sphere, as already experienced viewers, with thousands of viewing hours under their belts. Their interactions with most out-of-home agencies and institutions, and the contributions of those institutions to beliefs and behavior, are colored by that earlier exposure.

Third, television is more available and accessible than most other media. Unlike print media, television does not require literacy. Unlike theatrical movies, television runs almost continuously, and can be watched without leaving one's home and without payment on a per-program basis. Unlike radio, television can show as well as tell. Unlike the Internet, television does not require computer skills, (relatively) expensive equipment, or focused interaction from the audience member.

Most of all, Gerbner and Gross argued that television is different from other media in its *centralized* mass-production and ritualistic use of a coherent set of images and messages produced to appeal to virtually the entire population. Despite the growth of new technologies and the explosion of channels since the early 1970s, television remains the dominant purveyor of stories and messages shared across lines of class, gender, race, age, religion, geography, ethnicity, sexuality and so on. What were formerly the most mass of mass media, radio and magazines, now make profits by reaching (and cultivating) fragmented, sharply defined, specific audiences. The television audience has become more fragmented in the 1990s as well, but not nearly to the same extent, and the vast majority of the audience concentrates its viewing on a small number of channels showing "network-type" fare. For the advertiser, the story-teller, and the average audience member, television remains the medium that caters to the largest possible, most general audience.

A key factor is that television drama exploits a particular style of "representational realism," a dominant convention in Western narrative in general. Representational realism is the form of story-telling in which the hearer or viewer is convinced that, if certain assumptions are taken for granted, the events taking place could happen "in reality." Most sitcoms and dramas require a relatively simple suspension of disbelief to get to this state, other programs may be more fantastic, but virtually all programs share the characteristic that they present events as happening in a way that could really happen in a televised reality not too distant from our own. Thus, we can imagine Roseanne as our own mother or wife, or we can see Seinfeld's neighborhood as our own. Further afield, we might shake our heads at some depraved and tragic criminal act that the cops on *NYPD Blue* encounter, even forgetting that someone scripted the deed as we mumble about how dangerous our cities have become. And even though we know that *Star Trek* isn't "real" within the laws of physics as we know them, we have no trouble adapting its concepts, characters and morals to everyday reality, because the show is in fact more about today than the twenty-fourth century.

Of course, most viewers (even young children) know that they are watching fiction, that made-up stories have been produced by writers, actors, directors, technicians, etc. But no matter what happens in the foreground of the story, at the level of the surface plot, viewers demand (and expect) the *background* to be "realistic" – that is, to fit conventional criteria for what is *considered* to be "realistic." That background offers viewers a continuous stream of "facts" and impressions about life and the world.

Realism, as Gross (1977) submits, is a Trojan horse which carries within it a highly selective, repetitive and synthetic image of the facts of life. Even when we know that what we are watching is not "real," we may still not pay a great deal of conscious attention to the incidental, background information in a story. Gerbner and Gross (1976) illustrated this point by noting that much of what we "know" about the world is in fact derived at least in part from fictional but "realistic" symbolic representations. They asked:

How many of us have ever been in an operating room (awake), a criminal courtroom, a police station, jail, penthouse, corporate boardroom, movie studio, or other staple television locales? Yet how much do we "know" about such places, about what goes on in them, about the people who live and work in them? How much, indeed, of our images of the real world has been learned from fictional worlds? (p. 179)

What we learn – or what society in general teaches us and television most frequently reminds us of – is not only a store of "facts" but also the associated values and ideological assumptions which permeate the most stable and pervasive images of television drama. The presumed realism of the background – a background that is highly consistent across genres and over time – is critical in this process regardless of the degree of "perceived reality" we bring to bear on our viewing, no matter how aware we are of the fact that we are watching a made-up story, and no matter how much we refuse to suspend our disbelief. Through narratives and actions that take place against a highly realistic background, the stories television tells can help shape the deeper, invisible, rarely questioned assumptions all of us carry around; they do not "determine" our thoughts and actions so much as they color and help inform the meaning of what we think, say and do.

## A Thumbnail Sketch of Cultivation Methodology

In the following sections we present a methodological primer on cultivation research. First, we present details about some of the methodological mechanics of cultivation analysis. Then, we turn to a discussion of some fundamental conceptual problems that have arisen frequently in discussion and critique of cultivation results.

### Counting Messages

One way to explain the methodological approach of cultivation is to invoke an old parable: Imagine a person living all alone on a tiny deserted isle (or a mountaintop, or a cave, or a biosphere) with no contact with anyone or anything in the outside world besides what he or she sees on television. Everything this hypothetical hermit knows about "reality" is derived from the television world – a world that differs sharply from the "real" world in terms of demography, violence, occupations and so on, and a world in which motivations, outcomes, and many normally invisible forces of life and society are made clear. How would our recluse see the world? To what extent do heavy viewers see the world that way? Using our mythical viewer as a benchmark, cultivation analysis examines the extent to which heavy viewers learn lessons about the real world from the patterns embedded in the symbolic world.

The questions raised by this scenario do not have much to do with particular messages, programs, episodes or genres and their ability to produce *immediate* change in audience attitudes and behaviors. Now, of course, for any given individual, it is likely that specific images, stories, lessons and characters stand out in memory as vivid and important influences. In our own experience, for instance, characters and figures as diverse as Pee-wee Herman, John-Boy Walton, Captain Stubing, Archie Bunker, Rod Serling, Marcia Brady, Perry Mason, Steve McGarrett, Big Bird, Laura Petrie, Murphy Brown and Kramer stand out as having been particularly entertaining or memorable. And every person can think back on their own experience with TV and say something similar. Based on this, one might conclude that individual messages, lessons and characters *are* very important, and for the individual, they certainly are. But cultivation steps back from the individual level, because it often happens that one person's Edward R. Murrow turns out to be another person's Howdy Doody.

Thus, cultivation analysis should always begin by identifying the most recurrent and stable patterns in television content, emphasizing the consistent images, portrayals and values that cut across most program genres. This is accomplished either by conducting a message system analysis or by examining existing content studies. In general, message system analysis illuminates four dimensions of content: existence (what *is* in the symbolic world?), priorities (what is important?), values (what is right or wrong, good or bad, etc.?), and relationships (what is related to what else, and how?). These dimensions yield corresponding measures of attention, emphasis, tendency and structure, which together illuminate the symbolic functions of how things work in the world of story-telling. Although hypotheses concerning television's contribution to viewers' conceptions about social reality cannot be formulated or tested without reliable information on the most consistent content patterns and portrayals presented, this rule is sometimes bent slightly in practice; sometimes it is grossly violated. There are times when "reasonable" extrapolations from available content data can be made, yet there are also studies in the literature where no conceivable empirical content basis for a presumed cultivation hypothesis exists. In these cases, the theoretical boundaries of cultivation are strained beyond their carrying capacity.

### How is Cultivation Measured?

Although cultivation is a phenomenon that unfolds at a macro-social level, it is necessary to measure it by collecting observations from individuals. This presents some conceptual and theoretical problems, though these problems are common in social science and not unique to cultivation. That is, while cultivation is more than just the sum of individual reactions to TV messages, it is quite difficult to measure those reactions without cumulating data from individuals.

Cultivation typically uses survey procedures for examining relationships between exposure to television and reactions to those messages. The survey questions used to tap into people's conceptions of social reality are of several types. Some questions juxtapose answers reflecting the statistical "facts" of the television world with those more in line with reality; the response choices are referred to as the "TV Answer" and the "Real World Answer," with the former more in line with the way the world is presented on television. Other questions do not contrast the "facts" of the two worlds, but examine symbolic transformations and more general implications of the content data.

The questionnaires typically include questions relating to many aspects of social reality as well as measures of television viewing and demographic variables such as age, gender, race, education, occupation, social class and political orientation. Some of the questions are semi-"projective" (e.g., asking respondents to estimate some aspect of reality relative to their own situation), some use a forced-error format (e.g., asking respondents to estimate the chances of being involved in a violent situation, where they must either guess too high or too low), and others simply measure beliefs, opinions, attitudes or behaviors. Using standard techniques of survey methodology, the questions are posed to samples (national probability, regional, convenience) of children, adolescents or adults. Secondary analysis of large-scale national surveys (for example, the National Opinion Research Center's General Social Surveys) have often been used when they include questions which relate to relevant aspects of the television world as well as measures of television viewing.

The substantive survey questions posed to respondents do not mention television in any way; if respondents are explicitly thinking about television, it could contaminate their responses by shading their perceptions toward (or away from) the images of television. As we will see in subsequent chapters, many other studies have not taken this precaution, which may put their data at serious risk. Also, the respondents' awareness of the source of their information is seen as irrelevant; cultivation is not about what people "think about" television.

Amount of television viewing is usually assessed by asking how much time the respondent spends watching on an "average day." The ideal measures, from the cultivation perspective, provide estimates of the average number of hours the respondent watches each day, as opposed (for example) to how many shows they watch regularly or what types of shows or channels they like most. These data may be used in their original form (a ratio scale) or may be reduced to relative viewing categories ("light," "medium" and "heavy" viewing). Viewing, when so categorized, is seen in relative terms; the determination of what constitutes "light," "medium" and "heavy" viewing is made on a sample-by-sample basis, using as close to a three-way split of hours of self-reported daily television viewing as possible (the goal is to equalize and maximize the number of respondents at each viewing level).

Although more specific measures of hours of viewing each day facilitate some data analysis procedures, from a conceptual standpoint, what is important is that there are basic differences in viewing levels, not the actual or specific amount of viewing. This "orthodox" cultivation doctrine on the measurement of television viewing has been frequently criticized, and many other types of measures have been proposed. From our perspective, however, the methods used to assess television viewing are less important than the fact that one can realistically distinguish between relative levels of viewing with few problems. The assumption is simply that (for example) those who say "four hours a day" do, on balance, watch more than those who say "two hours a day." It is taken for granted that this procedure misclassifies some people (as does the empirical measurement of any construct or phenomenon), but this only means that any observed cultivation associations are in fact underestimated.

All in all, cultivation analysis tests for relationships between amount of television viewing and the tendency to respond to survey questions in the terms of the dominant and repetitive facts, values and ideologies of the television world. Systematic differences in the outlooks of heavy and light viewers provide evidence of television's contribution to viewers' conceptions of social reality.

## What Counts as Cultivation?

Given knowledge of what TV says about reality and what people think about reality, cultivation's final step is a relatively simple one: what is the relationship between the two? The "standard" cultivation analysis may begin with simple cross-tabulations between television viewing (using a three-way split of light, medium and heavy viewing) and the answers to the substantive questions (categorized by the TV and non-TV answers). The percentage difference between heavy and light viewers is reported as the "Cultivation Differential" (CD). For instance, suppose 52 percent of heavy viewers think that they are very likely to be a victim of crime in the next year, while only 39 percent of light viewers think so. In that case, the CD would be "+ 13" and, all other things being equal, this difference between light and heavy viewers would be seen as supporting the cultivation hypothesis (Figure 2.1). With the data in the form of simple percentages, the power and direction of the association is indicated by measures such as the gamma statistic, which shows the strength of relationship for ordinal data.

Of course, people who regularly consume a great deal of television differ from light viewers in many ways besides how much time they spend watching. In the general population, light and heavy viewers differ by age, sex, income, education, race, occupation, time use, religion, social isolation, political orientation, and a host of other demographic, social and psychological variables. But they also differ in terms of the extent to which television dominates their sources of consciousness. Light viewers tend to be exposed to more varied and diverse information sources (both mediated and interpersonal), while heavy viewers, by definition, tend to rely more on television.

To deal with this, differences between the responses of light, medium and heavy viewers are routinely examined within specific demographic subgroups, and/or the effects of other variables are statistically controlled (following the philosophy of "elaboration," outlined in Rosenberg, 1968). The differences associated with amount of viewing are sometimes independent of, but usually interact with, the many social, cultural and personal factors that differentiate light and heavy viewers. In other words, the strength, shape and even direction of cultivation relationships (such as the hypothetical one described above between amount of viewing and per-

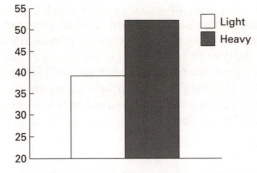

Figure 2.1 Percentage of light and heavy viewers giving "TV answer" to question about chances of being involved in violence (Gerbner and Gross, 1976)

ceptions of becoming a crime victim) may all vary considerably for different types of people and members of different groups at different social locations. Questions about the impacts of controls and the meaning of differential patterns of associations across subgroups have produced enormous conceptual and methodological controversy in cultivation research.

We will look at these issues and techniques in more detail throughout the book. For now, we would argue that cultivation has used fairly simple and commonsensical techniques of data analysis to make its arguments. Although cultivation research has increasingly used more sophisticated techniques, including multiple regression analysis, structural equation models, and other number-crunching implements, the gist of any cultivation analysis is still a comparison of lighter viewers against heavier viewers. Though the devil is in the details, each and every cultivation analysis can theoretically be compared against each other, because they all have the same essential nature.

To sum all this up: based on clear-cut, reliable evidence on how something is portrayed on television, cultivation analysts develop hypotheses about what heavy viewers (or our hermit) should be expected to think about the topic if they think about it the way it is presented on television. The researchers then collect (or find) survey data, asking people questions about the topic, and then they ask them how much time they spend watching television. The sample is divided to see if the predicted differences in the views of light, medium and heavy viewers show up, overall and within subgroups.

This approach turned many conventional assumptions and procedures of media effects research on their head. The following sections discuss some of the alternative assumptions advanced in their stead, especially the notion that overall, undifferentiated exposure is what accounts for cultivation. We also consider two key issues which have provoked much confusion and argument: the difference between cultivation and "causality," and the role of divergent interpretations ("readings") of media content. These next sections elaborate the conceptual underpinnings and rationale for the cultivation perspective; the empirical implications and permutations will emerge in later chapters through our review and meta-analysis of the research.

## The Bucket, not the Drops (or: the Messages are the Message)

As we have seen, a major shift brought about by the emergence of cultivation was to put aside the question of "effects" at the individual message or program level, and to concentrate on the level of the story system – which means thinking about messages in terms of their overall patterns and about the institutional structures which produce them. Simultaneously, this move changes the inquiry from running after short-term, immediate change to thinking about long-term stability and resistance to change. Others before and besides Gerbner have suggested that mass media may involve functions and processes other than overt change. Lazarsfeld and Merton (1948) argued that the primary impact of exposure to mass communication is not likely to be change, but maintenance of the status quo. Similar notions have been expressed since then by Glynn (1956), Bogart (1972) and Gitlin (1982). But Gerbner's emphasis on overall exposure to television, regardless of genre, channel or program type, is perhaps what is most unusual and important about cultivation analysis. And this insistence on overall viewing has been a major point of contention among cultivation critics.

It is not that cultivation theory blithely and simplistically asserts that "all programs contain exactly the same messages," although that is the straw caricature sometimes attacked. Cultivation theory does not go so far as to deny that programs can differ, that viewing can be selective, that variations in channels and genres can exist, that there can be individual and group differences in interpretive strategies or viewing motivations, or that any of these are important. All of these other issues, dealt with widely in the social scientific research on the effects of television, are relevant to questions that also concern us. But cultivation research brackets these as separate research questions, distinct from the central questions explored through cultivation analysis.

To focus only on selectivity and diversity (values privileged by the pluralist ideology of print culture) can blind us to subtle commonalities underlying superficially different program types. To focus only on specific types of programs or isolated messages is to risk losing sight (as in traditional media effects research) of what is most distinctive and significant about television as a *system* of messages and as the premier story-teller of our age: the cultivation of shared conceptions of reality and common terms of discourse among otherwise diverse publics. As Gerbner argues, television's messages form a coherent and organic whole; they are not simply unrelated facts in a universe without form or logic. The fact that its stories hang together as a system means that cultivation results not from any specific programs or genres but from massive, long-term consumption of centrally produced, repetitive stories among large and heterogeneous publics who never meet face-to-face and have little in common except the messages they share.

Specific programs may have important impacts, but at a different level of analysis from the consequences of cumulative exposure to the total world of television. There are numerous ways of studying the vast and flowing river that is culture. Some may choose to take small samples from the flow and analyze extensively their microscopic composition, or to explore a little-traveled stream flowing against and apart from the main current. Others may choose to monitor slow but broad changes in the rate of the main current, or its temperature, or even barely perceptible but immensely consequential shifts in its overall course. All of these together are useful, valid and necessary for a full understanding of the river; cultivation research chooses to focus its energy on the larger patterns, often more neglected and difficult to observe. Thus, cultivation researchers, though also carried along by the river in their own boats, seek to chart the strength and direction of the flow, despite the attractiveness of being carried off into interesting eddies or tributaries. Cultivation deals with the flow of the water, not the individual drops.

The commercial and institutional structure of the television industry encourages a great deal of derivative repetition, formula and homogeneity in content. Even television's surface novelty, its latest fads, begin to look rather homogenized from a historical perspective, notwithstanding changes in production values, slickness and "look." Is it a *Charlie's Angels* rerun we're watching or a new episode of *Baywatch*? Didn't *Seinfeld* steal that joke from Jackie Gleason? I could have sworn that I saw this story about aliens on both the *X-Files* and *The Outer Limits*. Indeed, relative to other media, television provides a comparatively restricted and recurrent set of choices for a virtually unrestricted variety of interests and publics. On the dominant channels, the variety of choices available to select from when most viewers are available to watch is also limited by the fact that many programs designed for the same broad audience tend to be similar in their basic make-up and appeal (Signorielli, 1986).

Amount of viewing largely follows the lifestyle and demography of the viewer, and the audience is usually the group available to view at any given moment. Viewing decisions depend more on the clock than on the program; outside of spectacular events, audience behavior is stable and predictable, flowing regularly according to the day of the week and the month of the year. Series and hits come and go, but viewing is integrated into styles of life in stable and consistent ways. Despite the never-ending proliferation of channels and alternative media "delivery systems" (such as cable, VCRs, DTH, WebTV, etc.), most programs are by commercial necessity designed to be watched by large and heterogeneous audiences in a relatively non-selective fashion. Network shares decline as "new" technologies promise (and allow) an expansion in diversity and choice, but this has been accompanied by decreased diversity in ownership and greater concentration of production and control, with little diversification evident in programming (see Chapter 9).

What is most likely to cultivate stable and common conceptions of reality, then, is the overall pattern of programming to which total communities are regularly exposed over long periods of time. That is the pattern of settings, casting, social typing, actions and related outcomes that cuts across program types and viewing modes and defines the world of television. No matter what they watch, most heavy viewers cannot easily avoid being exposed to those recurrent patterns, usually many times a day. Therefore, cultivation analysis interrogates the contribution of amount of exposure to that total pattern rather than only to specific genres or programs.

There may well be some "heavy viewers" who watch nothing but shopping channels, travel documentaries, golf tournaments, or weather forecasts (and this sort of viewing is now possible). But cultivation simply assumes that most regular and heavy viewers will, over time, watch "more of everything." Even in a 100 (or more) channel universe, the programs attracting large, heterogeneous groups of viewers are narrative in nature. As narratives, different genres of fictional programs tend to manifest complementary – although, of course, not invariant – basic features. It is likely that one will see more representations of police, crime and violence on action/adventure shows than on game shows or a cooking channel; but potential lessons about safety, vulnerability, victimization and the law are not limited to cop shows, and it is precisely the overall contribution of these lessons with which cultivation is concerned.

A researcher may find (as some have) that exposure to police/action shows contributes more to images of violence than does overall viewing, or that viewers seem to learn more about doctors from medical shows than from overall viewing (or from news shows or from cartoons or from sports, and so on). In such an event, we could say that "television" does not in fact cultivate any global image. But, as Newhagen and Lewenstein (1992) point out, looking at the isolated "effects" of different program types is problematic because viewers may not define genres in the same way as do researchers, and also because bizarre and nonsensical associations often emerge. There is a danger of reaching such trivial and irrelevant, though potentially true, conclusions, as "heavy viewing of the Home and Garden Channel 'cultivates' awareness of when to plant different bulbs."

From the point of view of the cultivation of relatively stable and common images, what counts most is the total pattern of programming to which communities are exposed over long periods of time. Research that does not focus on overall television exposure as a measure of absorption of TV's systemic messages is not really about cultivation.

In sum, no matter what impact exposure to genre X may have on attitude Y or belief Z, cultivation argues that the consequences of television cannot be found only in terms of exposure to isolated fragments of the whole. The project is an attempt to say something about the more broad-based, ideological consequences of a commercially supported cultural industry celebrating consumption, materialism, individualism, power and the status quo along lines of gender, race, class and age. None of this denies the fact that some programs may contain some messages more than others, or that these messages may change somewhat over time.

### Cultivation and Causality: Chickens and Eggs

Another nagging point of contention among critics of cultivation concerns the crucial conceptual difference between "cultivation" and "causality." In traditional empirical social research, to find a correlation between an independent variable (X) and a dependent variable (Y), measured at the same point in time, might mean three things: (1) that X caused Y (which is, presumably, the initial hypothesis), (2) that Y caused X (i.e., a case of "reverse causality"), or (3) that X and Y only appear to be correlated, and some other variable is the true cause of both (i.e., X and Y are in a "spurious relationship"). There are other variants and possibilities (such as intervening or antecedent variables and processes), but we will focus on just these three for now.

If a relationship is found between two variables (i.e., if the null hypothesis is rejected), then researchers typically try to determine, conceptually and empirically, which of these three possibilities best fit the data at hand in order to decide whether the core hypothesis ($X \rightarrow Y$) can be supported. Sometimes, the second explanation (reverse causality) can be automatically ruled out, especially if the independent variable is temporally prior to or cannot logically be affected by the dependent. For example, if we find a relationship between age (X) and political party membership (Y) – say, that older people tend to identify with the Republicrats and the younger people are mostly Demoblicans – it is pretty clear which is "causing" which: someone's age cannot easily be "caused" by the party for which he or she votes.

But even if we feel confident about concluding that age is the causal engine here, we don't know if the older people in the sample *were* Demoblicans when they were younger and *changed* their political allegiance over the years (which implies that the current younger people will also switch to the Republicrat side as they age, an inference which chalks up the observed difference to maturation), or if these older people *always* tended to be Republicrats, even when they were younger (which attributes the observed association to a historical or cohort effect). Of course, either way, things may be different for men versus women, or for people with more or less education, or for different racial or ethnic groups – or for multiple combinations of these other variables.

In complex social situations, as most are, a "simple" association such as the one between age and party membership can therefore become quite complex very quickly – and it can also spin off some interesting and unanticipated multilevel interwoven patterns. But underlying the various permutations in this example – and in the epistemology of most social research in general – is the acceptance of "causality" as a meaningful construct in the first place. Yes, the hammer might "cause" your thumb to smart, the doorbell's ring might "cause" you to get up from your comfortable chair, and a television show might "cause" you to be upset for quite some time about what you saw. But, as we will soon see, this linear, sequential, before/after model of stimulus-response "causality" cannot be universally applied to complex cultural processes.

In most studies, evidence for cultivation is claimed to exist when there is some association or correlation found between amount of television viewing and some attitude or belief. For example, let's consider a "classic" cultivation finding (one that we will elaborate upon greatly in subsequent chapters): heavy viewers are more fearful and apprehensive about crime than are light viewers. According to the traditional models of scientific interpretation, that association might mean three things: (1) that watching violence on television leads heavy viewers to be more fearful, or (2) that being more fearful leads people to watch more television (perhaps fearful people stay at home more, where they watch television; this is the reverse causality explanation), or (3) the association is spurious because of some other factor or factors (e.g., perhaps older people or people who live in dangerous areas are more fearful, stay home more, and therefore watch more television).

Now, if the association holds up after controlling for relevant and appropriate third variables, cultivation researchers (admitting that the list of possible third variables is infinite; the possibility of spuriousness can never be definitively rejected) would argue that the association between amount of viewing and fear is evidence that television "cultivates" fear. Some critics have rejected that interpretation, charging that it is as (or more) plausible that fear generates greater viewing (i.e., reverse causality). The critic, however, is confusing cultivation with causality. Indeed, of the three possible choices considered here, the first one – that television somehow "causes" fear – is actually the *least* compelling or plausible. So, although the critic is correct in rejecting that first causal interpretation, that interpretation is not the assumption of cultivation analysis in the first place. This can be seen in numerous early works of Gerbner and the Cultural Indicators (CI) school where strict, mechanistic, causal interpretations were clearly avoided.

For television to be the "cause" of fear in the sense of the term as it might be used in experiments in the physical sciences, we would have to be able to speak of a time in which a person was free from any social influence, and then measure accumulated exposures to various relevant messages over a prescribed time. We would, for example, have to imagine some hypothetical person, without fear, having never been exposed to television. If such a person exists (very small infants fit the description perhaps) we would then be interested to see whether he or she would become fearful after seeing some quantity of violent or fear-provoking television.

The problem, of course, is that with real television viewing there is no "before" condition in any meaningful sense; accordingly, therefore there is no "after" and no "change" to observe. Television viewing is a social condition, not a behavior that can be separated from other social facts in a sterile way. Even the small infant can't really be used in this experiment, because the pervasive presence of television's messages will contribute to the grounding and bounding conditions within which the infant learns to interpret the meaning of terms like "fear." Cultivation presumes that social actions account for the construction of the very ability to process social messages. That is, we learn how to interpret messages in part from the very system which sends those messages. To disentangle "socialization" from "education" therefore becomes a circular question and ultimately a frustrating exercise in tautology.

Perhaps the only way to really get at the question from the causal angle would be to remove television from our social environment. Since that's not going to happen, it becomes evident that to speak about "causes" is to ask a largely meaningless question. (And as we pointed out earlier, this is the reason for choosing the cultivation metaphor in the first place.)

Still, the charge of causal ambiguity continues to be offered as a critique of cultivation work. But if we leave aside the reductionist variable-analytic world of traditional causal models and think about reality for a moment, it should be apparent that we certainly do not live in a world of unidirectional, mechanistic causality. Translated to cultivation, this means that *both* of the first two explanations ($X \rightarrow Y$ and $Y \rightarrow X$) are too simplistic and sterile to explain the observed relationship.

There is no reason to assume that these are exclusive, either/or processes. More conceptually appealing is the argument of cultivation: that fear and television viewing mutually support, replenish, reproduce, renovate and sustain each other in dynamic and reciprocal ways. Fearful people watch more, which maintains their fear, which fuels continued viewing, which simultaneously cultivates their fear, and so on. To cultivate is to confirm what people "already know."

The question of "which comes first" is misleading. Cultivation means long-term patterns of stability among systems of cultural images and practices, lifestyles, and belief structures. People are born into a symbolic environment with television as its mainstream. Children begin viewing several years before they begin reading, and well before they can even talk. Television viewing both shapes and is a stable part of lifestyles and outlooks.

As will be detailed in later chapters, the third possibility (that the association is spurious) can be tested by statistically controlling for likely "third" variables. Sometimes cultivation relationships are spurious and sometimes they're not, but controlling for third variables most frequently uncovers divergent – and often fascinating – patterns among subgroups.

The elements of cultivation do not originate with television or appear out of a void. Layers of social, personal and cultural contexts also determine the shape, scope and degree of the contribution television is likely to make. Yet, the "meanings" of those contexts and factors are in themselves aspects of the cultivation process. That is, while a viewer's gender, age, race or class (and so on) may make a difference in perspective, television viewing can make a similar and interacting difference. Viewing may help define what it means, for example, to be an adolescent female member of a given social class. That interaction is a continuous process (as is cultivation).

Thus, television neither simply "creates" nor "reflects" images, opinions and beliefs. Rather, it is an integral aspect of an ongoing, active process. Institutional needs and objectives influence the creation and distribution of mass-produced messages which create, fit into, exploit and sustain the needs, values and ideologies of mass publics. These publics, in turn, acquire distinct identities as publics partly through exposure to the ongoing flow of messages.

Many of those with certain social and psychological characteristics, dispositions and worldviews, and fewer alternatives as attractive and compelling, use television as their major vehicle of cultural participation. To the extent that television dominates their sources of entertainment and information, continued exposure to its messages is likely to reiterate, confirm and nourish those values, perspectives and ideologies.

Still, in contrasting cultivation with causality, it is important to stress that cultivation is not the same as simple reinforcement (although, to be sure, reaffirmation and stability in the face of pressures for change is not a trivial influence). Nor do we mean to suggest that television viewing is "merely" symptomatic of other dispositions and outlooks. And we also do not believe that change is *never* involved.

The "independent contribution" of television viewing means that the development (in some) and maintenance (in others) of some sets of outlooks or beliefs can be traced to steady, cumulative exposure to the world of television. Longitudinal panel studies, although they have important limitations, show that television *can* exert an independent influence on attitudes and behaviors over time, but that belief structures and concrete practices of daily life can also influence subsequent viewing (Gerbner, et al., 1980; Morgan, 1982, 1987; Morgan, Alexander, Shanahan and Harris, 1990).

The "independent contribution" also means that television messages are seen as functionally essential to the social system as we currently know it. Thus, although television messages may not on their own be seen as efficient causes of social phenomena, it is also true that the meaning of most social phenomena would be significantly different without the presence of television.

The crucial point is that cultivation is not conceived as a unidirectional but rather more like a gravitational process. The angle and direction of the "pull" depends on where groups of viewers and their styles of life are with reference to the line of gravity, the "mainstream" of the world of television. Each group may strain in a different direction, but all groups are affected by the same central current. Cultivation is thus part of a continual, dynamic, ongoing process of interaction among messages and contexts.

As successive generations grow up with television's version of the world, the former and more traditional distinctions established before the coming of television, and still maintained to some extent among light viewers, become blurred. Cultivation thus implies the steady entrenchment of mainstream orientations for most viewers and the systematic but almost imperceptible modification of previous orientations in others; in other words, affirmation for the confirmed, and indoctrination for deviants.

Some researchers have pointed out the affinities between cultivation and functionalism (Burrowes, 1996), and this relationship warrants some further exploration. A "functional" approach (in some quarters a dirty word but one regaining some respectability of late) explains a phenomenon by showing its consequences (see Kincaid, 1994). Functional explanations reason that phenomena can also be understood if it is known why they work (as opposed to just how).

Cultivation provides a remarkably poor explanation of how individual viewers interpret and process messages from television. Rather, it explains televised messages' effects based upon the consequences they have from the perspective of social control and stability, arguing that these messages are functional for the social and economic elites who control them (or, alternately, "dysfunctional" from the perspective of civil society).

A common criticism is that cultivation fails to account for the "mechanism" by which cultivation operates, in which the term "mechanism" is meant to point toward a "cognitive" understanding of the memory and mental processes which result in cultivation (see Chapter 9). Cultivation has eschewed this approach, generally adhering to the comments offered by Kincaid:

We can in fact have fairly good evidence for a functional claim without knowing the precise mechanism. To know that A persists because of its effects, I need to establish a non-spurious correlation between A's effect and its persistence. Spurious causation can be eliminated by controlling for all relevant possible causes that might make the correlation between effects and persistence spurious. We need not know the precise mechanism, whatever that means. (Kincaid, 1994, p. 425)

While correlation may not imply causality, as should never be forgotten, there is still social meaning in some types of observed correlations. This has been the essential approach followed by cultivation: functional explanation tied to correlational data. If cultivation is a functional/critical claim, there is little call to criticize it from a mechanistic causal perspective, unless one discounts functional explanations entirely. Although cultivation researchers recognize the validity of research which develops and tests hypotheses about individual uses and responses to television, the specific relevance of such research to cultivation is sometimes unclear.

Altogether, then, cultivation analysis is not a substitute for but a complement to traditional approaches to media effects. Traditional research is concerned with change rather than stability and with processes more applicable to media that enter a person's life at later stages (with mobility, literacy, etc.) and more selectively. Neither the "before and after exposure" model, nor the notion of "predispositions" as intervening variables, so important in traditional effects studies, apply in the context of cultivation analysis. Television enters life in infancy; television plays a role in the formation of those very "predispositions" that later intervene and condition (and often resist) other influences and attempts at persuasion. Cultivation does not imply a one-way, monolithic causal impact, but rather a contribution that is subtle, complex and intermingled with other influences, deriving from interactions between the medium and its publics, in (once again) dynamic and reciprocal ways.

## The Actively Passive Audience

Some critics assert that cultivation implies a "passive" view of the television audience, which is shorthand for assuming that viewers take messages at their face value and do not question or disagree with the positions presented, and that all audience members pretty much interpret all messages in pretty much the same way as the program's producers intended. Those who criticize cultivation for having such a patently untenable view of the audience, however, have never pointed to any specific evidence that this is, indeed, the assumption of cultivation analysis.

If cultivation did think of the audience in this way, then such criticism would be more than justified. Some might *infer* that this is the view of cultivation, based on oversimplified characterizations of the cultivation model, which equate it with crude, stimulus-response, persuasion research; but the fact is that Gerbner et al. have never explicitly said much of anything about the presumed activity or passivity level of the audience one way or the other. That is because the entire active/passive debate is not seen as especially relevant to cultivation.

On one side, no one could seriously promote the idea of the fully passive audience, numbly and obediently processing and acting upon all messages in uniform, consistent, and non-problematic ways. On the other side, to see the audience as all-powerful, with unlimited interpretive options and in full control of the meaning and impact of all messages, strips the media of any effectivity whatsoever and thereby makes their study a waste of time.

This is, of course, the core of the complex and long-standing debate over the relative power of "text" and "reader" in literary criticism and cultural studies. The view of cultivation researchers has been, implicitly, that they should not have to wait for others to resolve these questions before proceeding with their work. Yet, cultivation in effect eschews this argument entirely: it simply attempts to measure to what extent there is power resident either in text or reader, or both. Cultivation outcomes can be seen as indicators of the extent to which texts are powerful (or conversely, as the extent to which audiences willingly submit to texts). Audiences' acceptance of messages is seen in the congruity between the television worldview and audience belief systems. Data which show congruence between audience beliefs and television messages are functionally interpreted as serving needs and desires of the institutions which control messages. Audience "activity" does not need to enter into this equation at all.

Attention to empirical detail shows that reasonable cultural theorists need to reach a compromise position when thinking about the power of texts and the resistance of readers. As we will see, cultivation relationships account for a small amount of variance in any given test. Most of the variance is accounted by other factors, or simply cannot be accounted for. This in itself is a stunning proof that readers do indeed create variant readings, since attitudes which are derived from readings obviously do not correlate perfectly. Moreover, the enormous variation in cultivation associations across different demographic subgroups also shows that there is indeed a broad and diverse range of readings and interpretations to be enacted.

Nevertheless, the consistency and direction of cultivation findings over the years shows a residual power in a text such as television. This power accrues from repetition and ubiquity: it is the power to provide context and background for messages on which otherwise active readers will impose their will. That is, as readers encounter particular messages, they will certainly interpret them in a variety of ways. But these particular messages will always appear against the common-sense backdrop which is erected and maintained by the institution of television, along with other dominant social institutions. The particular messages, if they change over time, will be more or less faithfully interpreted against the less variant backdrop.

Moreover, the very notions of preferred, resistive, negotiated or oppositional readings were developed in terms of specific informational or persuasive messages, such as political news stories or commercials. These are very useful ways of thinking about how people make sense of these kinds of individual messages, but it not clear how they apply to massive floods of images that wash over us year after year. The question of audience activity must be completely reframed when the focus is on the *system* of messages.

Cultivation analysis is an attempt to say something about the more broad-based ideological consequences of a commercially supported cultural industry celebrating consumption, materialism, individualism, power and the status quo along lines of gender, race, class and age. Audience activity is a relevant question when it comes to persuasion or attitude change, but less so when the focus is on cultivation, seen as the process by which mass communication creates publics and defines the perspectives and assumptions which are most broadly-shared among those publics. In "Toward 'Cultural Indicators'" (1969), Gerbner wrote:

A message (or message system) cultivates consciousness of the terms required for its meaningful perception. Whether I accept its "meaning" or not, like it or not, or agree or disagree, is another problem. First I must attend to it and grasp what it is about. Just how that occurs, how items of information are integrated into given frameworks of cognition, is also another problem. My interest here centers on the fact that any attention and understanding cultivates the terms upon which it is achieved. And to the considerable extent to which these terms are common to large groups, the cultivation of shared terms provides the basis for public interaction. (p. 139)

Since the symbolic environment gives direction and meaning to human thought and action, cultivation is then the (continuous) outcome of interaction within the symbolic environment, assuring shared terms of discourse and behavior. The cultivation of "shared terms" and "collective consciousness," however, is not to be mistaken for *consensus*:

On the contrary, the public recognition of subcultural, class, generational, and ideological differences and even conflicts among scattered groups of people requires some common awareness and cultivation of the issues, styles, and points of divergence that make public contention and contest possible. (Gerbner, 1969, p. 138)

The point is not so much that cultivation occurs (it is after all the historic and universal function of all socio-cultural institutions and the stories they tell), but that the cultivation of collective consciousness is now institutionalized and corporately managed to an unprecedented degree. The critical issue is that the "dissolution of publics into markets for mass media conceived and conducted in the increasingly demanding framework of commodity merchandising is the cultural (and political) specter of our age" (Gerbner, 1958). For cultivation theorists, the political implications of this process were highlighted from the start:

The rise of cultural mass production, creating audiences, subjecting tastes, views, and desires to the laws of the market, and inherently tending toward the standardized and the safe rather than the diversified or critical, creates new problems in the theory and practice of self-government. (Gerbner, 1959, pp. 276–7)

Again, cultivation means that the dominant modes of cultural production tend to generate messages and representations which nourish and sustain the ideologies, perspectives, and practices of the institutions and cultural contexts from which they arise. This points to some important affinities between cultivation and the idea of hegemony (Stevenson, 1995) in ways that shed light on the still unresolved relationship between base and superstructure, given that television's feet are so firmly planted in both spheres. "Hegemony" (Gramsci, 1971) differs from overly deterministic theories of cultural production and control in the same way that cultivation differs from overly deterministic theories of media effects: the difference is that both hegemony and cultivation are theories of social management which allow for contradictions in social discourse, which do not assume that people are "duped" by cultural messages, and which do not presuppose "false consciousness." Like hegemony, cultivation is a theory of the power of culture over large social aggregates at the macro level, and not about how individuals think or behave.

In sum, cultivation research is concerned with the most general consequences of long-term exposure to centrally produced, commercially supported systems of stories. Cultivation analysis concentrates on the enduring and common consequences of growing up and living with television: the cultivation of stable, resistant and widely shared assumptions and conceptions reflecting the institutional characteristics and interests of the medium itself and the larger society.

Almost thirty years of message system analysis reveals a world defined by the prominent and stable over-representation of well-off white males in the prime of life. Women are outnumbered by men at a rate of two or three to one and allowed a narrower range of activities and opportunities. The dominant white males are more likely to commit violence, while old, young, female and minority characters are more likely to be victims. Crime in prime time is at least ten times as rampant as in the real world, and an average of about five acts of overt physical violence per hour involve well over half of all major characters.

Cultivation researchers have argued that these messages of power, dominance, segregation and victimization cultivate relatively restrictive and intolerant views regarding personal morality and freedoms, women's roles and minority rights. Rather than stimulating aggression, cultivation theory contends that heavy exposure to television violence cultivates insecurity, mistrust, and alienation and a willingness to accept potentially repressive measures in the name of security, all of which strengthens and helps maintain the prevailing hierarchy of social power.

In the next chapter, we tell the story of how these views emerged in the field of communication research. We describe the early message system work on television violence, and then show how this work led to the initial studies on cultivation. These studies provided a focal point for much of the intense debate in communication from the late 1960s right through to the early 1980s. They were among the most cited, most applauded *and* most criticized research endeavors associated with the study of mass media.

# 3    Methods of Cultivation and Early Empirical Work

## Overview

The earliest questions explored by cultivation analysis revolved around televised violence. Dozens (if not hundreds) of other studies have also, of course, dealt with this issue over several decades. Congressional investigations and hearings, boycott campaigns, debates over family viewing times, content ratings systems, and the V-chip, along with periodic news items about dramatic cases of apparently imitative violence have all kept public attention focused on the problem. As is evident today, these questions have never been adequately resolved. Partially this is because of the failure to acknowledge the implication of cultivation, which is that televised violence is not something that can be solved by tinkering with a few problem programs. Rather, the early research in cultivation argued that television has to do with lessons about social *power*. These lessons applied not only to violence but also to a broad range of interwoven issues that touch on race, gender and class.

But more than anything else, cultivation's early empirical research focused on how violent messages could be important to the social outlook of "heavy viewers." Issues such as "the mean world syndrome," mistrust, perceptions of who is victimized and who isn't, were all early concerns of cultivation research. This was a sea change from the focus of other research which had been rather exclusively placed upon documenting specific impacts, particularly the imitation or stimulation of violence. The heavily cognitive and experimental focus of much violence research had led most of the research community to conclude, indeed, that television does have impacts, but these were seen as the result of exposure to specific violent incidents. In contrast, cultivation took a more critical position by arguing that message *systems* also have impacts. While these are more broadly construed impacts, they are real, and they permit a critical analysis of television's messages, and the institutions that produce them, taken as a whole. This chapter summarizes these early studies. While many were flawed in some ways, they were seminal reports on the broad impacts of television in the social system, and among the first empirical demonstrations of the critical impacts of the message system of television.

## The Problem of Television and Violence

Like "Hansel and Gretel," "Mom and Apple Pie," or "Lennon and McCartney," the words "television" and "violence" are inextricably linked in the mind of the public. And with good reason; with violence occurring in approximately 70 percent of all broadcast network television programs, at a rate of about five violent acts per hour (more than twenty per hour on children's programs), and involving close to two-thirds of all major characters each week, even light viewers can have a difficult time avoiding substantial doses of symbolic mayhem. As has been so often noted, our children see about 10,000 acts of violence per year on television; by the time they graduate from high school, they will have witnessed about 18,000 violent deaths. These figures, promulgated by the American Medical Association and many others, may or may not be inflated, but violence is undeniably as much a staple of US television as is the laugh track or the commercial. Most recently, the "Mediascope" violence study found that 57 percent of programs contain violence, but that premium cable channels were far more violent (85 percent of programming was violent with the "highest risk of harmful effect," UCLA Center for Communication Policy, 1995).

Television violence serves both dramatic and commercial purposes. From Homer to Hitchcock, from Shakespeare to The Shadow, from Tolstoy to Tarentino, authors have used violence as a plot device to grab the audience and keep it attentive and fascinated. Within any given narrative, violence can generate excitement, build emotional tension, enhance a thrilling climax, and generally provide a satisfying vicarious experience for many in the audience. We enjoy our rituals and our formulas; justice triumphs, evil is punished, the good guy gets the girl, and all is right with the world (or not, which can also be quite effective, for novelty's sake).

Indeed, violence is a legitimate, effective, gripping, tried-and-true component of story-telling, and has (probably) been a reliable, stock narrative device in all cultures throughout history. Television certainly did not invent fictional violence; so why be concerned? After all, virtually any sampling of standard literary texts, modern or classical, would show that conflict and violence are necessary and perhaps mandatory components of interesting and compelling narratives.

The key difference is that television makes representations of violence far more pervasive, mundane, unremarkable, standardized and formulaic than has been the case with other media, in other cultures, or in other times. This is partly due to the fact that the amount of time we spend consuming mediated stories now is much greater than has ever historically been the case. To fill its day, television must tell a lot of stories, and violence can be a simple and efficient (and lazy and formulaic) way to develop or resolve a story within very tight time constraints (including constraints on production time). As a result, exposure to fictional violence – in portrayals which rarely depict the "real" physical consequences of violence – has become a daily ritual for millions of viewers.

Also, as Gerbner and other Cultural Indicators researchers have continually pointed out, *commercialized* violence is particularly problematic. When violence exists mostly to sell, and therefore merely to attract and hold audiences for a predetermined time, there is little visible constraint on the nature of violence shown other than that it must be sensational or formulaic (although there are many invisible constraints which serve purposes of social control). Though sensationalism is not itself new, television story-telling amplifies these tendencies.

Most fundamentally, then, violence exists on television for its assumed ability to draw sufficiently large (and demographically attractive) audiences that may be sold at a profit to advertisers. Violence also sells well on the international market, where crucial syndication profits are made; humor does not always cross cultural borders successfully, and violence can also reduce the expenses associated with dubbing dialogue into other languages. As Gerbner has pointed out, viewers do not by any means prefer violence to other types of programs (most of the popular programs on TV, for instance, are the less violent sitcoms), it's just that violence presents some economic advantages which are easily exploited in the international program market. These tendencies have been particularly evident in the feature film market over the years, but the increasing blurring of television and film economic boundaries means that over-the-air television is reflecting this dynamic even more.

Beyond attracting and keeping audiences interested, any effects that symbolic violence may have on viewers are largely unintended by those who write, direct, produce, act in, or otherwise make decisions about television. There is no "conspiracy" among programmers, writers and network executives to incite violence, to make our streets less safe, to breed mistrust, or to undermine anyone's standards of decency and morality. They simply are in the business of maximizing the corporate bottom line and shareholders' returns. Although we think that "elites" do encode their preferred messages into media material (in that messages reflect the priorities and interests of the institutions that produce them), we do not think this happens in intentional, conscious or devious ways.

But, this does not mean that the media business is just like any other, or that (in the cynical terms of Reagan's FCC Chairman Mark Fowler) television is just "a toaster with pictures." Governmental and network policy decisions about media licensing, ownership, content and so on, have profound social, cultural, political and economic impacts in this country and around the globe. Therefore, the functions and consequences of television violence are of immense social significance.

More often than not – and perhaps especially in the early 1970s, as cultivation analysis was germinating – public concern about television violence was driven by the fear that viewers (primarily children and adolescents, but occasionally "unbalanced" adults) would imitate what they saw, and would hurt or kill other people. Another worry was that young people would become jaded, unimpressed, bored and desensitized to violence both on television and in real life (which would require media violence to keep pushing the envelope, raising the body count and gore level).

Of course, these fears are nothing new: comic books in the 1950s, radio in the 1930s, pulp magazines and movies in the 1920s, and other storytellers in earlier centuries all have been targets of the same accusations. There is no narrative "golden age" in which all the stories were perfectly uplifting, original and self-expressive. But in the 1960s and 1970s, with real-world violence seeming to reach chaotic and near-psychotic levels, and with many fingers pointing at television, researchers dove in headfirst, conducting many dozens of laboratory studies that all played variations (some quite ingenious) on one basic theme: are subjects who are experimentally exposed to scenes of violence more likely to behave aggressively following that exposure than are others not so exposed?

These many studies (Surgeon General's Scientific Advisory Committee on Television and Social Behavior, 1972; Pearl, Bouthilet and Lazar, 1982) do indicate that seeing violent material *can* generate an immediate response in the form of aggressive behavior. There is disagreement over whether this stems from direct imitation, or from arousal, or from reducing viewers' inhibitions about behaving aggressively, or by way of other cognitive or emotional processes (and there is little sign that this continuing debate will be resolved soon). Whatever the mechanism, however, the intrinsic qualities of the experimental design mean that these results cannot be simply mapped on to the real world.

Let us explain why findings from experimental research are usually of limited relevance to cultivation analysis. For one thing, psychological experiments are usually carried out under conditions that do not approximate real-world viewing; outside the lab, people watch for hours at a time, intermittently, often in a social or family context (providing both distraction and reinforcement), whereas in the lab isolated subjects are usually exposed to brief, specially selected program fragments. The aggressive behaviors that serve as dependent variables do not (for obvious ethical reasons) correspond well to the serious types of criminal and violent actions with which the public is concerned. In other words, the "effects" examined are usually short-term, immediate changes in behavior following exposure to short clips; in the real world, people see hundreds and thousands of violent acts over long periods of time. In the real world, viewers are not usually given the opportunity to engage in direct imitation of what they have seen, and other behavioral factors (such as the possibility of reprisal, often present in reality) are rarely included in the lab. This is not a blanket criticism or rejection of psychological, laboratory-based research, which has indeed made some very important contributions to cultivation research (see Chapter 8); it just shows that television is a complex social institution, and watching it is a complex social practice. This complexity escapes many tempting attempts to limit and define it according to more convenient or conventional methodological strictures.

Still, the external and predictive validity of experimental results has been strengthened by much survey research reporting positive associations between amount of everyday exposure to television violence and aggression among adolescents. These relationships generally withstand controls for social class, sex, school achievement and other factors. Some studies have found that violence viewing in childhood relates to aggression ten or more years later (Huesmann and Eron, 1986). Only one major survey study (conducted by NBC; Milavsky et al., 1982) did not find comparable results. Altogether, a fairly massive body of experimental and survey research does demonstrate that television violence is not merely a source of harmless (or, as some have claimed, even beneficial) catharsis (Bandura, 1965; Centerwall, 1993; Liebert, 1982; McLeod, Atkin, & Chaffee, 1972a, b); the weight of evidence has for some time indicated that children and adolescents who see more television violence are more likely to behave more aggressively. But what does this mean for most viewers, most of the time?

## Enter Cultivation

Stepping away somewhat from the conventional discourse of public concern and academic research, Gerbner and Gross (1976) argued that television violence may generate critical repercussions that go beyond the stimulation of individual aggression. Gerbner blended European ideas about social criticism and theory with American techniques of empirical investigation (for a detailed examination of Gerbner's intellectual development, see Lent, 1995).

Gerbner and Gross pointed out that instances in which a serious act of violence appears to have been influenced by television are quite rare, even though those cases may receive a great deal of publicity. And although many children sometimes get riled up and pretend to act out the violent maneuvers of television super-combatants after (or while) viewing, that kind of imitation is usually at a relatively low level (see also Gerbner et al., 1979). Such unruly behavior may be annoying and unpleasant, but it is light-years removed from the kinds of serious social violence that demand remedial intervention.

Gerbner and Gross were not asserting that television violence has *no* disturbing behavioral after-effects. They granted that if even a tiny fraction of all real-world violence is "caused" by television, then when assessed over the entire population that still amounts to tragic human suffering and considerable social costs. The point is that a comfortable majority of the 90+ million Americans who sit down and watch several hours of television each evening are not subsequently driven to rob a bank or shoot or stab their neighbors. Most of the viewing public does not succumb to any temptation to pursue careers in criminal violence or terror. Nevertheless, living in a symbolic environment in which violence is so common and prominent may have other consequences, consequences that are simultaneously more subtle yet more far-reaching.

Given the amount of violence most viewers see on television, the amount of violence in society would be vastly higher if imitation were the most common and likely outcome; real-world violence would be a daily experience for all of us. If that were the situation there wouldn't be very much need for research. Nor is research needed to show that people do not generally nor directly imitate catastrophic and sociopathic instances of TV violence, whether cartoonish or serious, extravagant, gratuitous, gritty or ridiculous. Conceptually, moreover, the notion that viewing violence leads to violent behavior suffers from the oversimplified inadequacies of a linear, stimulus-response model of communication. Defining the potential "effects" of violence as only or primarily related to inciting aggression or threatening law and order has been a great media game that has insured that most violence studies, reports and hearings would be social and political dead ends. Most of the public and governmental debate about television violence constitutes a brilliant example of the adage that if people are preoccupied with the wrong question, you don't have to worry about the answer. In short, the primary hypothesis of most research on television violence is often nothing more than a political straw-person.

In contrast, the cultivation perspective approaches television violence in more general terms: as a dominant, integral aspect of the symbolic environment, playing a central role in enculturation and in the maintenance of the status quo. Gerbner et al. (1978, 1979) argued that television violence may more fruitfully be seen as a scenario depicting social relationships, as a *demonstration of power*, and perhaps most importantly as reflecting the power hierarchy of society and reproducing the social order.

The institutions of a society work overtime to maintain and protect the social structures and relationships which sustain them. Far from being "just a business," Gerbner and Gross argued that mass communication – with television as its mainstream – is the chief cultural arm of the existing socio-economic order. The primary social function of television (not to be confused with its primary personal function, which is a generally pleasurable mix of distraction, ritual, habit, relaxation and entertainment) is to reiterate, legitimize, sustain and uphold the established structures of power and authority.

When we look at television from this social rather than the more usual individual perspective, certain fears do not make sense anymore. Is it likely that the primary cultural manifestation of society's dominant economic and political interests would promote potentially disruptive, socially threatening endeavors? Not very. If television's messages encouraged wanton looting, destruction, rape and criminality, wouldn't that threaten the interests of the very elites who ultimately control media institutions? Why would the "ruling classes," who have the most to gain by keeping society as firmly cemented and controlled as possible, promulgate cultural materials that would tear apart the social fabric?

Unlikely as it seems when presented in such terms, this is indeed the doomsday scenario implied by those who see television violence *exclusively* as an antisocial phenomenon. Also, this may explain why public interest groups concerned with media violence can be so easily manipulated and dismissed: media industries take advantage of the fact that these groups fail to recognize that attention to lurid and graphic effects of media violence efficiently distracts us from looking at basic structural issues like media ownership and other factors limiting the dissemination of more democratic discourse.

Gerbner's perspective facilitated a different take on the issue. It becomes much easier to square the pervasiveness of television violence with the interests of dominant commercial and political institutions when symbolic violence (and, perhaps, television in general) is seen as a vehicle of *social control*. Cultivation theory casts television violence as a dramatic demonstration of power, as a material reflection of ideology, which communicates much about social norms and relationships, about winners and losers, about the risks of life and the price for transgression of society's rules. Symbolic violence vividly shows who can get away with what against whom. It tells us who are the aggressors and who are the victims.

Symbolic violence is a way for those *with* power to teach lessons *about* power: how to get it, how to have it, when it can be lost, when it can be used, and who can do so. And symbolic violence teaches these lessons in a fashion which most people see as innocuously entertaining. Again, as Gerbner has argued, one function of fiction and drama is to make visible and clear that which in the real world is often hidden, blurred or opaque. In the process, messages reflect and cultivate the terms on which they are premised. Violence is one convenient technique by which this is done, as it is a simple and cheap way for a system to demonstrate the rules of its game of power.

All this leads to a critical hypothesis of cultivation: if some people "learn" to be violent from watching television, then might not others learn to be *victims*? After all, there are more victims than aggressors in the television world; both roles are there to be learned by viewers. Apprehension, mistrust and fear of victimization may be more widespread and general (and subtle) impacts of television violence than occasional acts of imitative aggression. In this way, the fear that may be cultivated by symbolic violence may be an even more effective (and entertaining) mechanism of social control than actual violence.

So what's the problem? Society can be dangerous and violent, so why shouldn't people be concerned about being victimized? Should television hide the realities of violence from its audience? Probably a realist would answer "no." Yet, in important ways, that is exactly what television does; the leading causes of real-world injuries, highway and industrial accidents, can be curiously difficult to find in the symbolic world. Television violence has little to do with real-world violence but much to do with *real-world power*.

The problem is not simply one of individual psychology, i.e., that some people are made overly "paranoid" by television violence, with warped perceptions of their chances of being victimized that interfere with their ability to function as normal, productive members of society. Rather, the danger identified by cultivation is more on the aggregate social level. Gerbner and Gross reasoned that a heightened and widespread sense of fear, danger and apprehension can bolster demands for greater security; this in turn can mean greater legitimacy of the authority that can promise to meet those demands, creating conditions highly conducive to repression and undermining support for civil liberties. It can also mean greater acceptance of the use of violence as an appropriate means to solve disputes of international policy (as Lewis, Jhally and Morgan, 1991, found in the context of the Persian Gulf War), or greater habituation to violence and passivity in the face of injustice.

The problem is also, fundamentally, one of distribution. Decades of Cultural Indicators message system analyses show that those who have more power in society, in reality – such as white, middle/upper-class males in the prime of life – are more likely to inflict violence than to suffer it on television, compared to others who are less powerful in reality – women, minorities, old people – and whose ratio of violence received to violence committed is much greater. Overall, 130 characters are killed for every 100 killers (again, victims are more plentiful than are aggressors). But among African-American characters, 154 are killed for every 100 killers, and 200 Latinos are killed for every 100 who kill. Asian Americans, older people and women are also disproportionately victimized. Of course, television did not create these patterns of inequities, but it may play an important role in their survival (see Morgan, 1983).

Clearly, the implications of injecting massive amounts of violence into the symbolic environment go beyond the occasional sensational case of imitative aggression. The preponderance of victim roles may cultivate corresponding general perceptions of the likelihood of victimization and support for related protective measures; the exact distribution of those roles across the symbolic landscape may help perpetuate an unequal hierarchy of social power that many are working to reshape in more egalitarian and democratic ways.

In sum, cultivation's theoretical development did not and does not deny that instances of media-induced aggression do occur, nor does it deny that television might play a role in phenomena such as "desensitization" or "disinhibition" to violence. Indeed, specific psychological mechanisms showing relationships between message reception and processing might help explain how television audiences internalize power lessons. But the focus in cultivation is different than that found in most experimental or behavioral research. Cultivation frames the struggle over television violence in ideological and cultural terms, not merely as a question of what is "good" for children versus the alleged First Amendment "rights" of powerful corporations. Television violence cannot be separated from the medium's representations of gender, race, ethnicity, age, sexuality and class, as well as how it portrays the world of work, the "good life," the family, other countries and much more. That is, once again, why cultivation research sets its focus on the larger, aggregate level where everything is intertwined with everything else.

### Message Systems, Violence Indices, and other Assessments: Gerbner's Geiger Counter for the Television Background

Thus far we have argued that television's background is as important as its foreground, and that the messages within this background are fairly consistent and clear. But not everyone has accepted this premise, so we should spend some time looking at the evidence. Most of this evidence is found in the Cultural Indicators "message system analyses," which have been conducted on a yearly basis since 1967. The message system analyses are also a source of much of CI's infamy: most network executives and others interested in television's social role have been very familiar with Gerbner's message work over the years. Any empirical work is open to methodological criticism of course, and the message analyses attracted more than a healthy share. Beyond important debates over methodological choices, unfortunately, the message data have sometimes also been misunderstood, especially by those who think that CI, and cultivation in particular, are making the simple argument that television is too violent. Though a content analysis may on its own serve as a critique of television institutions, we would like to stress that the main purpose of a Cultural Indicators message system analysis is to establish how issues and people are portrayed on TV so as to facilitate cultivation analysis.

The "Violence Index" (VI) is perhaps the best-known product of the Cultural Indicators content studies. The VI is the cornerstone of the periodic "Violence Profiles" that monitor television's level of violence (Signorielli and Morgan, 1990). It was designed to provide a multidimensional descriptive cultural "indicator," sensitive to a variety of clear-cut criteria, which could highlight how the culture was doing in terms of various aspects of symbolic violence.

The Violence Index combines a few different measurements to provide an overall quick assessment of the level of violence in prime-time and weekend-daytime network television programs in any given year, across a variety of categories, and over time. The relatively simple formula sums five specific measures: the prevalence of violence in programs (expressed as a percentage of all programs in the sample with any violence), the rates of violent acts, both per hour and per program, plus the percentages of characters involved in violence and killing. Thus, the formula for the Violence Index (VI) is:

$$VI = \%P + 2RP + 2RH + \%C + \%K$$

where:

%P = Percentage of Programs with Violence
RP = Rate of Violent Acts per Program
RH = Rate of Violent Acts per Hour
%C = Percentage of Characters involved in Violence
%K = Percentage of Characters involved in Killing

The rate per hour measure corrects for variations in lengths of programs (i.e., a ten-minute cartoon versus a two-hour movie). The two rate coefficients are doubled because they are much smaller arithmetically than the others; doubling them increases the weight of their contribution to the Index. Analyses of the statistical properties of the Index revealed that its reliability was actually enhanced with this adjustment, compared to a variety of other possible manipulations (Signorielli et al., 1982).

The resulting value, for any given year, averages about 160 (ranging from 115 to 185 over the years), and simply provides a thumbnail account of the amount of violence in a given programming year. The number in and of itself has no intrinsic meaning, but it is useful for examining long-term trends and for making a variety of relative comparisons. That is, the number can be tracked over the years, over different types of programs (e.g., children's versus prime-time), over different networks, over different dayparts (e.g., before or after 9:00 pm), over different genres of programs (action adventure, situation comedy, etc.), and so on. Moreover, the components (which are directly interpretable) are always reported along with the composite Index score.

The periodic Violence Profiles tracked television violence more consis-tently and clearly than any research program before or since, and this consistency has, for many critics, slopped over into a perception of culti-vation as the "TV violence theory." Many tended to see Gerbner as a bean-counting "numbers guru" for TV violence, solely interested in totting up how many times cartoon characters were bopping each other over the head. But, the Violence Index is best seen as a *component* of the overall research program, of which violence was only one part. Thus, the most important conclusion about violence from the mountains of message system data was that violence levels do not change that much. Analyzing nearly twenty years of content data, Signorielli (1990) showed that variations in the VI are mostly random and insignificant. While the Index declines somewhat during years of acute attention to violence issues, it always pops back up later, showing that violence is an essential and resilient component of the TV message system.

It was this *consistency,* rather than merely the level of violence, that led cultivation researchers to adopt the view that, on issues of violence at least, television presented a fairly stable and coherent message system, rather than just a collection of discrete violent scenes and portrayals. The question was, did this consistency extend across issues other than the simple frequency of violence?

The answer is "yes," insofar as message system analyses have revealed a fair amount of consistency in patterns of victimization (socially disadvan-taged groups are more frequently victimized), in simple frequency of por-trayals of minorities (Gerbner's "diversity index" of the mid-late 1990s continues this tradition, comparing minority portrayals to population levels) and on a few other issues. Decades of message analyses also show stability in the demography of the TV world, in terms of the consistent under-representation of women, and the relative invisibility of older people and the working classes.

Thus, the most striking thing about the Cultural Indicators message system analyses was that they have revealed how little has changed in terms of the portrayal of violence and closely related issues. With all this in mind, it is important to remember that almost ten years of content analysis (including VI results) preceded the publication of the first culti-vation results on violence. The initial cultivation project was, as much as any other project before or since, grounded in extensive and detailed analysis of the television environment. The nearly three decades of accu-mulated descriptive data continue to inform the procedures and findings of newer cultivation projects.

### First Results

Building on the content data and the assumptions we have explored so far in this chapter, the first publications of cultivation results (e.g., Gerbner and Gross, 1976; Gerbner, et al., 1977) presented data suggesting that heavy viewers were more likely than light viewers to give "television answers" to survey questions about law enforcement, crime, trust and danger. They began by pointing out some blatant statistical discrepancies between the "real world" and the world as presented in prime-time network television (as revealed by the message system data); the patterns showed that television content was replete with images that exaggerated the prevalence of crime and violence well beyond their rate of occurrence in reality.

For example, 1970 US Census data showed that 1 percent of all working males had jobs in law enforcement and crime detection; in the world of work on television (from the content data), that figure was 12 percent. That is, television drama shows us a society with an over-abun-dance of cops, detectives and criminal lawyers (and again, note that this fact has changed very little across the years, showing consistency).

To see if television viewing contributes to people's conceptions of this particular aspect of social reality, the technique of "forced-error" ques-tions was used. These questions had two available responses: one response option – deemed the "TV answer" – was slanted more in the direction of the world of television, and the other choice was closer to "reality." So, survey respondents were asked whether the proportion of men so employed was closer to 5 percent (the TV answer), or closer to 1 percent (the real-world answer). The TV answer was lowered because it was thought that 12 percent would be considered ludicrously high, and respondents, always looking for a trick question or the "right" answer, would shy away from such a high figure; in contrast, 1 percent versus 5 percent seemed a more reasonable choice to offer.

The hypothesis, of course, was that if television viewing cultivates assumptions about the facts of life that reflect the medium's most recurrent portrayals, then heavy viewers should be more likely than light viewers to choose the higher number, i.e., to over-estimate how many people's jobs revolve around the pursuit and punishment of criminals. Sure enough, 50 percent of the light viewers, compared to 59 percent of the heavy viewers, gave the TV answer and said "five percent" (Gerbner and Gross, 1976). This difference – here, nine percentage points – was deemed the "cultivation differential" and was interpreted as indicating the difference that greater television viewing makes to a particular attitude, outlook or belief.

As another early example, Cultural Indicators message system data showed that almost two-thirds (64.4 percent) of the characters in prime-time and weekend-daytime network dramatic programs were involved in violence each week. In contrast, 1970 FBI data showed .32 violent crimes per 100 persons per *year*; 1973 police data placed the annual victimization rate at .41 per 100 persons (Gerbner and Gross, 1976). Even though such official figures may be grossly inaccurate and not strictly comparable to the message data, it is undeniable that, overall, one's chances of actually encountering violence in the USA are vastly lower than the risks faced by characters in the world of fictional television. In this case, respondents were asked if they thought if the number of people involved in violence each week was "closer to 1 in 10" (the TV answer) or "closer to 1 in 100." In this case, 39 percent of light viewers but 52 percent of heavy viewers gave the TV answer (1 in 10), a cultivation differential of + 13. Thus, as we see from these examples, cultivation research had begun to demonstrate that the pervasively violent TV portrayal of the world may have some relationship to how people see the world.

Yet, as always in life and in social science research, questions arose. For one thing, the validity of the "forced-error" question, where neither of the options offered is necessarily correct, was questioned by critics of cultivation. Potter (1994), for example, thinks they are "curious" and "puzzling." Presumably, the critics believed that respondents should have been given a choice between an absolutely correct number and an absolutely fictional one. Yet, these kinds of measures have a long and respected pedigree in social psychology (Hammond, 1948). Campbell (1950) provides a strong defense of the technique; he supports it not only on the basis of face validity but he also argues that it reveals systematic biases in ways that reflect "the essential practical meaning of attitude" (p. 19; see also Cook and Sellitz, 1964). Even if some respondents recognize that neither answer corresponds to "reality," it is their *relative* judgment which is interesting to cultivation researchers. Indeed, throughout cultivation research, there has been little attempt to establish that television figures prominently in respondents' absolute assessments of world-states, only that heavy viewers should be relatively more congruent to the TV worldview than light viewers.

In any case, the analysis involved more than the comparison of real-world and TV-world statistics. For example, similar patterns were found in terms of trust: when asked if "most people can be trusted," 48 percent of light viewers but 65 percent of heavy viewers responded that "You can't be too careful." From this confluence of evidence (and much more), the notion of the "Mean World Syndrome" was hatched, suggesting that television viewing cultivates a complex of outlooks which includes an exaggerated sense of victimization, gloom, apprehension, insecurity, anxiety and mistrust. Thus, violence was contexted as something more than just vicious entertainment: it had broader social functions to be served in promoting fear and distrust.

So, the differences between light and heavy viewers were noticeable, generally significant, and in the predicted direction. They were not enormous, but cultivation does not predict massive differences. One reason why cultivation differentials should be on the small side is that television exposure is so widespread among most of the population; even light viewers watch quite a bit, cumulatively, and interact daily with others who watch more. Indeed, statistically large "effects" would be suspect.

More importantly, variables that are powerful predictors of social beliefs and attitudes, such as race, education, income, gender and so on, are also typically closely associated with television in meaningful ways. For instance, higher income respondents and those with less education tend to watch TV less. Given this, it was recognized from the start that statistical controls were essential to sustain the inference that these patterns could be taken as evidence of cultivation: "The obvious objection arises that light and heavy viewers are different prior to – and aside from – television. Factors other than television may account for the difference" (Gerbner and Gross, 1976, p. 191). The most important of these were background factors that predict or determine both viewing levels and social conceptions (usually education level, occupational prestige and income, singly or in some combination), along with age, sex, race and other media use (e.g., newspaper reading, TV news viewing). As we shall see, many additional and non-demographic controls have been thrown into the mix over the years.

Therefore, following a classic "elaboration" strategy, these same percentage comparisons between light and heavy viewers were made *within* relatively homogeneous subgroups. With these factors controlled, cultivation differentials were compared for, say, those with and without a college education, males and females, and those under or over thirty years old (the former being seen in the mid-1970s as the first "television generation"). In most cases, the patterns were not affected very much by the implementation of controls; the baselines of the dependent variables were predictably higher or lower in different subgroups, and some groups showed weaker or stronger associations, but the general strength and direction of the cultivation differentials persisted. Certainly, the controls did not eliminate or explain away the associations.

All seemed simple and in order. Yet these apparently (and deceptively) straightforward patterns were soon to unleash a veritable firestorm of criticism, controversy and confusion. Every aspect of measurement, coding, sampling, controls, question wording, scaling, reliability, techniques of analysis, and more, were to come under intense scrutiny. With such a simple hypothesis and a straightforward set of results, one wonders why? In hindsight, we believe that cultivation research was striking some sensitive nerves. The stridency of some of the critics (as we will see) was high, given that cultivation was, at this early stage, advancing some rather commonsensical propositions. With the benefit of twenty years, we now see this as a political phenomenon. Cultivation was calling into question the political premises of much mainstream American media sociology and communication research (along with the prevailing wisdom about the "effects" of violence and how they should be studied, and long-cherished beliefs about the importance of selectivity, genre differences, and variations in individuals' interpretations). Thus, cultivation research, perhaps inevitably, "politicized" the debate on media effects. Along with the greater political stakes, the confrontational nature of the discourse increased.

This is not to say that the critics did not address important problems with the early cultivation work. But much more data appeared before the battles were to begin. Soon after these initial results were published, Violence Profiles 8 and 9 (Gerbner et al., 1977, 1978) extended the number of samples used, adding both secondary analysis of national survey databases (especially the General Social Survey, conducted by the National Opinion Research Center) and several convenience samples of adolescents, including a six-wave, three-year longitudinal panel study of junior and senior high school students from suburban/rural New Jersey. The range of dependent variables also expanded, to include approval of the use of violence; buying a dog, or a gun, or putting new locks on windows or doors, all for purposes of protection; feelings of anomie and alienation; and outlooks on international affairs (i.e., whether the USA should be active in world affairs, and whether it was expected that the USA would "fight in another war within the next ten years").

Around the same time, message system and/or cultivation analyses began to appear that focused on other issues besides violence. These included studies on sex-role stereotypes (Gross and Jeffries-Fox, 1978), political orientations (Jackson-Beeck, 1979), news (Gerbner and Signorielli, 1978), women and minorities (Gerbner and Signorielli, 1979), older people (Signorielli and Gerbner, 1978), and occupations (Jeffries-Fox and Signorielli, 1979). Ideas about international extensions and cross-cultural comparisons were also being developed (Gerbner, 1977).

Thus, in early cultivation research, the issue of violence generally received the most attention, but the most fundamental concerns in studies on all issues (including violence) revolved around the notion of social power. This point was sometimes lost (by both sides) in the battles that were soon to come. (It continues to be lost in some contemporary critiques.) Not only do those with power in society control the production and distribution of cultural stories, but the stories they tell reflect, express, and reproduce – i.e., cultivate – specific patterns of power in material ways. Thus, whether the issue at hand was violence, sex-role stereotypes, aging, occupations, or anything else, the real concern was with whether television helps maintain a social power hierarchy marked by an unequal distribution of resources, opportunities and security, differentiated according to gender, race, age and other key markers of "difference." Critiques that attack cultivation on only technical method-ological points usually deflect attention away from these larger issues of social power and cultural policy.

The early work was replete with the standard social science caveats and disclaimers. Still, some critics accused cultivation researchers of indulging in rhetorical excess and exaggerating television's impact. This despite the fact that, in terms of television's role in perpetuating a hierar-chy of social power, Gerbner et al. (1978) were careful "not to assert that television alone is responsible or necessarily decisive, only that it makes a contribution" to perpetuating an unequal social power hierarchy (p. 194). Important to this argument, as discussed in Chapter 1, the very notion of "causality" was explicitly rejected, as were models of "effects" that are more appropriate to experiments in the physical or biological sciences and which imply law-like, linear, stimulus-response conceptualizations. But the notion that television has a role to play in maintaining social power hierarchies is often interpreted as "effects." So the debate was joined on that basis.

Again, the preponderance of associations reported in the early studies remained statistically significant, even under controls. Gerbner et al. argued that cultivation relationships "usually cannot be explained by social or personal characteristics, although [those factors] make important contributions to baseline levels of criterion variables and to differences in the strength and intensity of television's apparent role in cultivating certain assumptions" (Gerbner et al., 1978, p. 195). In empirical terms, these early studies emphasized the extent to which associations between amount of viewing and various dependent variables held up across a wide variety of subgroups, while acknowledging the undeniably obvious fact that "television makes somewhat different contributions to the perspectives of different social groups" (p. 206). Yet, the phenomenon of these clear variations in the size (and sometimes in the direction) of cultivation differentials, along with developments in the ways in which controls were applied, would soon become springboards for fierce controversies.

# 4   Criticisms

Until 1978, public criticism of the Cultural Indicators project had mostly come from researchers who worked for the television industry, and was focused on various aspects of message system analysis. Not surprisingly, these critiques were directed at the definition and measurement of violence (industry critics thought the CI definition was too vague and too liberal), along with sample size, sample universe, reliability, validity, coding procedures, unitization and numerous related issues. Several lengthy colloquies ensued in the pages of the *Journal of Broadcasting* (see Coffin & Tuchman, 1972–73a, 1972–73b; Eleey, et al., 1972–73a, 1972–73b; Blank, 1977a, 1977b; Gerbner, et al., 1977a, 1977b). The industry had an obvious interest in discrediting the research, in wanting to declare that its estimates of the amount of violence on television were grossly overstated. So they focused on such issues as whether "comic" violence and "accidents" should be included (as if there are ever any "accidents" in fiction). At times, both sides adopted indignant and antagonistic tones, but these interchanges were mild in comparison with what was to come over cultivation.

By the late 1970s, the cultivation method was established as a strategy for assessing the contribution of television's messages to conceptions of issues relevant to social power. Not everyone interpreted it that way, however, and basic disagreements over what cultivation was saying began to contribute to a rising tide of discord, discussion and diatribe. We now turn our attention to some of the specific criticisms. Though some of these debates are now almost twenty years old, they have not yet been fully resolved, as many communication researchers still return to them when evaluating modern cultivation research.

## A "Humanistic" Critique

Newcomb (1978) started the ball rolling with what he called a "humanistic" critique of cultivation, based in part on alleged differences between a quantitative and qualitative approach. In effect, Newcomb anticipated some of the concepts and processes that concern contemporary cultural studies and semiotics in terms of the polysemy of media texts as sites where hegemonic meanings are enacted, negotiated, resisted or opposed. The issues he raised remain important to communication research today.

He argued that "violence" has had many meanings in US history and culture, and that all viewers do not interpret an act of violence in the same way. He defended the value of in-depth analysis of individual programs against the Cultural Indicators focus on aggregate patterns. Especially, he emphasized the role and extent of *differences* – differences in context, differences in programs, differences in viewers. These differences, he argued, mean that no program, much less *all* programs, can have a single invariant meaning that is unproblematically and "correctly" perceived by all audience members. That is, he questioned whether viewers would "get" the message that Gerbner and Gross (1976) claimed they should from exposure to television violence.

A moment of reflection on our own personal experiences with media texts will doubtless reveal that Newcomb's basic position is clearly correct. Symbols *are* complex, and the layers of meanings we generate and construct as we interact with them are multiple, varied, unpredictable and slippery. Nevertheless, there is nothing in Newcomb's view that contradicts or invalidates the basic precepts of cultivation. To say that audiences' interactions with media texts produce enormous diversity and complexity does not negate the possibility that there may be important commonalities and consistencies as well. To explore those commonalities, as cultivation does, is not to deny that there are indeed differences; similarly, the examination of differences need not (and, arguably, *can* not) deny the possibility of shared meanings in a culture. To glorify or privilege *only* the fact of polysemy is to risk removing any vestige of articulatory or determinational power from the text – and thereby to render culture impotent as well.

Indeed, the structure of semiotic systems themselves shows that communication is a multileveled phenomenon. There is nothing inherently contradictory in proposing that some of television's messages, while potentially producing a riot of individual and even intra-individual thoughts, perceptions and attentions, must eventually also be understood in some common ways. If not, our concepts of language, culture and communication are themselves sterile.

In response to Newcomb, Gerbner and Gross (1979) justified their focus on the broad similarities that cut across program types by arguing that programs are more like formulaic, market-driven, assembly-line products than like uniquely crafted works of individual expressive artists (although even "high" art, of course, must eventually be interpreted in terms of dominant cultural attitudes). Most of all, they pointed out that the relationships observed between amount of viewing and various beliefs are in themselves the test of whether the patterns and "meanings" inferred from message data are indeed absorbed by viewers at a broad, collective level. The imperfection of the cultivation relationships observed is, of course, itself a proof of the operation of individual readings. Thus, cultivation can and need not mean that every act of violence observed on television means the same thing to every viewer.

Potter has more recently reiterated Newcomb's position by asking how cultivation researchers can "be confident that their designated television world answer has taken into account all the factors" that influence viewers' inferences from television content (1993, p. 11). Obviously, they can't. Once again, the extent to which viewers internalize or absorb the arrays of facts and values in the manifest and relatively unambiguous patterns revealed by message system analysis is exactly what cultivation actually *tests*. The evidence to support the theoretical and interpretive assumption is simply assessed in the degree to which heavy viewers are more likely to give responses which are demonstrably emphasized in the television world. Taking "all the factors" into account is both impossible and beside the point.

Ultimately, then, "Newcomb's big question, 'what does violence mean to the respondents' is not only irrelevant but distracting" (Gerbner and Gross, 1979, p. 227). Individual texts and programs and individual variations in interpretation are interesting, valid and valuable things to study, but cultivation research is more concerned with the bucket of beliefs and conceptions within which individual and idiosyncratic interpretations are but drops. That is, cultivation is designed to illuminate broad patterns across large groups of people, not the fine textures of minute variations. The distinction is not "humanism" versus "social science" or even "qualitative" versus "quantitative"; more simply, it is nothing more than macro versus micro.

## A Challenge from Britain

Around the same time, Wober (1978) published the results of some British research (conducted by Gallup, and sponsored by the Independent Broadcasting Authority) that failed to replicate what he called the "paranoid effect of television." This was one of the first studies to be widely cited as an empirical disconfirmation of cultivation, and was the first of many cultivation-related studies based on IBA data that Wober authored. The apparent lack of evidence for cultivation in Wober's data may reflect important cultural and structural differences between the

United States and Great Britain; British heavy viewers see less violence than do US light viewers (Pingree and Hawkins, 1981) and the institutional mechanisms and controls of British television ensure a more diversified and balanced flow of media messages that are not driven entirely by commercial interests (Wober and Gunter, 1988). If this is the case, then this study may actually strengthen the case for cultivation in the US context, since exposure to a message system less dominated by violence indeed should not cultivate a heightened sense of apprehension and mistrust. That heavy exposure to largely nonviolent television did not turn out to have a "paranoid effect on viewers" should not be seen as especially damaging to the idea of cultivation.

Also, Wober measured beliefs about fear and violence differently than the Cultural Indicators team. In order to gauge the so-called "paranoid effect," Wober used a "security scale" compiled from the following two survey items:

– How unsafe do you feel? During the next year, how likely is it that you will be robbed? (Extremely/very/fairly/not very/not at all likely)

– How trustworthy do you think people are? Out of 10 people chosen at random, how many do you think you could trust? (Any number, 0–10)

The two items were added together: "the scale therefore runs from 1 (least secure – trusts nobody and feels extremely likely to be robbed) to 15 (most secure)" (Wober, 1978, p. 319).

At first glance, this scale may appear to be a reasonable approximation of the kind of Mean World indicators employed by Gerbner et al. It is, however, marred by some technical, methodological and conceptual flaws that should be considered. First, the two items have very different response scales (five points versus eleven points); because they are simply added together, the second variable is in effect assigned double the weight of the first, skewing the scale much more in favor of the second variable. Also, the question that focuses on robbery is a bit difficult to reconcile with questions from early US cultivation research, which focused on perceptions of violence in general; and no message data were invoked to demonstrate that robbery is highly over-represented on British television.

More importantly, the combined scale blurs two phenomena that are conceptually rather different. On the one hand, we have respondents' perceptions of the *likelihood* of their being victimized (i.e., how likely they feel it is that they will be robbed). But they are also asked to express the extent to which they have an explicit *fear* of being victimized, in terms of apprehension for their own personal safety (how "unsafe" they feel). This is not mere hair-splitting; subsequent research often showed these to be two distinct dimensions that are related to amount of viewing in different ways (Gerbner et al., 1981b; Pingree and Hawkins, 1981; Sparkes and Ogles, 1990; Wakshlag, Viol and Tamborini, 1983). Here, combining them may well have obscured differential patterns of association with viewing levels.

Most of all, as Neville (1980) pointed out, Wober's own data show that the working classes scored *higher* on this "security scale" (i.e., they expressed greater feelings of security than did the upper classes), a finding which runs directly contrary to previous social stratification research and which creates great doubt as to the meaning and validity of this measure.

Of course, virtually all survey research can be criticized for these kinds of measurement uncertainties. Yet, one further critical problem may be at work here. The data were collected under the auspices of the Independent Broadcasting Authority and the survey was presented to respondents as being about "Attitudes to Broadcasting." Thus, from the start, the interview said "television" all over it. Is this a problem? Gerbner and his colleagues have always been careful not to introduce the notion of "television" in any way before respondents are asked about their conceptions of social reality (Gerbner and Gross, 1976; Gerbner et al., 1994); if they have any control over the survey instrument, "television" is never mentioned in any way until the viewing measures are reached late in the questionnaire or interview. The concern is that *any* prior mention of television may either subtly invoke some of the medium's images in respondents' minds when they answer the social reality questions, or sensitize them to the purposes of the study.

Others besides Wober have put their data at risk in this way. Rubin et al. (1988) told respondents "that the study concerned television viewing and communication with others" (p. 129). Weaver and Wakshlag (1986) started off their questionnaire with a television viewing diary, and then presented respondents with a battery of fourteen crime-related items. Potter has published many papers which purport to provide persuasive critiques of cultivation, but he used data that came from a survey entitled "Estimations of TV and Society" (e.g., Potter, 1991a, 1991b). In all these cases, the validity and import of the data, regardless of what they may suggest about cultivation, may be reduced accordingly. In our meta-analysis, we treat such "contamination" as a variable across studies, to see to what extent it has produced differences in reported cultivation results.

## Spuriousness or Specification?

The next major critique to appear after Wober's was Doob and Macdonald's (1979) study of the role of neighborhood crime rates in the cultivation process. The conclusions from their research have been cited many dozens of times; Tamborini and Choi suggested that it may even be "the most widely cited research challenging the cultivation hypothesis" (1990, p. 168). Yet, unwittingly or not, most scholars who have dealt with this research have misinterpreted the study's actual findings. To this day, Doob and Macdonald are routinely invoked as having demonstrated that the relationship between television exposure and "fear of crime" is spurious, an artifact of actual neighborhood crime levels. In fact, their data show nothing of the sort.

The hypothesis developed by Doob and MacDonald is conceptually appealing. Perhaps, they reasoned, people who live in high crime and/or urban areas are more afraid of crime because of where they live, and this would also lead them to spend more time indoors – where they would be more likely to watch television. That is, heavy viewers may be more fearful precisely because they live in objectively more violent and dangerous environments. Accordingly, the researchers drew samples from four areas of metropolitan Toronto: high crime/city, high crime/suburb, low crime/city, and low crime/suburb. The rationale, of course, was that if the relationship between television exposure and perceptions of violence was actually due to neighborhood crime level, then controlling for that "third variable" would explain away the association, such that "within neighborhoods . . . the effect should be substantially reduced or eliminated" (Doob and Macdonald, 1979, p. 171).

Respondents were given a newspaper listing of all available TV programs and asked which ones they had watched during the previous week. This question came first in the interview; as noted above, this may sensitize respondents in ways that can contaminate the data. The measure reflects the total number of programs seen the previous week, not the amount of time usually spent viewing. In any case, respondents were then asked thirty-four closed-ended questions dealing with a variety of issues related to their perceptions of crime, violence, danger and victimization. Factor analysis isolated nine of these items (out of the thirty-four) as representing the statistically dominant dimension, and the authors interpreted the resulting index as one measuring "fear of crime."

Overall, the fear of crime index and the television program measure were significantly correlated ($r = .18$, $p < .01$). The correlations varied widely across neighborhoods, however, as seen in Table 4.1.

Two things are especially noteworthy about these data. First, the relationship is *magnified* (and significant) in the high crime/city area; the relationship between television viewing (although weakly measured) and "fear of crime" is sharper and more pronounced among people who live in high crime urban areas. Second, the relationship in the high crime/suburban area ($r = .16$) is essentially the same as it is in the overall sample

Table 4.1 *Fear of crime findings (Doob and Macdonald, 1979)*

|           | High crime        | Low crime          |
|-----------|-------------------|--------------------|
| City      | 0.24* (N = 83)    | −0.06  (N = 71)    |
| Suburb    | 0.16  (N = 69)    | −0.09  (N = 77)    |

*Note:*
* = p < 0.05

(where $r = .18$), but it fails to reach significance because of the greatly reduced sample size (there are only sixty-nine people in this cell).

Doob and MacDonald did note, in passing, that the relationship held up in the high crime urban area, but they claimed that it disappeared in the other three (including the high crime suburb, according to them; p. 173). Most of all, they emphasized that the average of these four within-area correlations was only .09. On the basis of this averaged correlation, they concluded that "there is essentially no relationship between media usage and fear of crime when the effect of neighborhood is removed" (p. 173).

Their assertions, however, are wrong. The arithmetic average of the four within-neighborhood correlations is not the same as a partial correlation of amount of viewing and fear of crime with the effects of neighborhood "removed" (which could have been done by transforming nominal variables into dummy variables). The averaged coefficient is non-meaningful and misleading here; it suggests that the subgroup correlations average near zero when in fact they vary a great deal. Working from the above coefficients, r-to-z transformations show a significant difference between the two extreme correlations (i.e., the high crime/city and low crime/suburb; $z = 2.04$, $p = .02$), and a nearly significant difference in the correlations for the high versus low crime suburbs ($z = 1.48$, $p = .07$). The associations within the high crime areas, therefore, are reliably different from what was found in the low crime suburb; throwing them all into the same averaged pot masks this important difference. In contrast to the way these findings are usually presented, these data do not show a spurious association; if they did, the relationships would be essentially zero in all four areas. Instead, they show a theoretically vital *specification* – although the relationship disappears or is even reversed in the low crime areas, it persists or is even boosted in the high crime areas.

Gerbner et al. (1980a) interpreted the stronger association between television viewing and fear of crime among residents of the high crime urban area as an example of "resonance." Television's messages about violence may be most congruent with the lived worlds of residents of high crime areas; for them, television's images may "resonate" with everyday reality, producing a "double dose" of complementary messages, and thereby amplifying cultivation. Television's messages are not consumed in a vacuum; cultivation takes shape in the context of a wide range of personal, social, family and other factors. Television should be least influential where the realities of that context provide first-hand, unmediated, steady flows of contrary information. By the same token, when there is either no conflict or when one's environment reinforces ("resonates with") the television view of things, then exposure may make an even stronger contribution.

There may well be other explanations for these subgroup variations; the point we cannot stress enough is that Doob and Macdonald did *not* show that neighborhood crime rates *account for* the relationship between amount of viewing and fear of crime. The within-group correlations between viewing and fear were not reduced to zero; thus we see that neighborhood *mediated* the relationship. This difference between spuriousness and specification is crucial, and will come up again in other critiques.

Also, the conceptual distinction we noted above, between (a) general estimations of the amount of violence in society and (b) explicit personal fear of being victimized, plays an important role in this study. Most authors who cite Doob and Macdonald's evidence of spuriousness tend to forget that the fear of crime index only included nine of their thirty-four items. But later in their article, Doob and Macdonald also report that for fourteen of the remaining twenty-five items, significant pooled (overall) correlations with amount of viewing remained significant and/or comparable in magnitude even when averaged across the four types of areas. Why the difference? These other items were seen as dealing with "matters of a more factual nature" (p. 179) than personal fear levels; Doob and Macdonald attempt to reconcile the two sets of findings by noting that television "may well act as a source of information with regard to questions of fact, whereas it does not change people's views of how afraid they should be" (p. 179). In terms used elsewhere, they were in effect claiming they found evidence for "first-order" cultivation but not for "second-order." Regardless, this conclusion is wholly congruent with cultivation theory, which posits that television will teach us societal-level lessons about what "the world" is like, but not necessarily impact our perceptions of our own personal reality, where a much wider range of influences and everyday non-mediated experiences may play a stronger role (see also Tyler and Cook, 1984).

Doob and Macdonald did not present the within-neighborhood correlations for these fourteen other items; all we are given is the overall and the average of the four within-area correlations. Therefore, unfortunately, we cannot tell if these items produce resonance patterns between neighborhoods as well. Also, no controls at all were implemented with these other items. (The fear of crime index was also examined in regression analyses which included sex, age and other media use, although controls were never applied *within* each neighborhood.) This limits what we can say about the results for these other items, but does not in any way diminish this critical point: the results for the "factual" items go sharply *against* the most-often cited version of this study's findings (that neighborhood crime rates show cultivation to be spurious), even using the authors' own criterion of the averaged correlations. It should also be noted that this study took place in Toronto, Canada, so its relevance to the USA is uncertain.

Despite these problems, Doob and Macdonald produced an intriguing, innovative and provocative study that helped develop general awareness of the fact that cultivation patterns can vary significantly across subgroups. It also specifically contributed to the formulation of "resonance" as one model for what differential subgroup patterns might look like. Yet, despite the way it has gone down in history, it should be clear that the study did *not* demonstrate that cultivation patterns are the spurious result of neighborhood crime rates. Thus, as with Wober's work, we contend that it should not be construed as disconfirming cultivation.

### Measurement Artifacts

One other study from the 1970s should be mentioned, because it points to some methodological problems that continued to plague later efforts. Fox and Philliber (1978) examined how television viewing contributed to perceptions of affluence in a sample of 595 adults in greater Cincinnati. The rationale was that since television over-represents wealth, high status occupations and the privileged classes, heavy viewers could be expected to over-estimate the degree of affluence in society.

Respondents were asked seven open-ended questions inquiring "how many Americans out of 100" own a luxury car, belong to a country club, can afford a built-in swimming pool and so on. A significant relationship with amount of viewing was found (heavy viewers gave higher estimates of affluence), but the association was eliminated by controls for income, occupational status and (especially) education. Perceptions of the veracity of television (i.e., perceived realism) had no noticeable impact on the relationship. Fox and Philliber concluded that after social class is taken into account, television viewing has nothing to do with people's perceptions of affluence.

There are two problems, however, which call this conclusion into question. First, they measured amount of viewing by asking, "On the average, how many evenings a week do you watch TV at least one hour?" (p. 107). This is, it should be obvious, a very weak measure, if only because it provides no way to differentiate between "regular" and "heavy" viewers. Moreover, someone who watches four hours a night, six days a week, would be classified as a medium viewer, while someone who watches an hour every night would be classified as heavy. Also, the fact that the data were collected during the spring *and* summer may mean that normal seasonal fluctuations in viewing levels (during the two seasons when amount of viewing is at its lowest) account in part for whether one was categorized as a light, medium or heavy viewer. This is measurement noise beyond the usual.

More problematic, though not at first blush, is the nature of their dependent variables, which were based on open-ended percentages. The seven items are clearly reliable, in terms of internal consistency; they produce a Cronbach's alpha of .85. But we are skeptical of the *validity* of this type of measure. Unpublished, internal Cultural Indicators staff documents, describing data from a telephone survey of 355 adults in Philadelphia conducted in 1978, determined that to ask people such open-ended percentage questions is to ask for trouble. The respondents were asked what proportion of the population are children, elderly, nonwhites, teachers, women, police, judges and professionals, as well as what percent of the population fit into each of four income categories (a total of twelve items). The resulting matrix of sixty-six correlations revealed a striking pattern: all of the coefficients were positive, sizable (more than fifty of them exceeded .30), and only three were not significant. If people were responding in a valid way to the manifest content of these items, then few of them would be related. Yet, estimates of the percentage of the population comprised of "teachers" and "police" correlated at .71, and estimates of "children" and "judges" correlated at .42. Even the correlation between estimates of the percentage in the lowest and highest income levels was .36.

We can envision only one reason why all of these distinct estimates are so inter-related: that is, they simply tap a tendency to give consistently high (or low) responses to open-ended percentage items. (And they do so quite reliably; the alpha for these twelve items was .87 – even higher than Fox and Philliber's). These kinds of measures, then, seem to reflect little more than the systematic tendency to exaggerate proportions that are elicited by open-ended questions without baselines. People with less education respond with higher percentages across-the-board. So do heavy viewers; they give higher estimates of the proportion of the population that are very young *and* very old, and they give higher percentages for the proportion of people in *every* income category. It is therefore quite reasonable (and unremarkable) that controlling for education eliminates the relationship of such variables with amount of viewing (but not always; see Hawkins et al., 1987).

The relationship – and the explanation of spuriousness – therefore applies to the tendency to answer with high percentages, *not* necessarily to perceptions of affluence. This artifact might have been apparent if Fox and Philliber had also asked about how many Americans out of 100 are on welfare, receive food stamps, are below the poverty level, can't pay the rent and so on. This could have allowed them to evaluate the validity of their measure (assuming that higher perceptions of affluence would indeed imply lower perceptions of poverty, if we have to add up to 100 percent). Indeed, Shrum et al. (1991) found that viewing was positively related both to estimates of the percentage of Americans who are millionaires and to estimates of the percentage who earn less than $15,000 a year. In all probability, Fox and Philliber's heavy viewers would have also given higher estimates on perceptions of poverty; equally likely, education would have eliminated that association as well. Without counter-balancing poverty measures, of course, we cannot say for sure. However, the pattern in the Philadelphia data is unmistakably strong and persuasive. Discrete, conceptually independent open-ended percentage items are in fact highly inter-correlated, which suggests that such measures have low validity.

Many studies (e.g., Carveth and Alexander, 1985; Potter, 1986, 1988, 1991b; Potter and Chang, 1990) have used these problematic measures. Potter (1993) explicitly urged researchers to use them, and even refers to Fox and Philliber's items as an example of "good scaling"; ignoring their weak validity, he assumes that the unidimensionality and internal homogeneity of the seven items mean they are "a consistent measure of an underlying factor of perceptions of affluence" (p. 14). Most recently, Carlson (1993) has directly adopted Fox and Philliber's measure, with predictable results: a highly reliable index (alpha = .87) and failure to support the cultivation hypothesis for affluence. Using a forced choice scale to measure support for "capitalist values," however, Carlson found support for cultivation.

All these (and other) early critiques from the 1970s are still, at the end of the 1990s, often cited as having provided credible, definitive disconfirmations of the cultivation hypothesis. Yet, as our discussion should demonstrate, these efforts had as many conceptual, methodological, and analytical drawbacks as the studies they are alleged to refute. We are not playing fast and loose with double negatives here; pointing out the limitations and flaws in these critiques does not, by implication, necessarily lend greater credence to those studies that produced evidence supportive of cultivation. Rather, our point is simply that the case against cultivation is not convincingly made by any of these studies. Yet the research community of the time was fairly speedy in its acceptance of these rebuttals to cultivation, as a barrage of further critiques soon emerged.

## The Early 1980s

Sparked by the regular publication of cultivation findings in dependably annual Violence Profiles, and building on the momentum generated by the critiques discussed above, the research discourse of the 1980s cast cultivation into a massive wave of replications, attacks, responses and rejoinders. There were some independent confirmations of cultivation results and some extensions into other issues and methods (e.g., Bryant et al., 1981; Buerkel-Rothfuss and Mayes, 1981; Haney and Manzolati, 1981; Volgy and Schwarz, 1980), and many dissertations and unpublished reports (some are discussed in Gerbner et al., 1980a; Hawkins and Pingree, 1982) were helping to enlarge the literature base of cultivation. There was also some "friendly" criticism, offered by researchers who were generally sympathetic to cultivation but who felt it would benefit from various theoretical and methodological modifications. These included issues such as whether cultivation should use overall viewing measures or exposure to specific types of programs, and the role of perceived reality (Hawkins and Pingree, 1980, 1981; Slater and Elliott, 1982).

Then came the well-known reanalyses by Hughes (1980) and Hirsch (1980, 1981a) of NORC data which had been analyzed and reported in Violence Profiles 8 and 9 (Gerbner et al., 1977, 1978). Hirsch's reanalyses in particular led to fierce, prolonged battles, occasionally acrimonious and vituperative. The controversies consumed literally hundreds of pages of scholarly journals; the repercussions were felt at academic conferences and even spilled over into such popular media as *Time* magazine.

These battles have been characterized as everything from healthy scholarly exchanges to scathing exposés to vicious and unprofessional spats. Regardless, they attest to the timely prominence of cultivation theory and to the fact that cultivation analysis was not a static research approach, but one that evolved and developed in numerous ways, making it more complex and intricate but also more dynamic and intriguing. The conflicts also produced significant new issues and questions for cultivation analysis, many of which were still being developed and pursued a decade and a half later (cf. Tapper, 1995).

Why all the fighting? We cannot review all the charges and counterarguments in detail here, but it seems safe to say that the most fundamental issues of contention revolved around questions of spuriousness and the proper use of statistical controls. The majority of early published cultivation findings took the form of percentage comparisons, shown across light, medium and heavy viewers, overall, and within key demographic subgroups – and the subgroups were examined one at a time. That is, the results were presented for males, older people, those with less education and so on, separately. There were some exceptions; partial correlations with multiple simultaneous controls were used as early as Violence Profile No. 8 (Gerbner et al., 1977). But the majority of results were presented in simple cross-tabular form, in single subgroups (i.e., controlling for one "third" variable at a time).

Not surprisingly, numerous researchers soon began taking another look at the publicly available NORC General Social Surveys, trying out other techniques and data manipulations and bringing in other dependent variables and controls. All at around the same time, Hughes, Hirsch, the Cultural Indicators research team and others (e.g., Stevens, 1980) were independently finding that many of the relationships reported earlier using NORC data looked quite different under multiple controls applied at the same time.

In retrospect, the fact that earlier cultivation studies did not routinely report simultaneous multiple controls was indeed a problem, but this did not stem from any attempt to misportray data. The comparison of patterns across single subgroups was emphasized because it is simple, comprehensible and informative. Most importantly, it clearly illustrates the relative baselines and the relative "effect size" (i.e., cultivation differentials) across subgroups, in intuitive terms. Above all, it is perhaps the only way for the analyst to "see" the basic patterns. As Potter (1991b) notes, simple percentages can reveal powerful effects that multivariate coefficients can obscure. They do not tell the whole story, of course, but they are remarkably useful for depicting and elaborating the general shape and contours of relationships.

Still, various reanalyses of the NORC data, including those performed by Cultural Indicators researchers, all came to essentially the same conclusion: the application of multiple simultaneous controls (i.e., controlling for age, sex, education and so on, all at once) tended to reduce or completely eliminate relationships that had appeared between amount of viewing and a variety of dependent variables and that held up in subgroups examined one at a time. (Hughes also brought in additional controls, such as church attendance, club membership and hours worked per week.) The general interpretation was that it was insufficient to report that a given relationship held up under a series of controls applied one at a time; it could be that each individual control explained only a small portion of the apparent relationship, and all controls applied together would make an association disappear. This is in fact what the reanalyses purported to show, and led some investigators to conclude that cultivation relationships were spurious, mere artifacts of co-variation of demographic controls with both amount of viewing and dependent variables.

There are two problems with this conclusion. First, not all cultivation relationships were rendered spurious by such controls. Second, that conclusion does not recognize that relationships may persist *within* subgroups. As Hawkins and Pingree (1982) note, the application of multiple controls "may mislead us by removing relationships that are *conditional* on third variables" (p. 236, emphasis in original). This was the essence of Gerbner et al.'s rebuttal to these reanalyses; simply, if an overall relationship disappears under multiple (or even single) controls, that does *not* mean that there are no non-spurious and theoretically meaningful associations *within* specific subgroups (Gerbner et al., 1980a, 1980b, 1981a, 1981b, 1981c). Thus, "wholesale controlling can obfuscate potential conditional relationships" (Hawkins and Pingree, 1982, p. 246).

As noted, early cultivation research had emphasized the widespread and shared nature of television viewing. Clearly, the best-case support for cultivation theory would be a sample-wide relationship between viewing and a given dependent variable. But there was little problem in adapting to the notion that television viewing, while still a macrosocial behavior, could produce different consequences in social groups which differed for a variety of other reasons. Early on, variations in the magnitude and even the direction of the associations across groups were noted, without any clear interpretive model, but as a phenomenon deserving more attention. Again, a broad range of demographic, social and personal factors shape our experiences with television and how we relate to its content; they also impact on our conceptions of social reality. Given the complex nature of most social processes, it was inevitable that these issues would emerge in cultivation analysis.

This discovery (that relationships may persist in certain subgroups even where they seem to disappear under multiple controls for a sample as a whole) had profound conceptual and analytical implications for cultivation theory, and ultimately led to important refinements and enhancements. The most central of these was the idea of "mainstreaming," first noted in research relating to conceptions about sex-roles (Signorielli,

1979). Briefly, it was observed that differential cultivation associations across subgroups often took on a particular pattern, such that the relationship held up for the subgroup that "otherwise" (i.e., as light viewers) was least likely to give the "television answer." For example, as a group, less educated people showed no relationship between amount of viewing and scores on the "mean world" index of interpersonal mistrust; their scores were high regardless of amount of viewing. But a significant relationship persisted for those with more education, even under (within-group) multiple simultaneous controls. More educated people scored lower on the mean world index *unless* they were heavy viewers. Among heavy viewers, the impact of education was reduced, and the responses of people with more education "converged" with the responses of those with less education.

Thus, mainstreaming means that heavy viewing may absorb or override differences in perspectives and behavior which ordinarily stem from other factors and influences. Differences found in the responses of different groups of viewers, differences that usually are associated with the varied cultural, social and political characteristics of these groups, are diminished in the responses of heavy viewers in these same groups. As a process, mainstreaming represents the theoretical elaboration and empirical verification of the argument that television will cultivate common perspectives. It represents a relative homogenization, an absorption of divergent views, and an apparent convergence of disparate outlooks upon the overarching patterns of the television world.

Conceptually, the idea of mainstreaming helped elaborate the view of cultivation as a "gravitational," rather than a unidirectional, process. The angle and direction of the "pull" depends on where groups of viewers and their styles of life are with reference to the center of gravity, the "mainstream" of the world of television. The enormous diversity of potential subgroups and their differential relevance for specific dependent variables makes it difficult, if not impossible, to predict *a priori* precisely where and when mainstreaming will occur (Cook, Kendzierski and Thomas, 1983). This is not necessarily a problem, as some have alleged (Tapper, 1995), since general mainstreaming expectations can be formulated and tested in numerous areas (Gerbner et al., 1982, 1994; Morgan, 1986; Morgan and Shanahan, 1995; Shanahan, 1995; Signorielli and Morgan, 1990). This question is addressed in more detail Chapter 7.

Mainstreaming is not the only potential interaction pattern (Gerbner et al., 1981b, 1994); again, the results of Doob and Macdonald (1979) were interpreted as an example of "resonance," where television's messages may have a special salience for some subgroup (Gerbner et al., 1980a). But mainstreaming is by far the most commonly observed, and it has been found in studies dealing with political orientations in the USA (Gerbner et al., 1982) and in other countries (Morgan and Shanahan, 1995; Piepe, Charlton and Morey, 1990), as well as in studies of sex-role stereotypes, interpersonal mistrust, health, science and other issues (Gerbner et al., 1994).

But Hirsch's criticisms of cultivation theory were not muted by the introduction of the notion of mainstreaming, as he accused Gerbner et al. of "distorting scientific reality" (1980, p. 418) in their failure to properly report and analyze data. Hirsch charged that mainstreaming was nothing more than a *post hoc* refusal to let cultivation be falsified: "Each reformulation has been announced as a 'refinement' of the basic argument, rather than as a qualification or admission of earlier error and overstatement" (1981a, pp. 4–5). He attacked mainstreaming as pseudo-science, saying that the ideas presented in the CI team's responses were "irrefutable and untestable" (1981a, p. 5). He felt that cultivation theorists ought to have predicted which groups specifically would be likely to manifest stronger cultivation, something that was not done in the data to which he originally responded. Related to this, he saw mainstreaming as a "peculiar" type of "post hoc proposition" that "converts the statistical artifacts of ceiling effects and regressions toward the mean . . . into a statement of support for findings counter to predictions from the Violence Profiles' content analyses" (1981a, p. 25).

The debate was indeed acrimonious. Gerbner et al. and Hirsch traded accusations a few times until the debate cut itself off. Gerbner et al. cried that "We are particularly affronted by Hirsch's insinuation that we have intentionally misreported data" (1981b, p. 54), and they wondered "what compels the gleeful and sarcastic hostility in Hirsch's two pieces? . . . Hirsch's vituperations are embarrassing, unbecoming, and serve no scientific purpose; we regret if he has provoked harsh treatment from us" (1981b, p. 68). Hirsch himself charged that the researchers had failed to learn from their own mistakes, that they used proprietary surveys so as to hide data from the research community, and that they impugned the quality of GSS data, among other allegations.

Many of Hirsch's specific claims and the responses from the Annenberg team are tangential to the essential issue, which has to do with whether mainstreaming and other specification patterns are legitimate theoretical formulations or simply *post hoc* defenses against an overpowering critique. Although we deal with mainstreaming in more detail in Chapter 5, we note here that some early cultivation research dealt with this dispute in ways that might have answered Hirsch's critique. For instance, Hirsch argued that Gerbner et al. had failed to demonstrate any relationship between victimization on TV and a tendency to demonstrate higher cultivation relationships (and indeed, this was not done in the data which Hirsch was critiquing). However, not soon after the debate had begun to simmer down, Morgan published data (1983) showing a fairly conclusive correspondence between the likelihood of a group's victimization on TV and its tendency to demonstrate cultivation. That is, those demographic subgroups who were more likely to be victimized on TV were also more likely, in real life, to show stronger relationships between viewing and beliefs about violence. This finding refuted one of Hirsch's key charges – that patterns of cultivation had nothing to do with victimization patterns in the content analyses.

These developments made it clear that cultivation is a far more complex process than it may have appeared at first. Clearly, the critiques contributed to this theoretical refinement. Yet the fact that significant interactions and meaningful conditional associations can be found even when an overall relationship disappears goes a long way towards resolving some of the major objections raised by these reanalyses. But a variety of other criticisms and concerns have been voiced, by these and by more recent studies, and these are discussed in the next sections.

## The "Non-Linearity" of Cultivation Patterns

Both Hughes and Hirsch reported that relationships they examined were non-linear under controls. Hirsch went even further and broke out the usual light/medium/heavy viewing scheme into two additional categories – non-viewers (those reporting "zero hours" on "an average day") and extreme viewers (those watching over eight hours a day). He found that the "non-viewers" were more alienated, anomic and fearful than were the light viewers, while the "extreme" viewers were less so than the heavy viewers.

At first glance, this would appear to dramatically contradict what cultivation would predict, which would be a generally monotonic pattern across all viewing levels, no matter how many there are. Yet, both of these extreme groups are quite small (about 4 percent of the sample) and idiosyncratic. As Hawkins and Pingree note, they "are unusual enough that they probably differ from other groups on possibly relevant third variables," and to see the results as disconfirming cultivation "seems to us unreasonable" (1982, p. 235). Moreover, Gerbner et al. (1981b) conducted tests for linearity on the same variables Hirsch used, across Hirsch's five viewing categories; seventeen of the twenty-two tests showed significant linear trends while only *one* showed significant non-linearity. Thus, there was no convincing evidence in Hirsch's analysis that cultivation relationships are indeed non-linear; if the extreme groups are eliminated – a practice that some statisticians recommend should routinely be done (Hunter and Schmidt, 1990, p. 207) – then the associations become even stronger for the remaining 90 percent-plus of the NORC respondents.

A decade later, Potter (1991a) also claimed to show that cultivation relationships are non-linear, based on data from 308 students in grades 8 through 12. Dependent indices were constructed from five-point Likert scales on four topics: crime and law enforcement (six items), working females, affluence, and health (three items each). Potter does not provide any information whatsoever about the *content* of these dependent variables, so it is not very easy to determine the extent to which, if at all, they reflect any typical program patterns as might be revealed in message system analysis. Also, as noted above, the fact that respondents completed a questionnaire entitled "Estimations of Television and Society" means that the data may be contaminated by making "television" more salient.

Potter divided the viewing distribution in four different ways: (1) the closest approximation of an even three-way split (the method preferred by Gerbner et al.), (2) a split based on the standard deviation, (3) quintiles and (4) stanines (nine equal sized groups). He then compared the means of the dependent variable across each viewing group, and also examined the *correlations* of amount of viewing and the dependent variables *within* each viewing group. He then regressed the dependent indices on demographics and various transformations of the viewing measure: total viewing, total viewing squared, the square root of total viewing, the reciprocal of total viewing, and the log of total viewing.

Potter's conclusion that cultivation is non-linear rests on the correlations computed within the quintiles and stanines, which fail to be consistent in size or direction. But these correlations are misleading. With $N = 308$, the stanines each represent thirty-four cases at most; such small samples are certain to produce highly unstable coefficients, and no correction was made for curtailment of variance; variance for the viewing measure will of course be inordinately restricted within groups defined by viewing levels, and especially with such fine distinctions (nine levels).

This study raises important issues about how television viewing should be handled as a variable, although his measure of television viewing – Potter generally asks adolescents how many hours a week they watch each of twelve or so different genres – raises our eyebrows. Asking respondents how many hours *per week* they do certain things seems like a fairly demanding task, especially when the researcher's program categories are imposed upon them. Nowhere does he offer any information on the reliability of such measures over time. The data are probably weakest if used as measures of amount of exposure to the specific "types" of programs, but in this particular study the twelve genres were summed to provide an overall exposure measure.

In any case, overall exposure measures are only meaningful when they are seen as *relative* indicators of more or less exposure to television. That is why Gerbner et al. use the consistent method of dividing the sample into three groups of equal size regardless of the actual sample distribution or cutoff points. Contrary to Potter's assertion (echoing Hirsch) that the "theorists feel free to alter cut points at will across studies" (1991a, p. 570), the same technique *is* consistently used in all cases. To use the same exact hour cutoff points for all samples would be both impractical and indefensible; to use the criteria for typical adult samples with children and adolescents would be to end up with an unusable sample of mostly heavy viewers. Variations in question wording, response options, coding and the age of the sample all produce different distributions, and mean that the number of actual hours reported is less relevant.

Potter further questions why respondents are put into viewing categories at all, arguing that more powerful tests can be conducted if the data are kept in continuous form. Yet the whole point of categorization is to illustrate the nature and shape of the relationship, including baselines, in ways that correlational statistics cannot reveal (an argument also made by Potter, 1991b). Cultivation analysts may examine the simple percentage patterns within subgroups, but more rigorous multivariate techniques (based on the data in continuous form) are usually applied as well. It is important to examine the data both ways because, strictly speaking, correlations should *not* be used with television viewing in the first place; even though is it measured as an interval-level variable, it is usually not distributed normally.

Assumptions of normalcy are routinely violated in agreed-upon ways in social science, of course. Yet, although he chastises those doing cultivation studies for sometimes dividing the sample into light, medium and heavy viewers, Potter tosses out (but does not pursue) the observation that his viewing measure "would probably be better treated as a categorical variable from a statistical point of view because the distributions do not meet the assumptions of normalcy" (1991a, p. 574).

Examination of grouped patterns *and* more rigorous multivariate analysis of continuous data each have definite advantages and disadvantages; each clarifies some issues and obscures others. That is why studies by Cultural Indicators researchers so often use *both* sorts of analyses. (Potter, 1994, p. 27, also seems to believe that Pearson correlations are computed with the trichotomized, collapsed, ordinal exposure measure; this would indeed be a problem if it were true, but it isn't.)

Notwithstanding the methodological problems noted above, the key conceptual problem with Potter's arguments (and in some ways, Hirsch's) stems from trying to read a level of specificity and precision into the viewing measures that they cannot be expected to sustain. Overall exposure measures such as these can only indicate *relatively* more or *relatively* less exposure to television. Potter's conclusions might be convincing if hours of viewing were measured in extremely accurate terms; his manipulations assume that measures of viewing themselves are perfect, completely reliable, with no error variance whatsoever. We see these as unwarranted assumptions.

Volgy and Schwartz (1980) noted that many of their "medium" viewers (determined by the number of hours of viewing reported) also indicated watching a lot of specific programs on other measures; they suggested that this group may include both "real" medium and many "real" heavy viewers. Internal Cultural Indicators analyses of the ORC 1979 national sample showed that 15 percent of those claiming to be "non-viewers" also listed "watching television" as one of their favorite leisure activities. Further slippage is evident in the 1993 General Social Survey, which included measures of how often respondents watch "TV dramas and sitcoms," "TV news," and "Shows on public broadcasting" in addition to the regular question on hours of viewing. The data for the sixty-one self-proclaimed "non-viewers" (3.8 percent of the sample; total $N = 1,586$) are quite intriguing (see Table 4.2).

Most striking is that less than a third of the "non-viewers" actually say they "never watch" any of the three types of programs. Close to one in five (18 percent) say they watch dramas or sitcoms at least several times a month. A third of the "non-viewers" say they watch PBS at least a few times a month. Over half say they watch the news that often, and 13 percent of the "non-viewers" say they watch it every day!

We suspect that the measurement error in viewing is more random than systematic. Regardless, the obvious slippage makes dose-specific, mechanical, linearity tests such as Potter's beside the point, and may also partly explain Hirsch's findings. Most of all, rough approximations of general patterns are all that cultivation analysis assumes, pursues or requires. We want to know if it's warm or cold, not if it's 68 degrees or 69 degrees. The functional form is heuristic, and just cannot be tightly calibrated given available measurement techniques. Potter's analysis implies a level of pseudo-scientific precision that his measures cannot justify or sustain.

Thus, we stipulate that cultivation's preferred measure of television exposure, like any other measure of social phenomena, does not perfectly tap real-world viewing behaviors. This is, at most, what Potter has

Table 4.2 *Viewing patterns of "non-viewers" (percentages):*
*(columns = 100%)*

| | Percent who watch | | |
| | TV drama or sitcoms | TV News | PBS |
| --- | --- | --- | --- |
| Daily | 0 | 13.1 | 1.6 |
| Several days a week | 1.6 | 16.4 | 14.8 |
| Several days a month | 16.4 | 21.3 | 19.7 |
| Rarely | 52.5 | 27.9 | 34.4 |
| Never | 29.5 | 21.3 | 29.5 |

*Source:* NORC 1993 – Total $N = 1,586$   Non-viewers: $N = 61$ (3.8%)

demonstrated. This does have implications for how much "certainty" we want to apply to results based on imperfect measurement. Measurement error often implies that observed correlations are smaller than what one would find with perfect measurement, unless there is a more systematic source of error. To be sure, non-monotonic associations *do* appear in the cultivation literature from time to time (as do associations of no clear direction at all), but there is no convincing evidence to date that such patterns are either common or important. (Non-monotonic and non-linear are not the same, but they are often conflated.)

Importantly, Potter (1991a, 1993) offers no conceptual guidance as to what we might make of the non-linear pattern he claims to have demonstrated. What does it mean? What should we do with it? How should we interpret it? What specific kinds of non-linear associations might make sense? And what would they tell us about any relevant or critical consequences of television viewing? Hawkins and Pingree observed that curvilinear relationships with viewing "demand further explanation – not the simple negation of the original simple hypothesis" (1982, p. 236). Tapper (1995) has proposed a model wherein such patterns might be explained, but that model awaits empirical test. So far, though, no reason to expect cultivation to be non-linear has been proposed, nor has any explanation of such patterns, when allegedly observed, been offered by those who insist that cultivation is non-linear.

## Where Cultivation Stood

It should be clear, by now, that cultivation stood in a fairly embattled position in the early 1980s, having been subjected to several major critiques from both within and without the discipline of communication research.

But in many ways the field was only getting started. New graduate students continued to show interest in the area, even as other schools continued to downplay and critique cultivation as methodologically unsound and perhaps as too "political."

But the atmosphere of the 1980s was ripe for further cultivation work. During the Reagan years, with the distinctions between left and right cast in unusual clarity, the idea that TV could have pseudo-propagandistic effects on viewers (effects well suited to the purposes of capitalist media owners) did not seem that divorced from reality, and in fact, despite the noise and the verbiage, the field was ready to explode into a period of intense productivity (which we explore in the next chapter).

As for the critiques, most people more or less agreed to disagree. Cultivation is still taught in most universities as a watershed approach to media questions (indeed, it is one of the few theories that is almost universally taught) even as new generations of scholars prepare their own revisions to the theory. Neither have the critiques lost their force; discourse on cultivation is often still contentious. Nevertheless, in a few short years (1976–1981) cultivation had opened up a remarkably rich and controversial dialogue on the role of television in American (and global) life. In the next chapter, we explore some of the main themes of that dialogue as it evolved and developed.

# 5    Advancements in Cultivation Research

In this chapter we look at work that advanced cultivation beyond the initial volley of studies and critiques described in Chapter 4. We begin with some further historical recounting of the milestone studies that contributed to the important theoretical advancements. Primarily we examine two ways in which cultivation theory was pushed ahead: (1) through development of the concept of "mainstreaming" (briefly discussed in the previous chapter) and (2) through the expansion of the range of topics which cultivation examined.

### Advancing Cultivation

One can look at early Cultural Indicators and cultivation research (from 1967 to roughly about 1980) as the statement of a theme, followed by a critical response. The "theme" was the profferment of a hypothesis: that the nature and contours of the symbolic cultural environment – and the amount of time we spend living in it and absorbing its messages and lessons – have a relationship to how we think about the world. Attendant to the statement of this thesis was the political and critical argument that mass media institutions, especially television, were playing something less than the freedom-protecting role that a democratic society perhaps optimistically envisions.

One response to this statement, as seen in the previous chapter, was that cultivation couldn't be properly measured and therefore was probably not real; or, if real, it had not been convincingly demonstrated using sufficiently rigorous scientific techniques. Corollary to this line of criticism was the idea that television and other mass media were institutions whose effects are too complex to assess along a single dimension, least of all by means of the global, undifferentiated, overall exposure measure which cultivation theory favors. Fundamentally, although not always explicitly, the criticisms tended to cast doubt on the idea that mass media messages and institutions played any demonstrable or significant role in processes of social control.

As a result of these skirmishes, cultivation emerged into a unique and interesting spot within the academic community. Many mainstream social scientists tended to conclude that the work had been seriously damaged by the onslaught of critiques; again, it is not unusual to see Hughes, Hirsch, Wober, and Doob and Macdonald cited as having definitively refuted the claims of cultivation. And indeed, many specific alleged criticisms were not fully dealt with by cultivation theorists until our meta-analytic work began in the mid-1990s (Morgan and Shanahan, 1997).

Meanwhile, many scholars in the critical/cultural research community tended to see cultivation as tainted, trivial and trifling, owing to its use of quantitative, empirical survey research techniques, somehow inevitably associated with imperialist American research enterprises (Ruddock, 1997). Among critical cultural purists cultivation found little purchase as critical work moved more toward a postmodern fascination with "difference," the "text," and how audiences used media for their own various purposes and pleasures, often resisting hegemonic intentions. This changed somewhat as time marched on, first with those interested in political economy recognizing some affinities inherent in cultivation arguments. Later, other cultural studies scholars found more points of agreement than originally recognized (Lewis, 1991), but this rapprochement has been slow in coming.

Cultivation researchers were left in a strange and perhaps unenviable middle spot (which had been identified early on by authors such as Slack and Allor, 1983), not quite critical enough for some (there were all those numbers to deal with, after all, and Gerbner et al. went so far as to accept funding from federal agencies) and yet not clearly "administrative" or "positivist," either (there were all those assertions about democracy, power, freedom and social control). Cultivation theory and research thus seemed to represent a disconcerting kind of "critical liberal-pluralist" amalgamation that no one knew how to categorize or handle – it was scorned by the empiricists as "not scientific" and blinded by ideology while simultaneously rebuked by the critical camp for naively falling for the myth of quantitative objectivity. Yet despite these unsettling ambivalences, the simplicity and elegance of the cultivation hypothesis provided enough glue for a loose aggregate to emerge as a "community" of scholars who focused on ideas about cultivation. It was this community that enabled the work to continue and progress as much as it did, despite the challenging conditions of the mid-1980s. With funds for social research drying up in the Reagan years (indeed, Ronald Reagan came out of and was nurtured by the corporate media community which cultivation challenged) and with the communication research institutions changing themselves, it was more difficult to support one's work in cultivation (though not impossible).

It was in this period of challenge, after the thesis and antithesis described above, in which the real work of cultivation began: to produce a synthesis in which the critical insights and underpinnings of cultivation could be sustained by a more sophisticated research procedure. Thus cultivation, despite attracting much criticism, also catalyzed new research, both among the initial researchers and among the various recruits who were moved by the insights cultivation could bring, as well as by those who were unsatisfied with audience "activity" models which stripped media of any power whatsoever. And, to be clear, critiques also continued to emerge (for instance, from Potter, 1994). In short, cultivation was evolving from a rudimentary, embryonic and controversial area of scientific inquiry into a mature, far-reaching – and still controversial – area of scientific inquiry.

In this turbulent atmosphere, many different approaches were taken to cultivation. We will examine some of these approaches in further detail below. Yet for those who were slogging through the trenches of cultivation data, no idea was more important than mainstreaming. Here, we show how the concept was elaborated in the second "wave" of cultivation studies, and we also look at some of its implications for the issue of social control.

## Mainstreaming and its Implications

The idea of mainstreaming could well have been a natural outgrowth of cultivation research all on its own, even if no one else had bothered to challenge or critique the research. That is, it was evident that few cultivation analyses revealed results in which "unidirectional" cultivation patterns persisted across-the-board, invariantly for all subgroups in massive populations. Yet coming as it did, concurrently with the batch of critical reflections on cultivation's results, mainstreaming has often been seen as a kind of desperate, *post hoc* "response" to the critiques. Nevertheless, we would argue that mainstreaming is better seen as a synthesis of the original work and the important issues raised by critics, as well as a turning point in the organic development of cultivation work itself.

Some interpreted mainstreaming as a falsification of cultivation theory, because mainstreaming suggested that cultivation might only be present for particular (and unspecified) groups under particular (and unspecified) conditions. On the other hand, because mainstreaming ideas were developed at around the same time as the forceful and conspicuous critiques of cultivation were emerging, some thought that cultivation researchers displayed too much of a willingness to revise their original hypothesis, and refused to let cultivation be falsified.

Hirsch, in particular, argued that mainstreaming was nothing more than an attempt on the part of cultivation researchers to get around his penetrating critique. As we saw in the previous chapter, Hirsch found that some of the cultivation differentials reported in the early studies disappeared under multiple controls. In response to Hirsch, Gerbner et al. argued that the persistence of a relationship within significant portions (i.e., subgroups) of the sample, in directions predicted by cultivation, were enough to sustain cultivation as a theory, even in the face of Hirsch's reanalyses.

For Hirsch, this was evidence of unwillingness to let cultivation be falsified, and he practically accused Gerbner et al. of willingly distorting data and going out of their way to simply "win" the argument. But Gerbner et al. argued that mainstreaming was already implied in early cultivation work; in a sense, it was a finding waiting to happen:

The foundations of mainstreaming were implicit in our early theoretical and conceptual considerations of the role of television in our society. We stressed television's role in the mainstream of the culture, its celebration of conventional morality, and its potential for promoting homogeneity by crossing class, age, ethnic, and other boundaries. The repetitive pattern of television's mass-produced messages and images forms the mainstream of the common symbolic environment that cultivates the most widely shared conceptions of reality. (Gerbner et al., 1981b, pp. 46–7)

Gerbner et al. went on to note that even the early findings focused on cases in which cultivation was stronger for one group or another, though most of the attention was given to the strongest cases: where all groups were equally cultivated.

Hirsch admitted that cultivation relationships held up in higher education, higher status groups, but he wrote this off as essentially an artifact of regression to the mean. That is the phenomenon well-known from experimental research in which, if experimental groups are selected for unusually high or low scores on some test, they are statistically likely to regress toward a more average score on a subsequent test. Gerbner dismissed this assertion in several ways: most notably by observing the fact that in mainstreaming different groups are being compared (in typical regression cases, it is the same group compared at two times which demonstrates the phenomenon).

More importantly, Hirsch insisted that mainstreaming was not falsifiable; that it was developed simply to offer cultivation a way out of a critique beyond which the theory could not be carried. But, as Gerbner et al. noted, mainstreaming offered not just a new way to analyze data, but

an explanation that was fully in line with the earlier theoretical developments. And Gerbner went further, suggesting that Cultural Indicators
was an ongoing and flexible research effort which was, in the best sense of
the term, "speculative" (characterized by intellectual curiosity). Thus, for
Gerbner, the fact that mainstreaming emerged after Hirsch's critique was
not in itself problematic. But for Hirsch, any attempt to rework theory
and data analysis "after the fact" was cast as a sign of scientific weakness
to be purged from the annals of research. For Gerbner et al., mainstreaming admittedly was not tested in early theories, but that was no reason to
give up on a promising line of investigation (and cultivation research
along these lines has continued well after Hirsch's criticisms). In order to
see whether mainstreaming is indeed falsifiable and in what ways, we
need to explore it in further depth.

In the strictest sense, the concept of mainstreaming is a very substantial
enhancement to (and not just a revision of) the overall cultivation
approach. However, from a wider and (to us) more appropriate perspective, to understand the social importance of mainstreaming requires the
same assumptions (or propositions) that "simple" cultivation requires
(see our discussion at the end of Chapter 1). Thus, mainstreaming did
not do away with the "social meaning" of cultivation-inspired thinking (in
fact, it may have deepened it); it only permitted better explanation and/or
prediction within the original model. Although the idea of mainstreaming
introduced technical revisions to the crude version of the cultivation
"hypothesis," it was most of all a strengthening of the original theory.

As implied above, there are many suggestive hints about mainstreaming embedded in the earliest conceptual treatments of cultivation.
Although the precise analytical explication of mainstreaming was a
significant development, it did not, so to speak, come out of left field.
From the start, for example, television itself was defined and studied as
the *mainstream* of the culture; mainstreaming is simply the hypothesis that
television "cultivates common perspectives." Very early on, Gerbner and
Gross (1976) wrote about how television "transcends historic barriers of
literacy and mobility," providing "for the first time since preindustrial
religion, a strong cultural link between the elites and all other publics."
They stressed that television "has become the primary common source of
everyday culture of otherwise heterogeneous populations," as it spreads
common, shared images "from penthouse to tenement," and "from the
cradle to the grave." Thus, we can see that mainstreaming meant that cultivation was turning back to, not away from, some of its most fundamental
assumptions.

Let us look at some specific findings, with an eye toward seeing how
mainstreaming makes for a more exact examination of the cultivation

process. As we saw in Chapter 3, Violence Profile No. 11 (Gerbner, Gross, Morgan and Signorielli, 1980, "The 'mainstreaming' of America") was a milestone study for cultivation research. This study defines the mainstream as a relative "commonality" of outlooks that television tends to cultivate: "By 'mainstreaming' we mean the sharing of that commonality among heavy viewers in those demographic groups whose light viewers tend to hold divergent views. In other words, differences deriving from other factors and social forces may be diminished or even absent among heavy viewers" (Gerbner et al., 1980, p. 15).

At that historical juncture, mainstreaming may have seemed to be an interesting "corollary" to the overall theory of cultivation, but we can now see that this study was starting to outline a better cultural map over which the forces of television messages could flow. That is, we know intuitively that social, cultural and political issues are often presented in polarized ways, with culturally "valid" perspectives on those issues often falling in between points defined by traditionally "left" and "right" perspectives (especially in today's cultural landscape, where "traditional" left and right ideologies are increasingly converging upon each other). Though early cultivation research may have implied that TV messages would serve mainly politically "conservative" constituencies (and the implication may well have stemmed from the biases of most cultivation researchers), it became clearer that sometimes traditionally "liberal" issues might also be within the social mainstream and could also be "promoted" by television. Overall, though, even with mainstreaming becoming more important, TV was seen as a conservatizing force, especially in the sense that conservatism favors maintenance of the status quo.

Starting with this study, the experience with many different data sets revealed that television could be trusted most to hew not only to the right but to the supposedly safe and comfortable cultural center, where the playing field is seen as level and all nasty extremes are eschewed. One might even see television as operating within a marketplace in which an "invisible hand" guides it toward favoring representations that are maximally acceptable to (and seen as "normal" by) the widest number of people. But its role is not simply "reactive." Indeed, Gerbner's "three B's," emerging at this time, began to suggest that the impacts of television could be seen as "blurring" cultural, political, social, regional and class-based distinctions, "blending" attitudes into the television mainstream, and "bending" the direction of that mainstream to the political and economic tasks of the medium and its client institutions.

Particularly for the USA, which at least until recently has historically celebrated the melting pot of its homogenizing structures and its great mythical middle class, mainstreaming was a metaphor which did not have to work overtime when confronted with the realities of American culture. (In parallel fashion, it is noteworthy that much discourse has evolved to emphasize the "rainbows" of cultural differences as the proliferation of channels has fragmented the audience.) In contrast, simple "cultivation" did not always make sense to those who saw viewers as comprising an "obstinate," selective audience that well understands the distinction between fact and fiction. That is, mainstreaming was a concept that could include the possibility of diversity and disagreement within an overall project that still was interested in media "power." Moreover, mainstreaming suggested that it might be easier to effect social policy with a homogenized and stronger "center" of opinion than with a diverse and truly pluralistic public range of views and discourses.

Obviously, cultivation was not the first media theory to suggest that media as institutions were designed to function as "engineers" of consent (Lippman, 1922; Herman and Chomsky, 1988). But if mainstreaming works as proposed – and the data presented in Violence Profile No. 11 certainly suggested that it did – then homogenization of sociopolitical outlook is a consequence that implies that social control may be effected through cultivation. Further, mainstreaming also implies that social changes which do become evident over time might have been more radical or severe than would have been the case without television as a moderating force, especially in terms of changes that involved opening the mainstream to traditionally marginalized groups (women, African-Americans, gays and lesbians, to name a few).

Of course, other phenomena besides mainstreaming were noted. For instance, some studies have suggested that dominant television images may produce "boomerang" effects, in which "oppressed" minorities or social groups react with increased politicized resistance to mainstream images (Kang and Morgan, 1988). Other studies (including Violence Profile No. 11 itself) noted so-called "resonance" effects, in which TV messages that resonated with experienced realities were seen as producing especially strong cultivation. But empirically, it has been more common to see mainstreaming effects, and indeed they are most consistent with cultivation theory.

In hindsight, it makes more sense that cultivation might be stronger among the groups and classes which would "need" it more to "get to" (or gravitate toward) the dominant perspective. A functional analysis (discussed above briefly in Chapter 1) suggests that "effects" will be stronger in groups that "need" to be pulled closer to the "center" to establish social homeostasis. As an example, Violence Profile No. 11 showed that low-income respondents were more likely to think that "fear of crime is a very serious personal problem" (see Figure 5.1). TV viewing made little

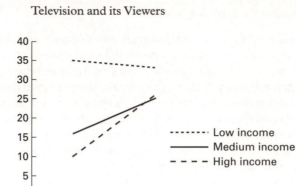

Figure 5.1 Mainstreaming among income groups for question "fear of crime is a very serious personal problem" (percentage of respondents saying "yes")

difference among this "already cultivated" group (and one might argue that, from a social control standpoint, it is important that this group be prone to a state of fear). In contrast, high-income respondents as a group were less likely to think of crime as a serious personal problem, which indicates a social "need" to bring them to the mainstream. Thus, cultivation differentials were much stronger within the groups whose attitude was furthest from the TV-cultivated version of reality, as revealed or suggested by content data. With respect to social control, then, mainstreaming suggests that the institution directs its messages where they are most needed (or that there is more receptivity to the messages where needed). Mainstreaming phenomena confirm cultivation most when groups tend to converge toward the "TV view." It would obviously confirm cultivation less if the counterpart subgroups converged "away" from the TV-sponsored view.

Another example of mainstreaming, again from Violence Profile No. 11, showed that whites and non-whites, who differed greatly on perceptions of social fear, demonstrated similar outlooks as heavier viewers. Compared to light viewers, white heavy viewers were more likely to express fear of crime, while non-whites were in fact somewhat less fearful as heavy viewers (see Figure 5.2). The paradoxical finding that non-whites would be less fearful as heavy viewers is resolved by noting that differences between whites and non-whites were smaller, with the result that heavy viewing respondents tend more toward agreement on fear of crime regardless of the very important social distinction of race identity. That is, the difference made by race in people's attitudes is attenuated by

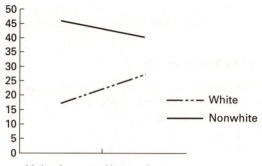

Figure 5.2 Mainstreaming among race groups for question "fear of crime is a very serious personal problem" (percentage of respondents saying "yes")

heavy viewing. In general, social groups' position relative to the mainstream determines the strength and direction of cultivation's gravitational power.

What explains this concurrence of views among otherwise divergent groups? Cultivation assumes that it is the "effect" of the accumulated messages, creating a more homogenized group experience of the world that brings individuals' perspectives closer together. Other explanations have also been offered, though. For instance, as noted above, some critics countered with the argument that mainstreaming was merely a "regression to the mean" artifact. Again, though, different groups are measured: there is no re-measurement based on extreme pre-test scores, and hence there is by definition no regression, only comparison. Others argued that apparent mainstreaming patterns might be due to other unexplained variance, to ceiling effects, to role incongruity, or to selectively reported random fluctuations, but as we will see, strict tests were marshaled to bolster the mainstreaming argument.

Mainstreaming, as noted, has turned up very frequently in the literature. Almost every important cultivation study, at least among studies conducted by Gerbner and associates, has presented findings confirming mainstreaming. Other authors have paid less attention to mainstreaming. We know, at the very least, that mainstreaming is a statistically resilient phenomenon, but it is only through the years that subtler theoretical readings of mainstreaming phenomena have been offered. These interpretations were developed as cultivation increasingly turned its attention to explicitly political and ideological issues. A look at some of the key research developments which contributed to the increasing "politicization" of cultivation results shows how direct attention to ideological issues raises the importance of understanding mainstreaming.

## The Politics of the Mainstream

"Charting the mainstream: television's contributions to political orientations" (Gerbner, Gross, Morgan and Signorielli, 1982) was the study which initially demonstrated that mainstreaming was not just a statistical accident, but a legitimate way to think about television's role in the nation's life of ideas. Gerbner et al. assumed, based primarily on results from the earlier studies, that television would cultivate "middle-of-the-road" perceptions with regard to political views, class position and income level. With ideological questions (where it would be difficult to "count" instances of anything in particular in content, because numerating ideology is different than counting, say, acts of violence) cultivation analysis was used as a way to confirm suspicions about larger symbolic transformations of general patterns in the content. What was tested here was not the cultivation of any specific attitude, but rather the logical extension of the concept of mainstreaming itself – i.e., that heavy television viewing should signal a general homogenization and a reduction in differences attributable to other social variables – applied to political outlooks, positions and identities.

Heavy viewers converged on a perception of themselves as "middle class." Responses of higher income and lower income respondents were closer to the mainstream when they were heavy viewers. Further, heavy viewers were more likely to gravitate toward a politically "moderate" self-perception. That is, when asked to designate their own political location on a seven-point continuum from liberal to conservative, heavy viewers ran from both ends of the scale, rejected both extremes, and firmly plopped themselves down in the "moderate, middle-of-the-road" mainstream.

In "The political correlates of television viewing," Gerbner et al. (1984) extended these results using different data from "Charting." The finding that heavy viewers self-identify with a moderate political position was replicated with striking consistency across nine different data sets. These associations were not to be seen for general media use (radio listening or newspaper reading), and were specific to television viewing. This study, taken together with "Charting," gave strong confirmation to the idea that television viewing engenders "moderate" perceptions and positions.

With respect to specific issues, however, the "Charting" paper found that heavy television viewing tended to generate mainstreaming toward

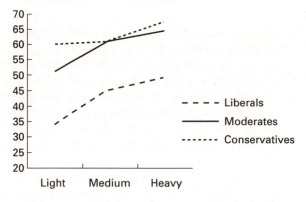

Figure 5.3 Mainstreaming among ideological subgroups for question "Communism is the worst form of government" (percentage of respondents saying "yes")

more conservative positions on social issues such as busing, interracial relations, "open" housing, rights for women, and sexual minorities, among a variety of others. With political self-designation used as a control, one pattern emerged over and over: the attitudes of self-styled "moderates" and "conservatives" were barely distinguishable from each other, and from the "liberals" who were heavy viewers. The only group "out" of the mainstream was the light-viewing liberals (see Figure 5.3). On variable after variable, heavy viewing indicated deep erosion for classically liberal positions on social issues. Thus, television was seen as restricting views that could otherwise contribute to a more participatory and pluralistic democracy.

Yet the authors also found that television viewing tended to cultivate support for *greater* government spending on a variety of what are often seen as "bleeding heart" causes (e.g., the environment, health care, the cities, education, etc.). Gerbner et al. interpreted this peculiar and potentially volatile mix of social conservatism and economic liberalism as a kind of "new populism," troubling in some ways for democratic principles and practices yet highly congruent with the consumption-oriented demands of commercial media institutions unlikely to promote "tolerance" or economic austerity.

By 1984 then, cultivation researchers had concluded that mainstreaming was not just a technical refinement, but an indication that ideological convergence and dissolution of differences represented a key hallmark of the cultivation process. Mainstreaming patterns were turning up with great regularity in all cultivation analyses, even in topical areas – such as health-related beliefs and practices (Gerbner et al., 1982) – less overtly charged with ideology. Still, the emergence of mainstreaming did help push cultivation in a more explicitly political and ideological direction.

The emphasis on mainstreaming and the political findings in these years can also in some sense be seen as a reaction to the critiques of the early 1980s, which had been catalyzed by the focus on TV violence. While media violence is obviously a political issue, as the discussion played out it seemed to drain politics out of the picture entirely. In some ways, cultivation, having been characterized only as a theory of violence and TV, was derailed at the start from its truer goal which was to examine the broader cultural and ideological effects of TV institutions.

One further twist on mainstreaming came from a paper by Morgan (1986), examining regional diversity in the USA. Morgan showed that responses to a variety of dependent variables in NORC's General Social Survey varied significantly by region. Generally speaking, the coasts were more liberal while the South and the interior were more conservative (as would be expected). Morgan tested whether heavy viewers were more similar across regions, as the mainstreaming hypothesis would suggest. He also tested trend effects, to see whether differences were narrower over time.

He found that, as predicted, variance was smaller for heavy viewers across region than for light viewers, and this restricted variance was interpreted as a mainstreaming effect. Further, he found that opinions and outlooks converged toward the generally more conservative views of Southerners. This despite the fact that television production centers were in the Northeast and West, and despite the worry that urban "degenerate" culture would be spread by means of the new television technology.

Thus, mainstreaming means that even regional differences are narrowed. While television could not by any means wipe out distinctive regional character, regional adherence to particular ideological stances may be somewhat loosened. Indeed, glacial but important shifts in regional political behavior have been critical to the consolidation of conservatism since the 1980s. The movement of a strengthened Southern ideology away from the "solid South" voting behavior of the past (and the development of ideological hybrids such as the "New Democrats") shows the degree to which previous regional ideological differences had been thrown up for grabs. At the least, television should be counted among those phenomena and forces that may be driving these displacements.

The political studies had suggested that the ideological dimensions underpinning televised entertainment – and the processes of cultural production it encapsulates – could be detected in the differential perspectives of lighter and heavier viewers, in complex but systematic interactions with other demographic factors. The implication was that escapist entertainment could have impacts on social sectors that had previously not been considered. If entertainment could contribute to our perceptions of social power, what would it say about politics, sex roles, images of different types of people and so on?

In the next few sections we examine cultivation research about "marginal" groups. In some cases, mainstreaming hypotheses were specifically tested, while other studies tested more basic exploratory notions about the intersection of television, ingroups and outgroups. In all cases, though, the studies contribute to an understanding of the location and resilience of the concept of the mainstream in American society.

## Television and the Margins

If mainstreaming suggests that TV strengthens the sociocultural cores of power, one immediately thinks about what is happening at the social margin. How are groups who are out of the mainstream dealt with in the TV world? If majority audiences are being cultivated toward middle-of-the-road positions, are they also being cultivated to view "outgroups" as marginal?

With this in mind, researchers began to look for other confirmations that cultivation processes would tend to provide, as we noted earlier, "affirmation for the believers, indoctrination for the deviants." This was a natural concern for cultivation. After all, much of the original concern with violence that emerged after the turbulent decade of the 1960s was subtly catalyzed by racial issues. But in the first five to ten years of its existence, cultivation had not paid much sustained attention to matters of race.

Thus, Gross' (1984) investigation of the cultivation of intolerance (which was carried out after the concept of mainstreaming had been developed) suggested that television's messages tend to produce negative consequences for socially marginalized groups. In a study very directly related to the issue of social control, Gross argued that "When groups, or ideologies, do attain visibility, the manner of their representation will reflect the biases and interests of those elites who make the basic decisions which define the public agenda" (1984, p. 345).

A decade after that statement was made, groups such as gays and (especially) blacks had attained a far greater degree of visibility in television programs. By 1995, African-American characters made up a full 11 percent of the prime-time population; given that they constitute 12.1 percent of the actual US population, their frequency of representation was running about 90 percent "accurate." (The exact qualities and characteristics of that representation are, of course, a different issue.)

Homosexual characters in 1995 accounted for 0.6 percent of the TV population (an accuracy rate of only 8.6 percent, figured on a real-world base of 7.0 percent), but gay characters and themes are certainly more prominent than in the past. Such media brouhahas as occurred in 1997 over whether the title character "Ellen" in a popular comedy was going to come out as a lesbian are miles away from the situation analyzed by Gross in 1984. So, obviously, social conditions for gays have changed somewhat (though we would still see them as marginalized in a good deal of mainstream media discourse; and for the most part, they are treated to gay representations designed for a straight audience, not a gay audience's images of or for themselves).

The fact that gays and some other minority groups have attained a degree of political power not previously held shows that television's tendency to hew to the mainstream is not "all-powerful" with respect to social change. Still, we would argue that social movements for change for groups such as homosexuals, blacks and women had to work harder to overcome the cultural barricades bolstered by the status quo-driven messages of TV. Gerbner (1978) and Tuchman (1978) discussed this process in terms of the "symbolic annihilation" that underlies the "dynamics of cultural resistance."

Taking a relatively firm position on the issue of social control, Gross concluded that the politics of the cultural "Leviathan" of television would mean that heavy viewers would tend to see blacks and gays as "out" of the mainstream, and would tend to favor policies restricting activities such as interracial marriage, acceptance of gays in society, etc. Further, Gross argued that television would mainstream differences present among light viewers. Liberals, accepting greater freedoms for socially marginalized groups, would be more restrictive as heavy viewers. Conservatives might converge toward a somewhat more accepting perspective, but the overall pattern was expected to reflect a conservatizing of opinion about these marginalized groups. This pattern, first discussed in "Charting the Mainstream," was becoming the preferred model for explaining television's cultivation of ideological issues: a narrowing of perspectives among heavy viewers, while bending the whole opinion structure rightward with viewing. If true, "outgroups" such as blacks and gays could be established as the social "scapegoats" for societal problems which would confirm the common-sense rightness of mainstream positions.

Thus, Gross' findings that heavy viewers were generally less accepting of civil and sexual rights on a variety of social issues was important confirmation for the emerging view of television as a "centrifugal" force plying the cultural mainstream, yet steering its own course toward the right bank. Again and again, the familiar mainstreaming pattern appeared, most sharply marked by the virtual disappearance of the classi- cally "liberal" view among heavy viewers.

The gradual increase in the number of African-American characters on television since the mid-1980s was not accompanied by any greater ten- dency to show blacks and whites interacting with each other. Later culti- vation analyses have continued to show that heavy viewers are more likely to endorse racial separation and express little enthusiasm for civil rights.

Moreover, there was another important change in the television land- scape for black images: namely, the rise of the upper-middle-class black television family, with *The Cosby Show* one of the most vivid examples. This change fits squarely with, among other things, the notion that in a culture of rugged individualism, TV messages might imply that any remaining racial and power inequalities in society are simply the fault of particular individuals and their weaknesses, as opposed to any systemic or institutionalized deficiencies. Thus, Kiecolt and Sayles (1988) thought that television's messages might intensify people's adherence to such "individualist" ideologies and that this could have negative consequences for majority perceptions about minorities. They found that exposure to crime drama appeared to depress white males' awareness of power inequalities between blacks and whites.

A sharp schism in African-American portrayals has developed, what Gerbner calls a "bifurcated image": blacks in entertainment programs (especially sitcoms) are even wealthier than whites, living in a luxurious world beyond racism. Yet, blacks in the news and in "reality" shows are predominantly criminals, vicious murderers and drug dealers. Thus, Armstrong and Neuendorf (1992), working with college-student samples, hypothesized and found that exposure to entertainment images correlated with a tendency to over-estimate blacks' socioeconomic attain- ments, while exposure to news images was associated with under-estimat- ing their socioeconomic position.

This complex combination of images suggests that television may be cultivating an exaggerated sense of the extent to which blacks have achieved economic success, implying that racism is no longer a problem, that blacks who don't "make it" have only themselves to blame, and that remedial programs such as affirmative action are now obsolete and superfluous.

This is very much in line with what Jhally and Lewis (1992) found in their study of *The Cosby Show*. They observed that blacks and whites took very different things away with them after viewing the program; they note that although a text may be polysemous, it can still function in ways that serve hegemonic purposes, in this case by deflecting attention from resid- ual institutional racism. Similarly, Matabane (1988) found that exposure to television was associated with over-estimation of racial integration among black audiences. Her conclusion was that "the effect of heavy television viewing seems most evident in isolating pockets of black dissidence among young and better-educated Afro-Americans and, to a lesser extent, individuals not active in their communities or in keeping informed about social events" (p. 29).

With all this in mind, let us return to the question raised at the start of this discussion: are majority audiences cultivated to view outgroups as marginal? The answer appears to be yes, but not always, given the twist that Gross foresaw: when marginalized groups become more visible, "their representation will reflect the biases and interests" (Gross, 1984, p. 345) of those who make decisions about the public agenda. Greater visibility can apparently also cultivate perceptions of lesser marginalization, but what can appear to be "positive" change can also be a two-edged sword. Even as certain new patterns emerge which are arguably desirable – an increase in the number of black characters, with more of them shown as upper-middle-class professionals – the cultivation of an exaggerated sense of blacks' economic success may be a side-effect with subtle but dangerous repercussions.

## The Marginalized Majority: Sex-Role Traditionalism

While Gross was documenting the marginalization of certain social groups, Morgan was examining the contribution of TV to children's sex-role perceptions (1982). Essentially, cultivation theorists have also viewed women as a marginalized social group, given their under-representation and over-victimization in the symbolic world of television. Cultivation assumed that television would tend to "traditionalize" women's roles, while privileging the place of men in the society, in the economy and the polity. Morgan's study was unusual in that it used longitudinal data rather than cross-sectional surveys to make its points. Longitudinal panel data were used, in part, to address the common criticism of cultivation research that correlational data do not provide evidence of causality (despite the fact that cultivation has skirted causal explanations), although there could be problems with assuming that longitudinal data would be "spaced" properly to catch differences, or that television's causal effects might be located within a specific time interval, or that they might be continuous over time. Nevertheless, Morgan's study provided some clues into how cultivation might work over time, especially with regard to mainstreaming.

Morgan determined that girls' viewing at an early time could be linked to greater sexism at a later time (even controlling for earlier sexism). For boys, however, he found that early sexism predicted later television viewing. For boys, relationships were small and slightly negative. Morgan argued that this was consistent with the phenomenon of mainstreaming, a temporal demonstration of the convergence of outlooks among disparate groups. Thus girls, with less "natural" reason to believe in a variety of sexist positions, were cultivated to accept these over time if they were heavy viewers. This is perhaps the only demonstration of the operation of mainstreaming over time.

Morgan (1987) explored these issues further (with another longitudinal sample) in a paper which concluded that there were no direct effects of television viewing on sex-role *behavior*. However, television viewing in this study was implicated in playing a role in the congruence between sex-role attitude and behavior. That is, heavy viewers tended to show more consistency between sex-role attitude and behavior than did light viewers. Thus, heavy viewers were more likely to specifically and "correctly" identify their position on sex-role issues.

Of course, public outlooks on sex-roles have changed a great deal since cultivation research began, and it is no longer questioned by most people that women should have opportunities outside of traditional family life. Although real-life sex-roles have changed dramatically, television lags behind, and continues to portray men and women unequally (by at least a 2–1 margin). Thus, studies continue to show that media messages contribute to conventionality in sex-role beliefs. Even though the spread of more progressive attitudes about women may make it more difficult to detect sex-role cultivation in the future, mainstreaming patterns continue to pop up frequently in the literature (Signorielli, 1989). Sometimes these patterns hint at what Signorielli calls a "liberating" effect (in which more conservative subgroups are cultivated toward a somewhat more non-traditional perspective) while at other times they reflect simple cultivation of traditionalism. But despite important changes in the social climate on sex-role issues, the data show that television is still playing an important role.

## More Ideology

Within the explosion of studies (and expanding range of topics examined) in the late 1980s and into the 1990s, probably the most important stream of thought had to do with a more direct examination of cultivation's ideological nature, and with the question of social control. Cultivation's contribution to political theory can be seen most clearly in work on issues related to "authoritarianism" and problems related to civil liberties. The relevant question in studies such as these was whether TV messages tended to promote political views and orientations that would benefit authority structures. Without asserting that television would function as a massively powerful propaganda machine, the idea was that subtle effects should be noticeable if indeed television fosters views amenable to those of elites.

Why would cultivation assume such a possibility? To answer this question, we must come back to issues of social control. Earlier on we looked at propositions about the relationship between cultivation as a media effects theory and as a theory of social control. Now is the time to recall those propositions, as we review cultivation's findings that bear most directly on questions of social control.

One useful illustration comes from a study of Argentine adolescents which is also probably one of the larger and more comprehensive cultivation efforts. In this research, Morgan and Shanahan (1991b, 1995) explored the ideological consequences of television viewing for adolescents, with extensive series of questions on political ideology and authoritarianism. These studies were particularly important for investigating social control because of the political situation in Argentina when the data were gathered. Having just emerged from the notorious "Dirty War" in which authoritarian principles were taken to an extreme, respondents were extremely sensitive to issues of democracy and civil liberties. Yet, they were also becoming used to a media system that was newly privatizing, offering the benefits and attractions of an entertainment-oriented media scheme. This offered cultivation a unique opportunity to test notions of authoritarianism in an environment where such questions were foregrounded. The combination of a US-modeled media system working in a country where authoritarian tendencies and habits were more manifest and tangible provided a valuable context for exploring cultivation as a theory of social control.

The studies showed that heavy-viewing Argentine adolescents tended to express authoritarian beliefs and to support authoritarian propositions. The questions used in the studies dealt with issues directly related to social control. For instance, heavy viewers tended to agree more with statements such as "the government should do what it thinks is right, even if it's not what the majority wants" and other statements reflecting support for government latitude with respect to civil liberties and free speech. The findings echoed those seen in Carlson's work (1985), although his studies focused primarily on perceptions of police and criminal authorities.

In particular, the Argentine results provided broad confirmation for the notion of political mainstreaming. With great consistency, groups of higher socioeconomic status (SES) and older respondents showed strong evidence of the cultivation of authoritarian beliefs, whereas lower SES and younger groups were more authoritarian across the board, regardless of viewing. This fit into a larger pattern of results on authoritarianism in social science, particularly those of Altemeyer (1988) who suggested that "social learning" approaches would best explain the appearance and maintenance of authoritarianism. Thus, the Carlson studies and the Morgan and Shanahan Argentine results were all confirming the notion that television tended to repress democratic support that might otherwise have developed among older adolescents and those of high socioeconomic status.

Shanahan (1995) examined this issue further with a sample of US adolescents, in a study specifically designed to examine this "retardation" hypothesis (Carlson was the first to use this term). This study used questions similar to those from the Argentine studies, but also provided for tests of abstract/cognitive ability. These tests were used to see whether intellectual skill would explain relationships between television and authoritarianism, since cognitive ability is directly related to both. The results showed that the predicted mainstreaming patterns emerged when SES subgroups were compared, consistent with most other examples of political and ideological mainstreaming. Further, these relationships were independent of abstract thinking ability. Thus, though one might have suspected that viewing's effects would have been negated by co-relations with cognitive ability, this was not the case.

## Religion, Science, Environment

The range of topics that could be addressed by cultivation is huge, and of course we cannot deal with all of them here. However, three areas in particular – science, the environment and religious issues – do help us to think further about the flow and boundaries of the mainstream. Religion is important because it has traditionally set the value standards by which the mainstream had formerly been judged, so it is valuable to know how television intersects with that institution. Science is important because of the factual claims it stakes out. Finally, environmental issues show how television deals with emerging issues which may be candidates for radical social change. All told, studies in these three areas help us to chart the mainstream more accurately.

To begin, Gerbner and other cultivation analysts have often argued that the American television institution functions as a kind of religion. This argument was developed as early as Gerbner's "Television: the new state religion?" (1977). The piece pointed out that television, like religion, provides a common set of repeated stories and rituals around which virtually an entire society can organize its life and daily understanding. The ritual and narrative nature of television was emphasized along with its aspect of service to the state. The idea that television presents a set of morals about daily life which lead to a creed of adherence to corporate realities is obviously not wide of the mark from what cultivation data were finding. But what did cultivation say about religion – and religious television – itself?

In a large-scale national study of 1,300 viewers and 1,300 non-viewers of religious programs, Gerbner et al. (1984) found that – consistent with earlier research – the audience for religious programs was more likely to live in rural areas of the South and Midwest, and to be older, less educated, of lower income, more conservative and more "fundamentalist" than the population at large. Dissatisfaction with the dominant moral climate (which often, of course, they encounter via television) drives them toward religious programs. Contrary to the concerns of some religious groups at the time, the study found that religious television did not pose a menacing challenge to mainline religion and local churches. Rather, the messages and worldviews cultivated by religious television were found to be in more direct competition with the world of commercial television; there were, in effect, two distinct, contesting "mainstreams" – the religious and the general.

Heavy general viewing and heavy religious viewing manifested distinctive profiles. Heavy viewers of religious programs, for example, described themselves as conservative, favored tougher laws against pornography, and voted in the most recent elections. Heavy general viewers claimed to be moderates, were not overly concerned about pornography, and tended not to vote. Most of the time, relationships between amount of religious television viewing and many political and social dependent variables held up across-the-board for most subgroups; in contrast, within-subgroup associations for general television viewing persistently revealed mainstreaming.

Hoover (1990) elaborated on these findings and also compared religious television viewing to "conventional" television viewing in terms of specifically religious beliefs and practices. He found that viewing religious television was highly predictive of emblematic religious behaviors, including Bible reading, praying, church attendance and so forth. That is, religious viewers tended to do religious things more frequently, as one would expect. On the other hand, "regular" TV viewing tended to have smaller and sometimes negative relationships with frequency of religious behaviors. Hoover concluded that "the religious role of contemporary television – as predicted by Gerbner – seems very much to be one of competition. If television is a kind of religion in contemporary life, we might expect to find what we did, that its viewers find it less necessary to participate in conventional religious behaviors" (p. 138). The implication is that general commercial television tends to supplant religious satisfactions in ways that lessen the importance of traditional religion for heavy viewers (see also Goethals, 1981).

Television even encroaches on religious subcultures that have traditionally been very resistant to modern communication. Umble's (1990) study of the impact of television on Mennonites shows that Mennonites who were heavier television viewers were much less traditional than their peers who chose not to watch. The data suggested that television represented a powerful force for the "moderation" of traditional religious practices in Mennonite life. This mimics the general conclusion of authors such as Mander (1991), who have suggested that television tends to dissolve traditional ways of life. It is worth noting that at the time Umble's data were collected, most Mennonites owned television sets; that is, set ownership was no longer in and of itself an indicator of a kind of "liberal" predisposition. Although one should not interpret these findings as suggesting that television just came along and scooped up unsuspecting Mennonites and secularized them, these data illuminate the dynamics of what can happen when strains of commercial television culture seep into traditional cultures.

So, clearly, television plays a role in how audiences understand religion, as hypothesized by Cultural Indicators. This influence also impacts on understanding of science. Gerbner et al. (1981d, 1985) reported that television disseminates a full range of familiar and conflicting cultural myths of science as weird and frightening, as omnipotent but dangerous, always progressing boundlessly but out of control, offering hope for the future, or even salvation, but also perhaps our annihilation. With similar complexity, scientists are shown as being important "authorities," yet working alone, socially isolated, very smart, often mad, sometimes evil. Compared to other fictional professionals, more of them are of foreign (non-US) nationality (which contributes to their "strangeness"), and they have a far higher failure rate. Proportionally more scientists are killed than any other occupational group – perhaps as a penalty for uncovering secrets better kept locked away, or by their own investigations run amok. Given these patterns, the cultivation work predictably showed that heavy viewers saw scientists and science as "strange" and mysterious, likely to do weird things and to be outside of the social mainstream.

Yet over time, a somewhat more nuanced version of television's impact on science has emerged. First of all, from a social control perspective, science is an institution that works hand-in-hand with corporations to develop new technologies, many of which have cultural and social implications. The idea of the military-industrial complex, for instance, rests upon science as providing access to new ideas that permit extended domination. Concurrent with our fear of science runs our adoration of technology and our wide-eyed faith it can solve any problems – sometimes, even the ones it creates.

Thus, one might hypothesize that if television were to function as propagandist for this elite social system, science would need to be "idealized" as a valuable and beneficent institution. Indeed, one prevalent image in media is that of the scientist as "omniscient" (Long and Steinke, 1996). At times scientists are portrayed as "heroic" figures (Lewenstein, 1989) who master malevolent forces (Hornig, 1990). They are all-knowing and are asked to comment on all topics, even those outside their expertise (Goodell, 1977). They are an elite and privileged group (Long and Steinke, 1996), wearing white lab coats or suits to differentiate themselves (Shortland, 1988) as belonging to a sacred field for which it is necessary to have qualified individuals as guides (Hornig, 1990). As Turow (1989) found, television (and other media) offers generally "authoritative" presentations of scientists and doctors.

But the picture is more complex. Across a variety of media, scientists are also sometimes portrayed as "powerless" (Goldman, 1989). They are easily manipulated or dominated (Basalla, 1976). They are often seen as pawns doing the dirty work for either big business or the military (Shortland, 1988), as seen, for example, in movies such as *The China Syndrome* and *Silkwood*. They are shown as different from other people, as eccentric and antisocial (Long and Steinke, 1996), as work-obsessed geeks (Basalla, 1976; Nelkin, 1990).

Thus, studies have identified several distinct images of science and scientists that tend to persist. This point is important because it is through media that much of the public encounters science, even (or especially) when they are not consciously seeking such information. How do these images contribute to public beliefs about science? As early as 1963, Davis found that the public held scientists in high regard. Scientists were described as intelligent, educated and dedicated. Most respondents felt that the world is better off due to science because of health improvements, a higher standard of living and technological advancements. The National Science Board (1991) maintains that 40 percent of Americans hold the scientific community in very high regard and are confident in its leadership. The public also believes that the benefits of scientific research outweigh the costs. Studies have also found that both teenagers and children see scientists as a force for good (Mead and Metraux, 1957; Potts and Martinez, 1994).

Most studies of media messages about science have considered only the impact of journalistic or "news" messages (Aukney et al. 1996;

Dornan, 1990; Hilgartner, 1990; Lewenstein, 1989). Following the prin-ciples of cultivation analysis, however, Gerbner, et al. (1985), looked at what heavy television viewers absorbed about science from regular viewing in general. In contrast to reading science magazines or watching science documentaries, overall television viewing appeared to cultivate *less* favorable, *more* skeptical and *mis*trustful outlooks on science, as well as the belief that scientists were odd, unsociable, impractical and generally peculiar people doing dangerous work. Heavy viewers were more suspi-cious of technological innovations, and more willing to tolerate restric-tions on the areas and problems scientists may investigate. Consistent with mainstreaming, all these patterns were strongest within groups (e.g., those with more education) whose members were science's greatest sup-porters as lighter viewers.

Thus, television's reliance on time-tested dramatic formulas and stock characters means that the medium continues to disseminate and sustain unflattering images of science – images which have deep cultural roots. These findings can also be contexted within the wider field of research on science communication, some strands of which are moving in the direc-tion of linking science beliefs to political beliefs. Specifically, "scientific authoritarianism" is an idea that can help explain apparent contradictions in the portrayal of science. That is, television's portrayals may serve to convince audiences that complicated and important scientific decisions need to be left in the hands of qualified scientists and experts. This can be compared to cultivation's argument about violence, which is that fear of violence induces society to be more accepting of social power structures to deal with the problem. Thus, in a world fraught with scientific danger and mystery, it may be that scientists are ever more needed to deal with problems that may be encountered.

As perceptions and beliefs about science are related to religious convic-tions, so too are they implicated in our opinions and assumptions about the environment. Coming after the intense wave of social concern about the environment that surged in the late 1980s, the question of television's role in suppressing or enhancing "environmentalism" represents the latest topical extension of cultivation research.

Although many people see TV as a potentially powerful force for improving environmental awareness, cultivation saw TV as a force to prevent such awareness and concern. The world of television drama (despite the alarmist nature of much news coverage) is one with few envi-ronmental problems (Shanahan, 1996; Shanahan and McComas, 1997), and the corporate sponsors of commercial entertainment certainly do not want to disturb viewers with upsetting images of environmental devasta-tion that may be linked with current consumption practices; neither do they want to draw attention to the environment as a *social* problem versus a domain that is up to individuals ("Don't pollute!") to protect. Moreover, given the proliferation of "green" packaging and environmentally "lite" products, a viewer may be tempted to believe that whatever environmental problems we may have once faced have now happily been cleansed away, thanks to the noble efforts of formerly polluting companies. (There is a parallel, of course, in the notion that television's portrayal of upscale, middle-class black families may lead some to conclude that we have solved our problems of racism, and that such policies as affirmative action are "no longer" needed.)

Shanahan (1993) initially demonstrated that TV exposure was negatively correlated with environmental concern. In later studies using GSS samples, Shanahan, Morgan and Stenbjerre (1997) showed more nuanced relationships, still suggesting that TV contributes to less support for environmentalism. In their comprehensive review of television's contributions to environmental beliefs, Shanahan and McComas (1999) conclude that television tends to place a "brake" on the speed with which society adopts environmental social change (a conclusion which mirrors the "retardation" hypothesis from the social control literature).

Shanahan and McComas also found that the environment and religion are often treated similarly by television; that is, they are marginalized. McKibben (1994) and other social critics have argued that religious beliefs are very important to establishing and maintaining environmental awareness and concern. In that respect, it is perhaps not surprising that television tends to undercut both.

Taken together, the complex of beliefs television cultivates about religion, science and the environment is congruent with the early Cultural Indicators notion that TV tends to "push aside" other institutions which have typically had a claim on the moral value systems of mass audiences. Of course, TV doesn't formally replace religion or science (though Shanahan and McComas argued that one of the most important effects of TV was to "replace" the natural environment). But even without actually eliminating such institutions, it becomes clear that television has played a very important role in how the institutions are experienced and interpreted. At the broadest level, TV can take what it likes from previously dominant institutions and remold those features into a more consistent ideological package, as predicted by Cultural Indicators theory. The cultivation of this specific mix of perspectives and orientations – including the supplanting of religion, the suspicion of science and the skepticism about environmental threats – seems, altogether, highly conducive to and congruent with the needs of a secular but conservative celebration of consumption.

### Where Does This Get Us?

After the early 1980s, cultivation clearly began examining a much wider variety of issues and focus areas, extending in many directions the earliest work on symbolic violence. Here we have summarized some of the work on ideology, politics, sex roles and other areas that complemented and extended the early work on violence and the mean world. There are many other studies that we have ignored thus far. Indeed, to discuss the results of all would take another two or three thick volumes (although we will mention some other studies in subsequent chapters).

Cultivation moved through the 1980s and into the 1990s with a more explicit and direct focus on politics, ideology and social control. Mainstreaming and its implications dominated the agenda, showing that the hegemonic contributions of television's messages were important to understand. Much of the social agenda of the 1980s and 1990s confirmed these thoughts. Although we should not focus too much on the tabloid issues of the day, the role of TV in framing debates on race (O. J. Simpson, Anita Hill), sex and the family (Murphy Brown) and politics (Iran–Contra, the Persian Gulf War) shows that important social questions are always dealt with within the context "already" provided by TV and other dominant media, even though television's messages don't uniformly "tell us what to think."

Thus, knowing how television discusses an issue is always a good clue to knowing how society at large sees the issue. If it can be discussed on television, the issue is "mainstream." If it cannot be discussed, or if an opinion would be mocked or marginalized on TV, then it is "radical" or "extremist." Thus, television makes it obvious what is "in" and what it is "out." Those looking at the medium have a reliable barometer for determining the cultural status of any given idea, position or practice; if they like, those on the margins have the information they need to make the changes necessary to bring themselves toward the political/cultural center of gravity. Indeed, cultivation's possible connection to the "active" audience notion is found precisely in this relationship; one need not assume a passive and atomized audience to see how mainstreaming might work: the audience might do the work for social elites by "managing" themselves to take on belief characteristics consonant with mainstream ideologies (in a manner similar to that posited by spiral of silence theory; Noelle-Neuman, 1993).

All this suggests several main conclusions from the more mature work performed by cultivation in the 1980s and 1990s:

1 issues of violence, although not neglected, became less central to cultivation work;

2 as cultivation focused on a broader range of topical areas, it increasingly confronted political and ideological issues more explicitly;
3 the idea of mainstreaming was cemented as the most important statistical test for judging the presence or absence of cultivation;
4 and finally, cultivation gradually began to leave behind the critique–retort format.

These conclusions allow us to return to the issue Hirsch raised: is mainstreaming falsifiable? We can now answer that question more completely. First, as we have argued, mainstreaming is not simply a statistical artifact. Its regular occurrence makes it noteworthy, if nothing else. Second, mainstreaming occurs consistently across many topic areas. Third, its specific pattern is fairly consistent, in that higher-status, higher-education and "liberal" groups have tended to show the stronger associations. If mainstreaming were mere artifact, then lower-status groups would equally merge toward a mean. Finally, mainstreaming is entirely consistent with the theory of cultivation, and can be falsified in one of two ways:

1 by a body of research which, adopting cultivation's basic assumptions and methods, finds consistently that mainstreaming patterns don't exist; or
2 by devising and testing a theory which accounts in another way for the continued observation of mainstreaming patterns.

Method 1 would require a good deal of research to match the twenty plus years of cultivation research. That is, a single study finding no mainstreaming is not acceptable, for reasons that will become especially clear in the next chapter. The second method would be the preferred method of falsifying mainstreaming, although no such effort has yet emerged. Still we should make clear that we are arguing for a relatively "weak" form of falsifiability; that is, mainstreaming predicts only the general nature and frequency of patterns to be observed. Mainstreaming should not be seen as some sort of "lawlike" phenomenon, appearing with complete consistency in every case. As with all social prediction, there are still many cases where we might expect to see mainstreaming but it does not occur. These instances demonstrate a need for further theoretical development and empirical testing.

If research moves in paradigms (rather than incrementally inching ahead through hypothesis and falsification), we would argue that the cultivation paradigm is still firmly entrenched and quite viable. But, as always, there are still other questions to answer. One major question, to be dealt with in the next chapter, is how all the separate studies might be summarized in a more "objective" way, less subject to the whims and preferences of any particular reviewer. We will do that, in the next chapter, using the techniques of meta-analysis.

# 6    The Bigger Picture

In the preceding chapters we examined the history of cultivation theory and analysis, providing a description of its major studies and critiques. Those chapters represent the story of cultivation as *we* tell it. Others may, of course, tell it differently. And this points up one important problem with any narrative evaluation of the results: other observers may not recognize the telling as "objective."

Although no account can be perfectly objective, in this chapter we try to get around the natty problems of objectivity (at least somewhat) by using meta-analysis, a technique that summarizes results from a different, non-narrative, perspective. Meta-analysis allows researchers to look at separate, independent studies as individual "data points" and to determine whether these studies can be seen as a single body of research which yields a single conclusion.

## What is Meta–Analysis, Anyway?

This section is for readers who do not have the slightest idea of what we mean by "meta-analysis." (Others may wish to read it anyway.) Earlier, we noted that, theoretically, any cultivation analysis can be compared against any other, because they are all testing essentially the same thing. This means that, with a little effort, we can look at the last twenty years of cultivation research as a single, unified inquiry into relationships between television exposure and people's beliefs about the world. And that is exactly the foundation on which this chapter is built. When researchers cumulate results from independent studies and attempt to reach a single concise and comprehensive conclusion, that is known as "meta-analysis" (Mullen, 1989). Meta-analysis is becoming increasingly important in the reanalysis of communication findings (Allen et al., 1995; Kim and Hunter, 1993; Herrett-Skjellum and Allen, 1996).

To explain how it works, let's take Anytown, USA, population 150,000, where the average person watches 3.2 hours of television a day. That is the figure we would get if we did a census (not a survey) of each and every person who lives in that town. In most cases, doing a census is too expensive and time-consuming, so researchers usually take data from samples. The average we get from the sample is an estimate of what the "true" figure is for the full population, a figure that we (by definition) do not know.

If we visit Anytown and draw a properly selected, representative sample of, say, 500 people, chances are that the average viewing figure we get from our sample should be close to the "true" figure of 3.2 hours – but it probably won't be *exactly* the same. It might be 2.9, or 3.3, or even 3.8. The difference between the sample mean and the (unknown) "true" mean is called "sample error." Since we don't know the true mean, the sample error is itself an estimate that we accept at various levels of confidence.

If we drew a succession of independent samples of 500 people each from the town, then some of the sample means would be right on the "true" figure and some would be quite a way off; but the *average of all those sample averages* would most likely (we can never be sure without a census) be very, very close to the "true" average. In other words, the average of all the sample averages almost certainly provides a better estimate of the true average than does any single sample average – that is, the average of the averages has less sample error, and the more samples are added, the smaller the sample error becomes.

Meta-analysis works on this same principle. Say that two variables are "really" related to each other, but the only way we would know this for sure would be if we were to conduct a census of the relevant population. Instead, we look at the relationship between two variables in a sample from that population. In any given sample – using any given test of a hypothesis – the relationship may or may not be seen, and it may appear to be stronger or weaker than it "really" is in the entire population. Not every test of a "true" hypothesis will show it to be true; i.e., there can be false negatives. Similarly, by chance, a study could suggest that a relationship exists that in the population "really" does not. But if there are many studies done on a topic, then – just as in the example of TV viewing in Anytown – the *average* results of all those studies together will provide a far better estimate of the "true" size of the relationship in the full population than will any individual test.

Stated more technically, meta-analysis provides an estimate of how much of the variation in results observed across studies simply reflects sampling error, along with many other corrections of a more technical nature (Hunter and Schmidt, 1990). This offers a major advantage over the traditional narrative review. That is, we can see how much of the differences in reported cultivation findings is "real" after the variation

expected due to sampling error is accounted for. And if any "real" variation is left, we can then determine if results vary across different types of
samples, different dependent areas, different methodological or analytical
strategies, and so on.

Perhaps the greatest justification for meta-analysis is that it takes *some*
of the subjectivity out of the review process. As we have seen, cultivation
research has been portrayed in extremely different ways, depending upon
the academic and political commitments of those doing the reviewing.
Given the divergences, one wonders at times whether the same studies are
being read. Although we do not assume that a mere aggregation of results
will somehow automatically provide "truer" evidence of cultivation,
meta-analysis does let us look at the existing data in a more systematic
way than previous reviews have allowed. Moreover, it lets a critical reader
make a more informed judgment about the literature being analyzed.

Meta-analysis corrects for many pitfalls of the traditional narrative literature review and reliance on the usual criterion of statistically
significant results. For one thing, the risk of making Type II errors (i.e.,
mistakenly rejecting a "true" hypothesis) is rampant when the reviewer
simply counts up the number of significant findings reported (Hunter
and Schmidt, 1990). Studies with small samples can report effect sizes
that are not "significant" but exactly the same as the "true" correlation
(as we saw with Doob and Macdonald, above). Meta-analysis can shed a
much clearer light on bodies of work that might otherwise be characterized as showing "inconsistent results."

In meta-analysis, each observed result is assumed to be a random sampling from a distribution whose mean represents the "true" effect. The
analysis thus gives a better estimate of that "true" effect, adjusted for
sample size, than does any individual study. But meta-analysis does more
than that. The cumulated data are examined to see if the set of relationships is homogeneous (using the terminology of Mullen, 1989), or to see
how much of the observed variation in results across studies reflects mere
sampling error (using the terms of Hunter and Schmidt, 1990). If the
findings are heterogeneous, or if there remains much unexplained variance after sampling error has been removed and other adjustments have
been made, then the meta-analyst can conduct a theory-driven investigation of the variables that might have *moderated* the observed effects.

Because there have been so many cultivation studies (and findings), it is
vital to begin to look at them as individual cases in a broader research
agenda. We need to examine what kind of forest has been grown out of the
trees of individual cultivation studies. Accordingly, we used the technique
of meta-analysis to help guide us through a different kind of assessment of
cultivation theory and its accomplishments in its first twenty years.

## Some Descriptive Data from Cultivation Theory

The conventional meta-analysis requires that data be collected and presented in certain ways. We describe these requirements as we proceed, though full details are given in our methodological appendix. These requirements mean we must jump a number of methodological hurdles before the data can be properly presented. Especially because cultivation findings have been presented in so many different ways, we undertook a variety of data "collapsing" exercises to help us compare often disparate studies.

To begin our analysis, we collected all published studies on cultivation since 1976. From each study, we coded all reported cultivation "findings." A finding is simply a statistical estimate of a relationship between hours of television viewed and some dependent variable. A finding (a simple correlation, a gamma, a beta and so on) can be reported either for an entire sample, or for a subgroup of that sample. Findings also include reports of relationships where controls were implemented. Dependent variables can be perceptions of crime, fear of violence, sex role perceptions, etc.

This exercise generated a database of 5,799 separate findings, derived from 97 studies/samples (some studies used more than one sample, so we used the "sample" as the ultimate unit of analysis). Thus, the average cultivation study reports nearly 60 "results" (findings), much more than in many other types of communication research (where a handful of statistics constitutes the results of a given research effort). This is because cultivation often reports not only "simple" relationships between television exposure and some other variable(s), but also reports relationships within subgroups (male/female, young/old, etc.) and with various statistical controls. Thus, most papers and articles present *many* separate findings; some present literally hundreds.

For instance, the first cultivation study, "Living with television" (Gerbner and Gross, 1976) reported twenty-five different findings relating television use to various perceptions of crime and violence. In that study, relationships were reported using percentage differences between light and heavy viewers. That is, as noted in Chapter 2, cultivation was measured by showing how many heavy viewers gave a "TV answer" compared to how many light viewers. The difference, in percentage terms, was seen as an indicator of cultivation. Of the twenty-five findings reported, three were "overall" findings (that is, they reflected the beliefs of the entire sample, as opposed to subgroups such as males or liberals). These three findings on average showed that heavy and light viewers' answers on perceptions of violence differed by about 13 percentage points (the

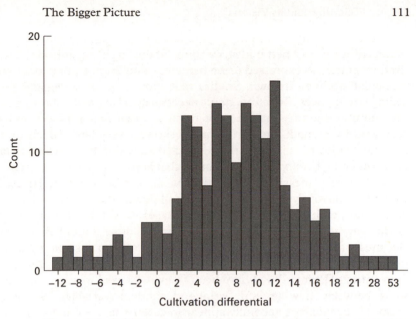

Figure 6.1 Cultivation differentials (CD) expressed as percentage differences (from overall dataset; average = 8%, mode = 12%)

cultivation differential). This thirteen-point difference would be counted by meta-analysts as one "observation" in an ongoing body of research.

As might be guessed, meta-analysts believe that one finding is suggestive but does not "prove" a case. Figure 6.1 shows the distribution of all of the overall percentage differences reported in our sample, gathered from all available studies, not just Gerbner's. It is interesting to note that, though Gerbner's study was the first cultivation study, its estimate of percentage differences between light and heavy viewers was close to differences reported in most of the studies that followed. The modal difference seen in Figure 6.1 is 12 percentage points. The average (mean = 8 percent; SD = 7.35 percent) is somewhat lower due to some negative outliers.

The figure shows two things. First, Gerbner's initial estimate of cultivation effects proved to be rather close to what subsequently gathered percentage estimates of differentials would reveal, on average. Second, the composite body of these differentials reveals a good deal of variety. What causes the variation? Even if measurement were perfect, we must remember that we are dealing with human beings, who do not always behave in predictable ways. Additionally, in cases where measurement is good and behavior predictable, there will always be a certain amount of variation in results due to sampling error.

Figure 6.1, though combining some findings that are not independent of each other, gives a better idea, we think, of the "true" magnitude of cultivation, at least as expressed using percentage differences, than does any particular study on its own. Studies that show smaller or negative percentage differences, therefore, don't necessarily falsify cultivation, rather they simply (due to sampling error or some other factors) have underestimated its strength. Similarly, studies showing very large effects don't prove that cultivation is larger than expected; they simply happened to fall at the other, higher end of a distribution that is (*ceteris paribus*) normal.

If all studies measured cultivation using percentage differences, it would be a relatively simple matter to "boil down" the differences across all samples, taking an average of the averages, to get some idea of how much heavy viewers differ from light viewers, all other things being equal. But most studies use more sophisticated methods for assessing cultivation. Three statistical techniques have dominated the literature. Correlations (Pearson's $r$'s) have been frequently used to assess relationships between viewing and various dependent variables. Similarly, "gamma" coefficients generally appear in cases where ordinal scales are used to measure responses for dependent variables. Finally, partial correlations, regression coefficients, and other techniques have been used when researchers wish to control statistically for other relevant variables. In the entire dataset, there are 706 $r$'s (12 percent), 2,331 partial $r$'s (40.2 percent), and 1,722 gamma findings (29.7 percent). The rest of the findings use other miscellaneous techniques.

The first study to use correlations for overall populations to measure cultivation was "Violence Profile No. 8" (Gerbner et al., 1977). In that study, four correlations measuring relationships between television viewing and beliefs about violence averaged .15. The findings from VP 8 suggested small positive relationships between viewing and beliefs about violence.

Once again, if all cultivation studies were measured using correlations, it would be fairly simple to average them all together to say how cultivation looks from the broad perspective. However, because different measures have been used, this kind of comparison is not always so easy. One revealing comparative technique is simply to examine distribution patterns for the various types of measures that have been used, to see if there is any comparability or consistency among them. We do this in Figures 6.2–6.4. These figures show the characteristic frequency curves obtained for the observed relationships in our database, using the three most common forms of estimating cultivation relationships.

The histograms show that these samples are distributed fairly normally, regardless of the type of measure, and that each distribution

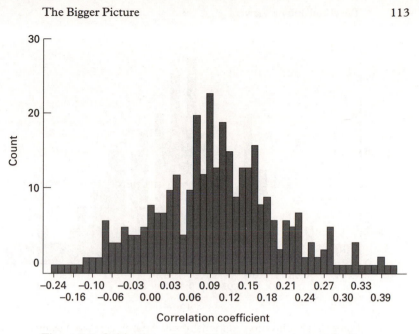

Figure 6.2  Cultivation relationships in dataset, measured using *r*

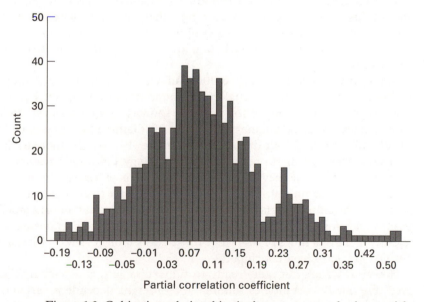

Figure 6.3  Cultivation relationships in dataset, measured using partial *r*

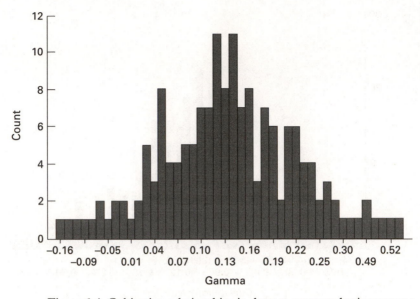

Figure 6.4  Cultivation relationships in dataset, measured using gamma

centers on a mean that is close to about .10. Again, the consistent appearance of this pattern suggests quite strongly that any particular cultivation finding from any particular study is simply *one* estimate that should not in and of itself be taken too seriously (again, *ceteris paribus*), no matter how strong or weak the results.

In the entire dataset of nearly 6,000 findings we accumulated, average simple *r*'s run about .10. Partial correlations would be expected to be lower (because they control for possible sources of spuriousness, they reduce many associations); they run about .09. Gamma measures usually run slightly higher; in our dataset they average .14. Mostly, though, the data show that regardless of measurement strategy, cultivation results do seem to be drawn somewhat systematically from a larger population whose mean is about .10. Thus, it might make sense to conclude at this point that the cultivation literature has demonstrated that there is a small positive relationship between beliefs about the world and exposure to television. This is more or less what most cultivation reviews – friendly, hostile or mixed – have concluded.

However, we are not quite ready to fully support that assertion. The preceding analysis combines findings for different dependent variables (violence, sex-roles, mean world, etc.). And it also combines findings that are not statistically independent of each other, because the overall database of 5,799 findings comes from a much smaller number of distinct samples. But as we will see they come close to the mark as an accurate description of what the body of cultivation research can tell us.

Table 6.1 shows average cultivation results from each of the individual studies in our dataset. As noted, some published studies use more than one sample, but for this table we've simply averaged samples together within studies, for ease of presentation. The table simply shows the average $r$ for the study, and the average $N$ of the sample in the study.

The table vividly shows that there is a good deal of variation across studies. But some individual results are interesting. Studies such as Potter's "linearity" study (1991a), which are framed as critical of cultivation, actually show average results close to what the entire sample shows. On the other hand, studies such as Hirsch's "scary world" re-analyses do show stronger negative findings (though a variety of technical points should be recalled on Hirsch's study, from Chapter 4). There are also examples of studies from proponents of cultivation that show results weaker than the average. If nothing else, all this shows that individual investigators can often reach startlingly different conclusions from similar results or even from the same data.

The individual studies show how much variation there can be in a body of research. Taking this larger perspective shows that it can sometimes be unwise to talk about whether a *particular* study confirms or disconfirms a theory. In any case, different readers might use different methods for deciding whether a study "confirms" cultivation. The meta-analytic method is to look at all the studies together, because individual samples can vary due to nothing more than sampling error. As Table 6.1 shows, the studies overall show an average of about .10 (weighted averages are slightly lower). For us, such a "meta" correlation can be interpreted as a general confirmation of cultivation's prediction that there will be small but significant relationships between exposure to TV and various beliefs. Yet others would say that such a correlation is too small to be meaningful – a correlation of .10 means that about 1 percent of the variance has been accounted for. Before going any further, therefore, the whole question of "effect size" as it relates to cultivation research needs some attention.

### Effect Size and Variance within the Sample

What sort of relationship should one expect between amount of television viewing and dependent variables of interest? What kind of relationship is strong enough to confirm the theory, or what would disconfirm it? As we pointed out in earlier chapters, any expectation of extremely large relationships should be ruled out on theoretical and statistical grounds. First

Table 6.1 *Summary of findings*

Note: In some studies, the average *r*'s are calculated from a fairly large number of findings; others use relatively few. See Appendix for procedures used to transform measures into common metric.

| Sample | Study | Citation | mean *r* | mean *n* |
|---|---|---|---|---|
| Aggregate of 17 data sets | Political correlates of TV viewing | Gerbner et al., 1984 | 0.04 | 651 |
| Arbitron data; 20-market adult sample | Religion & TV | Hoover, 1990 | 0.06 | 1,496 |
| Argentine adolescents | International cultivation | Morgan, 1990 | 0.10 | 406 |
| | Political attitudes in Argentina | Morgan & Shanahan, 1991b | 0.02 | 314 |
| | *Democracy Tango* | Morgan & Shanahan, 1995 | 0.03 | 443 |
| Arizona adolescents | TV and perceptions of govt | Berman & Stookey, 1980 | 0.07 | 600 |
| Baltimore; Korean immigrants | US Koreans | Choi & Tamborini, 1988 | −0.02 | 152 |
| Bank Street School children | Violence Profile 9 | Gerbner et al., 1978 | 0.28 | 60 |
| British adults (IBA data) | TV & personal threat | Wober & Gunter, 1982 | 0.17 | 322 |
| British adults (quota sample) | Politics & TV in the UK | Piepe et al., 1990 | 0.11 | 451 |
| California/Oregon adolescents | Perceived reality | Slater & Elliott, 1982 | 0.03 | 510 |
| Center for Political Studies, 1976 Election Data; National adult sample | Violence Profile 9 | Gerbner et al., 1978 | 0.06 | 1,142 |
| Chinese adolescents | International cultivation | Morgan, 1990 | 0.05 | 578 |
| Child Trends; Followup of national survey of adolescents | TV, family cohesion and control | Rothschild & Morgan, 1987 | 0.05 | 452 |
| Connecticut Mutual Report on American Values; National adult sample | Political correlates of TV viewing | Gerbner et al., 1984 | 0.03 | 1,610 |

| Sample | Study | Citation | Value | N |
|---|---|---|---|---|
| Dutch adults | Dutch cultivation | Bouwman, 1984 | 0.09 | 300 |
| Korean adolescents | International cultivation | Morgan, 1990 | 0.07 | 659 |
| Lansing, MI; Korean immigrants | US Koreans | Choi & Tamborini, 1988 | 0.10 | 86 |
| Madison, WI adults | Cognitive processing | Hawkins et al., 1987 | 0.25 | 100 |
| Mennonites | Mennonites and television | Umble, 1990 | 0.10 | 3,591 |
| Mid-Atlantic children | Kids, TV & chores | Signorielli & Lears, 1992a | 0.04 | 307 |
| Mid-Atlantic adults | New media study 1 | Perse et al., 1994 | 0.23 | 81 |
| Midwestern adolescents | Perceived reality | Potter, 1986 | 0.00 | 237 |
| Midwestern adults | Local TV News & Involvement | Perse, 1990 | 0.11 | 300 |
| Midwestern adults | New media study 2 | Perse et al., 1994 | 0.04 | 510 |
| Midwestern undergraduates | Perceived reality | Potter, 1986 | 0.17 | 92 |
| Midwestern undergraduates | Soap viewing patterns | Perse, 1986 | 0.20 | 458 |
| Minnesota adolescents | Impact of new TV technologies | Morgan & Rothschild, 1983 | 0.18 | 153 |
|  | Political correlates of TV viewing | Gerbner et al., 1984 | 0.10 | 294 |
|  | Cultivation, perceptions of marriage | Signorielli, 1991 | 0.07 | 1,355 |
| Monitoring the Future, 1985; National adolescent sample | TV and perceptions of work | Signorielli, 1993 | 0.12 | 1,064 |
| "Myth and Reality of Aging"; National adult sample (Louis Harris) | Aging with TV | Gerbner et al., 1980 | 0.15 |  |
| New Jersey adolescents; Panel Data | TV & enculturation | Gross & Morgan, 1985 | 0.18 | 100 |
|  | Sex-role stereotypes | Morgan, 1982 | 0.21 | 216 |
| New Jersey adolescents; Wave 2 segments | Aging with TV | Gerbner et al., 1980 | 0.21 | 431 |
|  | Be when grow up? | Gross & Jeffries-Fox, 1978 | 0.18 | 323 |
|  | Violence Profile 8 | Gerbner et al., 1977 | 0.16 | 466 |
|  | Violence profile 9 | Gerbner et al., 1978 | 0.11 | 256 |
|  | Violence profile 10 | Gerbner et al., 1979 | 0.13 | 249 |

Table 6.1 (cont.)

| Sample | Study | Citation | mean r | mean n |
|---|---|---|---|---|
| New Lincoln (NY) Schoolchildren | Violence profile 10 | Gerbner et al., 1979 | 0.21 | 62 |
| NORC 75 | TV blacks & gays | Gross, 1984 | 0.05 | 467 |
| | Violence Profile 9 | Gerbner et al. 1978 | 0.12 | 606 |
| NORC 77 | Political correlates | Gerbner et al., 1984 | 0.05 | 1,530 |
| | TV, blacks & gays | Gross, 1984 | 0.07 | 467 |
| | Violence Profile 9 | Gerbner et al., 1978 | 0.06 | 695 |
| | Mainstreaming of America | Gerbner et al., 1980a | 0.09 | 486 |
| NORC 75/78 | Mainstreaming of America | Gerbner et al., 1980a | 0.07 | 1,132 |
| | Scary world | Hirsch, 1980 | −0.07 | 1,364 |
| NORC 78 | Political correlates | Gerbner et al., 1984 | 0.09 | 1,532 |
| | TV, blacks & gays | Gross, 1984 | 0.04 | 467 |
| NORC 75,77,78 | Violence Profile 9 | Gerbner et al., 1978 | 0.10 | 2,200 |
| | Charting the mainstream | Gerbner at al., 1982 | 0.08 | 1,099 |
| | Health portrayals | Gerbner et al., 1982 | 0.04 | 1,640 |
| | TV and sex-roles | Signorielli, 1989 | 0.05 | 1,796 |
| NORC 80 | Charting the mainstream | Gerbner et al., 1982 | 0.08 | 1,220 |
| | Mean World syndrome | Signorielli, 1990 | 0.10 | 640 |
| | Political correlates of TV viewing | Gerbner et al., 1984 | 0.08 | 1,468 |
| | TV, blacks & gays | Gross, 1984 | 0.11 | 559 |
| NORC 82 | Mean World syndrome | Signorielli, 1990 | 0.05 | 640 |
| | Political correlates | Gerbner et al., 1984 | 0.03 | 1,506 |
| NORC 83 | Mean World syndrome | Signorielli, 1990 | 0.08 | 640 |
| | TV & voting | Morgan & Shanahan, 1992b | 0.11 | 1,450 |
| NORC 85 | Mean World syndrome | Signorielli, 1990 | 0.08 | 640 |
| | TV & voting | Morgan & Shanahan, 1992b | 0.15 | 1,450 |

| Sample | Topic | Reference | | |
|---|---|---|---|---|
| NORC 86 | Mean World syndrome | Signorielli, 1990 | 0.09 | 640 |
| | TV & voting | Morgan & Shanahan, 1992b | 0.08 | 1,450 |
| NORC 88 | TV & voting | Morgan & Shanahan, 1992b | 0.13 | 1,450 |
| NORC 89 | TV & voting | Morgan & Shanahan, 1992b | 0.11 | 802 |
| NORC 90 | Growing up with TV | Gerbner et al., 1994 | 0.06 | 401 |
| NORC 93 | Cultivation and the environment | Shanahan et al., 1997 | −0.06 | 683 |
| NORC 94 | Cultivation and the environment | Shanahan et al., 1997 | −0.07 | 398 |
| NORC 80, 82, 85 | Mean World syndrome | Signorielli, 1990 | 0.08 | 2,042 |
| NORC 83, 85, 86 | TV and sex-roles | Signorielli, 1989 | 0.05 | 1,596 |
| NORC 80 + composites | Charting the mainstream | Gerbner et al., 1982 | 0.06 | 1,417 |
| NORC 88–91 | TV, sex and AIDS | Bosompra, 1993 | 0.01 | 3,300 |
| Northeast college students | Soaps and cultivation | Carveth & Alexander, 1985 | 0.16 | 233 |
| Perth children | Australia | Pingree & Hawkins, 1981 | 0.14 | 990 |
| | Cognitive processes | Hawkins & Pingree, 1980 | 0.19 | 640 |
| Philadelphia children | Cultivation and group affiliation | Rothschild, 1984 | 0.19 | 33 |
| Potter adolescents, 2 | 3 strategies | Potter, 1988 | 0.10 | 82 |
| Potter adolescents, 3 | Linearity | Potter, 1991a | 0.10 | 308 |
| | Psychological perspective | Potter, 1991c | 0.04 | 308 |
| RI adolescents | Prime time crime | Carlson, 1985 | 0.10 | 374 |
| RI adults | Affluence & capitalism | Carlson, 1993 | 0.07 | 297 |
| Roper, national adult sample | Views on crime | O'Keefe, 1984 | 0.04 | 1,188 |
| Science and Technology; national adult sample | Political correlates of TV viewing | Gerbner et al., 1984 | 0.07 | 1,635 |
| Southern adolescents | Adolescent occupational expectations | Ryan et al. 1988 | 0.12 | 480 |

Table 6.1 (*cont.*)

| Sample | Study | Citation | mean r | mean n |
|---|---|---|---|---|
| Southern communication undergraduates | Soap operas & cultivation | Buerkel-Rothfuss & Mayes 1981 | 0.20 | 290 |
| Southwestern adults | TV & sociopolitical attitudes | Volgy & Schwartz, 1980 | 0.29 | 176 |
| Starch 1973 national adult sample | Violence Profile 8 | Gerbner et al., 1977 | 0.16 | 573 |
| Swansea, MA adolescents, 1985 | International cultivation | Morgan, 1990 | 0.06 | 500 |
| Swansea, MA adolescents, 1988 | International cultivation | Morgan, 1990 | 0.11 | 360 |
| Toronto adults | TV and crime in the city | Doob & Macdonald, 1979 | 0.10 | 192 |
| Trinidad adolescents | TV in Trinidad | Phekoo et al., 1996 | 0.22 | 418 |
| Virginia Slims data; | Health portrayals | Gerbner et al., 1982 | 0.06 | 1,637 |
| national adult sample | TV and quality of life | Morgan, 1984 | 0.11 | 3,944 |
| (Roper) | Political correlates of TV viewing | Gerbner et al., 1982 | 0.02 | 3,944 |
| Washington, DC African-Americans | Blacks and the mainstream | Matabane, 1988 | 0.12 | 81 |

*Note:* This table shows results for studies where overall correlations were reported, for purposes of comparison. Studies with results in other metrics (such as partial correlations, regression coefficients, etc.), are not shown here.

of all, very commonly used and influential variables such as age, income and education typically show correlations no larger than .30 with most cultivation dependent variables, and frequently they average around .15. So even variables that are commonly thought to be powerful predictors do not reveal very high correlations. This is due to the random nature of much human behavior and the vagaries of measuring such phenomena; there is a lot of variance we simply can't, and never will, explain.

Cultivation theory certainly accepts, and common sense predicts, that TV viewing will play a smaller statistical role than major demographic variables, so it is no surprise that the average cultivation relationship is less than .20. Also, television viewing tends to co-vary in significant ways with important demographic variables, so that tends to restrict the variance we can detect as well. Judged within those parameters, and by the parameters of social science generally, then, a significant and consistent relationship of .10 is something important, even though it is not a "large" effect size. Particularly when one considers that TV viewing's effects are cumulative and repetitive, a relationship of .10 is something that can make a difference over time. Slow but consistent effects can also have noticeable and important influences.

Indeed, think about the many ways in which 1 percent can make a difference. If your weight increased every year by 1 percent, you wouldn't notice it at first, but before long the disturbing and long-hidden trend emerges: you're getting fat! If you weighed 150 pounds at age 25, a 1 percent yearly weight increase (hardly noticeable, perhaps best described as a "small effect size") would have you weighing 200 pounds by age 55. Then the importance of small differences could become apparent.

Now at other times, small differences are not important. The weight example is meant to suggest that small differences and small correlations can be important when they result from phenomena which work *consistently over time*. In our view, exposure to television messages can be seen as such a phenomenon. If 1 percent of the variance in various dependent variables is consistently associated with television viewing, that means that there is a chance for the meaning of messages to sink in slowly and in the background, not necessarily in the foreground of attention. Indeed, the fact that cultivation theory argues that this is where effects will emerge is consistent with small effects, not large ones. This is why most cultivation theorists would be very surprised to see large correlations between viewership and dependent variables, except in extreme cases.

Other meta-studies in the communication literature reveal similar effect sizes. For instance, Herrett-Skjellum and Allen's (1996) meta-analysis of relationships between TV viewing and ideas about sex-roles

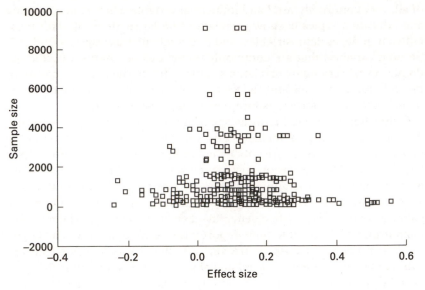

Figure 6.5 Funnel plot

reveals a relationship of .10 (essentially what we came up with, though some different studies were analyzed). O'Keefe and Figge's (1997) analysis of "door-in-the-face" persuasion strategies (well accepted in the literature as an "effective" means of communication) shows a similar effect size. So, small correlations are not unusual in the communication literature; it is part of the difficulty of doing social science.

Now let us return to the body of results. Why do they vary? One important answer is sample size. As Mullen (1989) points out, meta-analytic theory suggests that results from larger samples should be closer to the overall mean (i.e., the "true," unknown, mean) than results from smaller samples. That is, as samples get larger, other things being equal, they should be more likely to reflect the true population average. One way to examine whether this is the case is through a "funnel" diagram, which is a scatterplot that compares average findings against their sample size. If the sample of studies gathered reflects the behavior of the real population, then the scatterplot should reveal a "funnel"-shaped pattern, in which results far from the population average (either above or below) are found at lower sample sizes, while higher sample size studies should reveal results rather close to the true average. If the expected funnel pattern is not evident, it may indicate problems with the method in which the cumulative data were gathered. Figure 6.5 presents the results of a funnel diagram for our data.

The expected funnel pattern is apparent. The larger sample size studies do cluster about an average effect size of about .09–.10 (with one or two outliers), again suggesting that this is likely to be a good approximation of the "true" population average. The generally funnel-shaped nature of the data shows that the body of literature varies in ways that statistical theory would predict: it does not look, for instance, as if different studies are studying different problems (which might be the case if different modes appeared in the data).

Also, the funnel diagram allows for a test of the "file drawer" problem, which occurs when a meta-analysis has unintentionally excluded studies with weak findings (often because such findings can be difficult to publish). If the file drawer problem were afflicting cultivation, then the funnel would be artificially "cut off" on the low side. Also, it allows for a test for the reverse of the file drawer problem, which we will call the "hypercritique" phenomenon, in which strong findings are absent from the literature because the field views a theory critically. In this situation, the funnel would be artificially cut off on the high side. Because the distribution of our findings is close enough to the expected funnel shape, it is not likely that either of these problems is occurring (although cultivation has certainly received its share of criticism).

These informal, preliminary findings support the contentions of cultivation research over the past twenty years. That is, again, cultivation predicts small relationships between exposure to television and responses to a variety of dependent variables, and the data from the vast bulk of studies and samples do support that conclusion, at least on the bivariate level. In order to sustain that conclusion, and to deepen our understanding of it, we next move to a more formal and systematic meta-analysis.

### Meta-analysis of Cultivation Findings

A formal meta-analysis needs data that come from "independent" samples. The data shown in Table 6.1 do come from different samples (although some other analyses we will present are based on the full dataset of nearly 6,000 findings which, as noted, are not independent). In the principal analyses to follow, every finding comes from the accumulated dataset made up of independent samples. The analyses in this section, therefore, provide the most reliable indicators of overall cultivation strength, because each study is effectively randomly drawn from and stands for the larger population.[1]

---

[1] This analysis is based on and elaborates the analysis that originally appeared in Morgan and Shanahan (1997).

Using independent samples also allows us to test whether the cumulated body of studies can be viewed as significant, but not quite in the sense that "significance" is usually approached. That is, we'd like to know whether the observed correlation is strong enough to suggest that the result is not simply due to chance. Any individual finding may be wrong somewhat (i.e., it may provide a misleading – whether higher or lower – estimate of the actual effect size) simply by chance. So can one be more confident simply by adding up and averaging results from studies which are prone to error?

First, we note that our meta-sample includes tens of thousands of individuals. With such a large sample size, virtually any finding differing from 0 would be considered significant, so the quick answer is "yes." However, there is also a somewhat more complex and interesting answer.

Hunter and Schmidt (1990) point out that typical, routine tests for statistical significance are of limited value because they tend to under-appreciate the havoc that can be wreaked by forgetting about Type II errors (and this amnesia seems to occur with great regularity in social scientific research). Type II error results in a study when we erroneously accept the null hypothesis (i.e., when we accept a false negative). Researchers, using textbook procedures to assess statistical significance, control very well for Type I error (falsely rejecting the null hypothesis), but the risk of Type II error is often overlooked. As a consequence, as Hunter makes clear, there can be many wide variations in a body of research that is normally considered "significant."

Hunter champions meta-analysis as a solution to this problem, and we agree. Rather than asking how "significant" the findings are, Hunter suggests that meta-analysts present statistics on variability in their findings, and then compare that variability to the variance expected from sampling error.

This means that the meta-analyst needs to show a few things. First, of course, comes the "base" finding which is the average of all the studies. Second, comes the amount of variance in the averages observed from the meta-sample, and third, the amount of variance one would expect simply from sampling error alone. If the analyst can show that there is not much more (or even less) variance than what one would expect from sampling error, then one can be rather confident that one has revealed a true, "unmoderated" effect in the meta-analytic data. If, though, there is more variance than what one would expect from sampling error, it may mean that other variables are moderating the relationship. Knee-jerk habits to the contrary, the question of significance is left aside in our analysis, since most meta-analyses usually measure responses from enough individuals to make significance a relatively trivial issue.

Table 6.2 *Summary statistics for meta-analysis*

| analysis | K | avg. effect | % var from error | $X^2$ |
|---|---|---|---|---|
| overall | 58 | 0.085 | 48 | 118.6*** |
| *Dependent variables:* | | | | |
| violence | 26 | 0.10 | 45 | 56.6*** |
| sex roles | 10 | 0.09 | 78 | 12.5 |
| politics | 27 | 0.078 | 30 | 87.7*** |
| *Gender:* | | | | |
| females | 29 | 0.081 | 77 | 37.0 |
| males | 29 | 0.079 | 43 | 66.3*** |
| *Research groups:* | | | | |
| core | 32 | 0.078 | 51 | 61.4*** |
| other | 26 | 0.104 | 51 | 49.9*** |
| *Sensitization to independent variable:* | | | | |
| yes | 8 | 0.116 | 100 | 6.86 |
| no | 34 | 0.079 | 46 | 73.1*** |
| *Sample size:* | | | | |
| small | 25 | 0.13 | 58 | 41.9* |
| large | 33 | 0.079 | 52 | 63.8*** |

*Note:* *** $p < 0.001$, ** $p < 0.01$, * $p < 0.05$

After we conducted our first meta-analysis of cultivation research (Morgan and Shanahan, 1997), we updated the data to include a few new studies. Our amended analysis shows that the average overall effect size for cultivation studies is .10 (with fifty-eight independent samples). Again, this means that, on average, cultivation studies (summing across all studies, all samples, all methods, all measures, and all dependent areas) have found a consistent, theoretically predicted relationship between exposure to television and beliefs about the world. When the correlations are weighted to allow larger samples sizes to contribute more to the overall average, the resulting weighted average is somewhat lower ($r = .085$; it was .09 in the original study). Some meta-analysts favor use of the weighted average, others use the raw figures. Either way, the majority of cultivation results supports a consistently small but positive statistical relationship (see Table 6.2).

Thus, though the effect is small by anyone's standards, it is present and in the direction predicted by cultivation theory. Now, Hunter and Schmidt (1990) say that if the mean effect size is at least two standard deviations larger than zero, then the "true" effect can be assumed to be "always positive," no matter what any specific single study might suggest.

Also, they suggest that if sampling error variance accounts for at least 75 percent of the observed variance, then one can conclude that observed relationship is "real" and unmoderated (that is, that there are no important differences in the body of results). In our data, we find that almost 50 percent of the overall variance can be accounted for by sampling error, and also that the doubled standard deviation is a bit larger than the average effect (.091).

One striking fact, then, is that almost half of the differences that have been so controversial in the literature are due simply to sampling error. This is enough to sober up any social scientist, whose efforts are constantly riddled with measurement error. Also, this means that there is sufficient variance in reported findings across cultivation studies to suggest the presence of one or more "moderators," a variable which may explain some of the *variance* in the observed relationships between TV exposure and other dependent variables – that is, the analysis suggests that there is a variable (or variables) which explains why some studies find larger effects and some do not.

### Moderators

At this point let us briefly clarify the difference between "moderators" in meta-analysis and "third variables" in individual studies. The term "moderator" refers to any factor that explains why findings vary among different studies; these are usually study characteristics relating to the way in which the studies were conducted, such as sample size, country of sample, etc. A meta-analytic moderator, therefore, is not the same as a third variable, which allows for assessing spuriousness between two variables in an individual study, sometimes pointing to stronger or weaker relations in subgroups (as in the case of mainstreaming). However, we should note that third variables may sometimes *point toward* the presence of moderators at the meta-analytic level, especially if it can be shown that study designs have varied with respect to demographic composition, the nature of groups represented, etc.

Age, socioeconomic status, gender, political beliefs, among many others, all may be sources of spuriousness in cultivation associations; but they may also moderate the relationship between exposure and beliefs about the world. Yet although these variables have been found to be important in many of the single studies, there has been no attempt to determine if they account for any consistent moderating patterns *across* studies. So the meta-analysis could help out by showing if results differed in any systematic ways in various subgroups.

We performed moderator analyses by meta-analyzing separate subsets

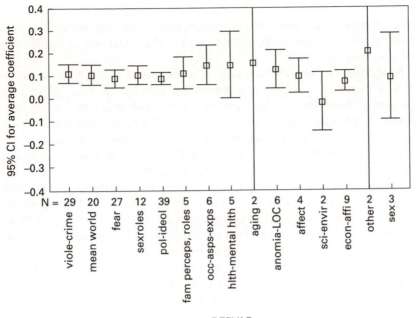

Figure 6.6 Error bar diagram, showing average cultivation effect sizes for various dependent variables

of the data for theoretically meaningful variables that might generate any differences in cultivation results obtained across studies. The ultimate goal is to find out why cultivation studies vary in effect size.

Given that cultivation analyses have been carried out in so many different substantive areas, does the strength of the observed relationships vary systematically by topic? For instance, effects for violence could be stronger than effects for sex-roles, or ideology, and so on. One way to get at this issue is simply to compare average effect sizes across dependent variables. We show the data for this comparison in Figure 6.6.

Figure 6.6 shows average cultivation effect size for overall findings, across dependent variable areas. Also shown are 95 percent confidence intervals for the figures. The data show that there is not a great deal of variation in the size of observed cultivation effects for different dependent variables; except for one or two outliers (based on small numbers of studies), the variations are essentially within error parameters and the dependent variables do not radically differ from each other in effect size. This suggests that dependent variable does not moderate cultivation (a fact that we reported in our first analysis of these data, 1997).

Table 6.2 shows the results for the meta-analysis across dependent variable. Published studies that dealt with more than one dependent area were treated as independent datasets, for the purposes of comparing effects across variables.

Weighting the data by sample size, we found an average effect size of .078 with political beliefs as a dependent variable (K = 27). About 30 percent of the variance in the magnitudes of the associations was explainable through sampling error. Meta-analyzing ten sex-role samples, we found an average effect size of .09 (essentially the same as Herrett-Skjellum and Allen's, 1996, finding of .101). For this group, 78 percent of the observed variance in effects can be attributed to sampling error. Herrett-Skjellum and Allen found significant heterogeneity in their sample of sex-role studies, also without a clear moderator. Finally, on the issue of violence, we found an average effect size of .10 (K = 26). With 45 percent of the variance explained by sampling error, we again conclude that these studies display heterogeneity. Despite some minor differences in effect size, the substantive focus of the dependent variable is apparently not a moderator of cultivation. Thus, the cultivation of beliefs about violence, sex or political ideas is all of a piece, at least in the sense that effect sizes are similar.

Although the focus of the dependent variable does not moderate the strength of cultivation results, it is possible that demographic characteristics might do so. First, we analyzed the findings separately for males and females, as shown in Figure 6.7.

This analysis again shows little difference. For females, the effect size averaged .081. For males the average was .079. However, Table 6.2 shows that there was less variance in the findings for females (as also seen in the figure). The evidence of cultivation for females is thus somewhat more consistent than that for males, though on average it is of about the same size. Thus, gender itself is not a moderator (the variance remained heterogeneous for males).

So neither the specific dependent variable nor gender proves to be much help in accounting for differences in cultivation results across different studies and samples. As we turned our attention to other factors, we consistently found that studies in various subgroups and across various study characteristics really did not differ that much. For instance, we also investigated whether education level (or parental education, for children and adolescents) functions as a moderator. It doesn't. Nor do age subgroups seem to make much difference.

Although demographic controls may produce wide discrepancies in cultivation patterns within any given study, the meta-analysis suggests few marked or recurrent demographic differences across studies, except

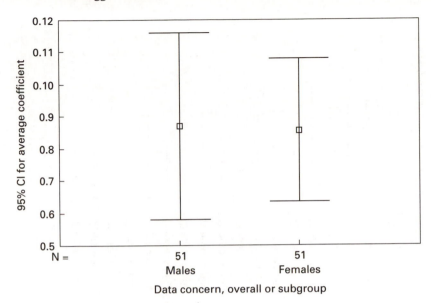

Figure 6.7 Error bar diagram, showing average cultivation effect sizes for males and females

for one, as we will see. Figure 6.8 shows how cultivation effect size has varied for different data subgroups. Many of these subgroups commonly appear in different studies (males and females are included again in Figure 6.8, for comparison).

The figure shows that cultivation effect size doesn't vary sharply by demographic characteristics. However, some interesting and suggestive patterns do emerge. For instance, older people, who did not "grow up" with television, show a somewhat lower overall effect size. Whites show a markedly higher effect size than non-whites. Those with college education and those higher incomes appear to be more susceptible to cultivation effects than those with less than a high school education or low incomes. With all these patterns, though, there is enough margin for error to be cautious when interpreting the differences.

Most noticeable, however, is the fact that liberals are more susceptible to cultivation than moderates or conservatives, even accounting for a fair degree of chance for error. Thus, self-identified liberals may be a very important group for helping us to think about why cultivation studies vary. The differences between liberals and other groups (along with the differences in income, education and, to some extent, age) are highly supportive of mainstreaming, and will be further explored in the next

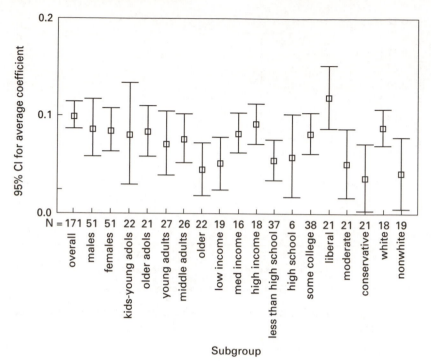

Figure 6.8 Error bar diagram, showing average cultivation effect sizes for various data subgroups

chapter. At this point, however, they do not show the presence of a moderator across all the studies.

### Study Characteristics

One prominent issue in cultivation is that many studies have been carried out by a core group of researchers (especially Gerbner, Gross, Morgan and Signorielli, who conducted many of the original cultivation studies in the 1970s and 1980s) and others associated with them. This includes those who attended the University of Pennsylvania as graduate students and those who later came into contact with members of the original team in places such as the University of Massachusetts or the University of Delaware. However, cultivation research has also been carried out by many outside of this core group, including critics, friendly amenders and so on. We were interested in whether results differed across these two groups, since methods have differed and been the focus of critical discussion. But again, and despite the efforts expended by critic and proponent alike, there doesn't seem to be much difference across the analyzed studies. Studies conducted by Gerbner and associates found an average effect size of .078, while those conducted by others averaged .10. Moreover, there was significant variance with each of these groups as well. (These data are shown in Table 6.2.)

Similarly, we also looked at whether measurement of the independent variable made a difference. A key issue in many critiques, of course, is that cultivation uses too broad, too gross and too unreliable a measure for assessing how people "really" watch television. Surprisingly, though, when we compared studies using different methods for assessing exposure (program diaries, genre viewing and other methods of estimation) we find that they all tend to reveal broadly similar effect sizes. Thus, as with many of the other findings focusing on study characteristics, it appears that methodological decisions about measuring cultivation do not play as big a role as was suggested in the literature.

We also compared whether a study informed respondents at the start that it was dealing with TV, potentially sensitizing the respondents. Though sensitization did not turn out to be a true moderator, it did emerge that studies risking sensitization by mentioning television at the start did in fact reveal somewhat *higher* effect sizes. Those studies following the method preferred by Gerbner et al. revealed more conservative estimates (as seen in Table 6.2).

The most noticeable difference was observed when comparing large sample size studies to small sample size studies. Larger, random and more representative samples are obviously preferred to smaller convenience samples. Smaller ($N < 600$) samples produce an average effect of .13; larger ($N > 600$) samples yield an average effect of only .079. Both large and small sample groups display heterogeneity of variance for effect size (see Table 6.2), so this cannot be considered a true moderator variable.

In none of the cases has the variance turned out to be homogeneous for all subsets within a given comparison of studies, which means that none of them can be considered as a moderator of variations in cultivation. Still, one consistent tendency is worth noting. Studies which have stuck more closely to the original design of the investigation – i.e., studies conducted by those associated with Gerbner, studies which use larger samples, and studies which make sure not to sensitize respondents to the purposes of the research – all tend to produce somewhat *smaller* estimates of cultivation. It is interesting that the findings produced by researchers and methods most connected to Gerbner have been, in a meta-analytic sense, more conservative than those of the critics and others, who have sometimes used smaller and less representative samples. Again, though, these patterns are merely descriptive and suggestive, since no true moderator emerges from our analysis.

In an important sense, then, if there is indeed any specific factor that explains why cultivation results vary across studies, that moderator remains "at large." Still, let us not forget that none of these analyses gets at what might be the most powerful mediator of cultivation findings: mainstreaming. However the data presented in Figure 6.8 do suggest that political ideology may be the most important mediating factor, an observation which would be highly congruent with cultivation theory.

Indeed, if the theoretical discussion offered in Chapter 5 is correct, mainstreaming is probably the best candidate for explaining variance in simple cultivation relationships. Mainstreaming theory would suggest that cultivation relationships would be stronger for groups more distant from the cultural "center" and less strong for groups closer to the center. However, it is not possible to measure this in a meta-analytic sense, because single studies do not routinely provide "baseline" figures for their cultivation estimates. However, it *is* possible to examine mainstreaming from a perspective somewhat different than that of the single study, which we take up in the next chapter.

### Control

Another weakness of meta-analysis at its current state of development is that it is not clear how to handle findings that have been controlled for possible spuriousness. That is, meta-analysis simply calls for an averaging of bivariate findings from a group of studies, and does not easily let us take control variables into account. These bivariate findings provide lots of information, as we have seen, but they don't do much to answer the question, what if the "cause" is not TV? One way to deal with this is to show how findings have varied in subgroups (as we have just done) but this does not take into account the possibility that the correlations meta-analyzed are spurious.

As previously noted, most cultivation studies do control for a variety of variables. The variables normally used are those that are (1) important demographic markers (sex, age, etc.), (2) related to television viewing (income, education) and (3) related to dependent variables (political self-identification, for example).

Despite the lengthy debates on the importance of controls in cultivation research, there has been little systematic attempt to examine which variables are most likely to attenuate cultivation patterns. This is important because the atheoretical application of numerous control variables to any observed relationship is likely to "cancel out" what might be meaningful associations. Absent a consistent and theoretically motivated account of how controls have been used in cultivation, we are confronted with an intricate and confusing picture. Here we try to reduce that complexity somewhat through a descriptive analysis of the impact of controls on cultivation strength.

One way to get a sense of the contribution of controls is to look at the overall control "structure" of cultivation findings. That is, some findings are "uncontrolled" or simple findings, whereas others are controlled for various plausible sources of spuriousness, singly or simultaneously. But the literature is marked by vast diversity; strikingly few cultivation studies apply controls in exactly (or even more or less) the same way, so it is difficult to forge exact comparisons across studies. To get around this, we looked at the presence or absence of each potential control variable as a predictor of cultivation strength.

First, we analyze whether cultivation associations are much lower in the presence or absence of a given control. Table 6.3 summarizes average values of cultivation findings with and without particular controls (comparing simple $r$'s and gammas with no controls to partial $r$'s with controls). This analysis does not compare particular findings before and after control; it merely sums the populations of studies either with or without controls. By necessity, these data come from the complete (non-independent) set of reported findings, and therefore depart from strict meta-analytic procedures. The table summarizes data for the seven most important and commonly used demographic controls, though data for many others were collected as well.

Table 6.3 shows the average effect size for findings with a particular control variable and compares this to the average size of findings without that control variable. The table shows that cultivation associations are normally somewhat lower in the presence of controls, as shown in debates about the early work. However, though the overall differences in some cases are not extremely large, three variables (political self-identification, education and income) reduce cultivation more significantly. Again, though, we should remember that such reductions in effect size can reflect either of two phenomena: spuriousness or specification.

Of course, one problem is that studies do not always report each and every correlation with each and every control, so we often do not know which control most reduces or specifies the overall finding (more often it is all the controls taken together which reduce associations). The usefulness of our meta-analytic database, from this perspective, is that we can use control variable "structures" as independent variables to see how well their presence or absence predicts cultivation strength. Thus, we do not

Table 6.3 *Impact of control variables on cultivation results*

| Control variable | Findings with ($N$) | Findings without ($N$) |
|---|---|---|
| Sex | 0.074 (934) | 0.09 (3770) |
| Age | 0.073 (889) | 0.09 (3815) |
| Income | 0.054 (268) | 0.09 (4436)* |
| SES | 0.083 (642) | 0.09 (4061) |
| Political | 0.052 (148) | 0.09 (4556)* |
| Education | 0.065 (641) | 0.09 (4063)* |
| Race | 0.072 (432) | 0.09 (4272) |

*Note:*
* denotes that the presence of the control variable significantly reduces effect size, controlling for the presence or absence of other controls; $p < .05$

need to know the exact impact of each control variable; rather, its contribution can be estimated from the overall sample of findings which have it as a control.

By regressing effect size onto the presence or absence of controls in the data, we found three significant predictors: similar to the results noted above, they are political self-identification, income and education. The beta coefficients for these predictors are small (all under .06), which indicates that by themselves, control variables are not strongly related to cultivation strength, and taken together, our analysis shows that control "structure" explains about 1 percent of the variance in our sample of findings. If cultivation findings were heavily spurious, we would expect knowledge about their control structure to reveal severe differences in findings. Since this does not happen, we reject the argument that cultivation findings are "merely" spurious.

Still, however, some variables do make a significant difference, and we need to investigate these further. As seen in the previous chapter, the typical cultivation response to arguments about spuriousness has been to look for mainstreaming patterns. Often, these searches have been accused of being *post hoc* data-driven exercises, and the research has lacked a tool or criterion for specifying ahead of time where to look for mainstreaming. This problem is alleviated somewhat by noting that it is often the variables which seem themselves to indicate spuriousness that point the way to specification patterns of theoretical interest. For instance, and as we noted earlier, political self-identification is a particularly important variable because it influences other dependent variables and because it is not directly correlated with television viewing. But moreover, cultivation is apparently much larger among liberals. Thus, the fact that it reduces overall cultivation strength is probably not due just to spuriousness issues, but may hide a deeper and more important difference. We will explore this in the next chapter. The same thing might be said about income, which seems to be a somewhat weaker moderator of cultivation findings.

Thus, though it continues to be logically and empirically important to control cultivation findings for other variables, it is clear that, as a body, cultivation associations are not reduced to zero, even in the presence of multiple and simultaneous controls (and despite some of the early critiques). What is more clear is that relationships between TV viewing and other dependent variables are *partially* explained by demographic factors, as would be expected. But the data still show that exposure to television's messages plays a small but persistent and meaningful role in people's understandings of social and political issues.

## Summary

In this chapter we show that the entire "body" of cultivation research is consistent with the theory developed in the earlier chapters. That is, at the broadest possible level, the findings of the dozens of studies conducted in the past twenty years support the idea that cumulative exposure to television cultivates absorption of ideas and worldviews congruent with what is seen on TV.

We used both meta-analysis and more informal data cumulation techniques to make this case. The chapter primarily addresses the most basic type of relationship investigated by cultivation, the bivariate relationships between exposure to TV and beliefs about the world. Further, the meta-analysis suggests the presence of an undiscovered moderator of cultivation findings. That is, we know that cultivation is, in some sense, "real," but we do not fully understand why there is so much variance in the findings across studies beyond what would be expected from random variation alone.

But further analyses do turn up clues. Particularly, it looks as if political ideology, across the body of studies, plays a major role in mediating the findings. This is consistent with theory developed in Chapter 5. It suggests that, within samples, effects vary depending upon the political ideology of the respondents. Across studies, however, it may be that issues related to political ideology (how the questions are framed, who is in the sample, etc.) play a role in the "size" of the cultivation effect.

In the next chapter we build on these findings in two ways. First, we look at how mainstreaming explanations of cultivation hold over extremely large datasets. In particular we focus on ideological issues. Second, we look at cultivation over time. Again using large trend-oriented datasets, we see whether television has played a theoretically consistent role in social change across a twenty-year period.

# 7    Mediation, Mainstreaming and Social Change

In the previous chapter, we presented evidence for an overall cultivation effect, but we also found a considerable amount of variance across the studies. That is, there was more variance in the meta-sample than what we would expect if the observed differences in results across studies were due to nothing more than chance. Also, we did not find a specific moderator for cultivation relationships, although many plausible candidates were tested. However, cultivation differences across liberals, moderates and conservatives were suggestive. The "missing moderator" problem suggests that we need different data explorations to think about what might be causing some studies to reveal stronger or weaker results.

The theory we presented in earlier chapters suggests that mainstreaming analyses may provide one answer. Although mainstreaming explains differential cultivation patterns across subgroups *within* specific studies, it may also help shed light on variations in results *across* studies. But, as we have pointed out above, it is not really possible to deal with mainstreaming within the guidelines of a meta-analysis (because meta-analyses do not provide "baseline" estimates of responses to dependent variables; they only provide estimates of relationships between TV exposure and dependent variables). Thus, to see whether mainstreaming helps explain across-study variance, one needs access to data that *do* allow examination of baseline estimates. This chapter looks at data that can help us to answer these questions.

## "Third Variables" and Cultivation

Before we look at some data about mainstreaming, it will be useful to examine some of the different possible ways that third variables could affect cultivation relationships. TV exposure does not in many cases have "direct" effects in the sense normally studied by social scientists. Exposure often relates to dependent variables in concert with other variables. Theoretically, there could be several ways this might be happening. One way is that demographic variables might serve as "intervening

Figure 7.1  Intervening variable model

variables" between TV exposure and various dependent variables (see Figure 7.1).

In such a model, TV has "causal" effects on various control (demographic) variables, which themselves in turn affect dependent variables. For instance, those who think that TV viewing makes direct contributions to educational success might favor such a model. However, this model is not highly plausible, because TV exposure, though an important marker of social status, cannot be thought of as temporally "prior" to most demographic variables. It is true that children are raised with television programs years before their formal education begins, so in some senses TV does "come first," but we must also remember that education as a variable tends to stand for immersion in a variety of social processes which begin at the same time as television viewing begins and which help shape the television experience of the child. More reasonably, then, we would argue that the variables are temporally intertwined.[1]

An alternate pattern, in which TV exposure intervenes the effect of other demographic variables, is seen in Figure 7.2. This model is somewhat promising on logical grounds, but is not fully workable for two reasons. First, the time-order is ambiguous, though most people might be comfortable ordering demographic variables as "prior" to TV viewing. Second, in such a model, relationships between demographic variables and dependent variables should disappear when controlled for television exposure, and this normally does not happen in cultivation data.

This leaves (at least) two alternatives. One is that "third" variables may "account" for cultivation, marking the explanation as spurious. Such a pattern is shown in Figure 7.3. In such a case, TV exposure has relationships with dependent variables only by virtue of the fact that amount of viewing is co-related with third variables that are also related to the various dependent variables. That is, if the third variables did not exist, there would be no relationship between TV exposure and the dependent variables (Rosenberg, 1968).

This model was the one favored by cultivation critics such as Hughes

---

[1]  Of course, it is possible to conceive of mental processes as intervening between TV exposure and beliefs about issues, but here we are mainly concerned with social/demographic variables as interveners.

Figure 7.2  Antecedent variable model

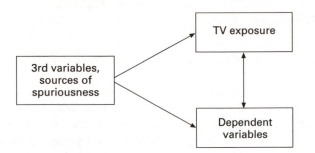

Figure 7.3  Spuriousness model

and Hirsch, and their interpretations were not completely inconsistent with the data (though see the fuller story in Chapter 3). However, a correlation that looks spurious need not be interpreted as such. As Rosenberg points out, associations conforming to the above model can be given theoretically meaningful interpretations. Technically, a relationship of the above type is termed "symmetrical," indicating that a causal order cannot be specified. However, symmetrical relationships may reflect other meaningful patterns. Although such relationships can be "spurious" (i.e., related only as an artifact of the third variable) it may also be that such variables are "functionally interdependent," meaning that the variables are correlated because they co-exist as part of a functioning unit (Rosenberg, 1968, p. 5). Our earlier arguments that cultivation works best as a functional theory (cf. Burrowes, 1996) should be recalled at this point.

Thus, for instance, if we find that TV exposure is related to perceptions of violence, but also that education makes this correlation disappear, it does not necessarily mean that education is the "cause" of the perceptions of violence. It may simply mean that education level and television exposure are parts of a wider system, whose co-relations may obscure pseudo-causal impacts on particular variables. Thus, from a systemic perspective, it can often be difficult to specify particular effects without knowledge of the entire system. Complex inter-relations do not negate that specific parts of the system play crucial roles, even if they are strongly correlated with other aspects of the system.

Mainstreaming (and resonance) can take us beyond these simple three

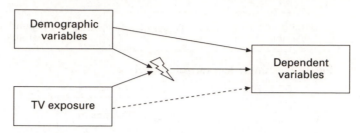

Figure 7.4  Interaction model

variable models by examining "conditional" associations, associations that are present only under certain conditions. Invariably in social relationships, assumptions that two variables will be related in clearcut ways often break down into more complex partial or subgroup relationships. Also invariably, these conditional relationships shed light on the original interpretation, and that is certainly what happened when the idea of mainstreaming was introduced.

Given the difficulties in determining causal order (and remembering that cultivation also favors a reciprocal causation process, which we admit is more difficult to measure or model well) we think the best overall model is one in which both TV and other third variables make independent and direct contributions to dependent variables, but in which they also interact. The model is depicted in Figure 7.4. That is, television viewing does make direct contributions to dependent variables, but they are sometimes negated by controlling for other factors (hence the dotted line). Demographic variables also make direct contributions; depending on the variable at hand they are generally fairly resistant to control (hence the solid line). Moreover, television viewing "interacts" with demographic and other control variables, and normally these interactions are significant within the context of multiple control, showing the existence of conditional associations (hence, again, the solid line). Most commonly, the interactions spark mainstreaming patterns.

Examples of this model abound in the literature. For instance, Shanahan, Morgan and Stenbjerre (1997) found that political ideology, television viewing, and an interaction between them, all made significant contributions to willingness to make personal sacrifices for the environment. In general the main effects of television viewing in such tests turn out be smaller than those from the demographic variables, but still large enough to matter on their own. Shanahan (1995) also found that television viewing predicts higher authoritarianism among adolescents, but that television viewing also interacts (along lines predicted by mainstreaming) with variables such as socioeconomic status. Also very

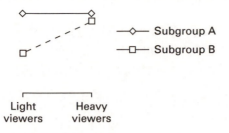

Figure 7.5  Schematic example of mainstreaming

common is the model seen in a variety of studies, and in many of the data examples to follow in this chapter, where the direct effects of television tend to disappear under control, while the interaction effects hold up.

Thus, we may embellish cultivation theory along the following lines: in situations where television can be shown to distribute messages consistently and cumulatively, the effect of television can be best seen in interaction with important demographic variables. That is, television does not necessarily mediate the demographics, nor is the reverse true. The two variables seem to work together in inculcating beliefs and outlooks.

Working from this perspective, we might best see television exposure as another "demographic" variable which helps mark out the nature of an individual's life experience. For instance, suppose we see race and gender as important demographic markers in a piece of social research. One would not necessarily assume that either variable predates or mediates the other's effect on some social variable. The same can be said of television: its influences, when not direct (which is fairly often) can still be felt in interaction with other "primary" demographic variables.

## Submitting Mainstreaming to Logical Tests

Thus, cultivation is to be seen mostly in interaction with other variables. Mainstreaming is the particular interaction in which cultivation is stronger for some subgroups, weaker or absent for other groups, *and* in which heavy viewers' responses are closer than those of light viewers (see Figure 7.5 for a schematic example). When these conditions are not met, mainstreaming is not present. But even within these constraints, there are a variety of explanations that might reflect mainstreaming. After we have observed mainstreaming, it becomes logical to ask which groups show cultivation, and when (i.e., under what conditions)? It is an important question, but one that has mostly eluded cultivation researchers, who have not tended to make specific mainstreaming predictions in advance (and this has not been lost on critics).

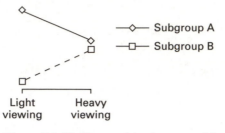

Figure 7.6 Uniform cultivation toward "average" position (Hypothesis 1)

We need an account that helps us better understand when to expect mainstreaming, and where to expect cultivation to be stronger and weaker. In this section, we look at several different possibilities for constructing more exact descriptions of and predictions about mainstreaming.

One idea (let's call it Hypothesis 1), is that mainstreaming uniformly pushes disparate groups toward "center" positions; that is, heavy viewing simply brings groups toward a socially "average" position representing the cultural mainstream. We might think of the position toward which heavy viewers are drawn as an "objective" social center, around which light viewers are more widely distributed than heavy viewers. This is seen schematically in Figure 7.6.

A second idea (Hypothesis 2) is that television messages will push or pull viewers toward more "conservative" or "traditional" positions, rather than to some arithmetic "middle." This argument gains some force from many cultivation studies which show that, while television does not have direct and observable conservative influences in every case, there does seem to be some evidence that television tends to work to "hold back" progressive social change, as well as the fact that most of the cultivation observed among liberals has been cultivation toward conservative positions. Under this assumption, mainstreaming moves in the direction of greater conservatism, regardless of where the social center is "objectively" located (see schematic example in Figure 7.7).

A third idea (Hypothesis 3), stemming from the functional notions we mentioned earlier on, is that mainstreaming should work on those groups "furthest" from the social center of gravity, regardless of whether the distance is in the conservative or liberal direction. This is based on the notion that groups most out of sync with the cultural mainstream pose the greatest threat to the stability (homeostasis) of the social system, and therefore demonstrate a "need" to be brought toward the center. Thus, if liberals were most out of sync with mainstream opinion, cultivation

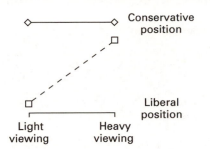

Figure 7.7 Schematic example of mainstreaming toward conservative position (Hypothesis 2)

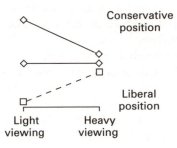

Figure 7.8 Mainstreaming toward cultural center of gravity (Hypothesis 3)

would proceed toward conservative positions. But, in cases where conservatives are more out of sync with mainstream opinion, cultivation would proceed toward more liberal views. Such a case is seen schematically in Figure 7.8. The figure shows groups flowing toward the more common, homogeneous, dominant stream regardless of whether the distance is on the liberal or conservative side. The difference between this case and that shown in Figure 7.6 is that here the "center" point is determined by cultural reality rather than just its mathematically average position between two divergent extremes. Thus, it would be better to think of this type of "center" position as an elite-defined "center of gravity" representing what the culture sees as "common sense."

A final hypothesis (Hypothesis 4) is that none of these ideas will hold and that mainstreaming will depend very much on the specific question(s) and the specific social circumstances being analyzed. Some theorists don't like this, because it is not classically falsifiable in the Popperian sense, but it may just reflect the complex and chaotic nature of social reality. Thus, though such an explanation is less theoretically parsimo-

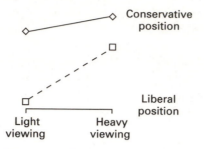

Figure 7.9 Mainstreaming, with both groups mainstreamed toward more conservative view

nious, it is by no means out of the realm of possibility, especially given the extent to which different subgroup audiences do react to (and interact with) different messages in different ways.

Playing out these ideas may be somewhat challenging, but it is worth the effort. First, let us look at the idea that television mainstreams toward the "objective" social center – that is, toward some mathematical average between two outlying groups. The best way to test this would simply be to see whether heavy viewers converge toward these "average" social responses on a variety of issues. If this were this case, we would expect to see conservatives and liberals demonstrate similar (though inverse) culti-vation effects (in terms of correlation magnitudes). Since we know this is not the case from the meta-analysis (liberals tend to show cultivation while conservatives don't), this first hypothesis can be rejected relatively easily. Thus, mainstreaming is not simply an "averaging" process; it appears to be a process with specific ideological content.

Hypothesis 2 may look more attractive because liberals are main-streamed far more frequently than either moderates or conservatives, but under Hypothesis 2 we might also expect conservatives to show some cul-tivation toward even-more conservative positions, as in Figure 7.9.

The situation pictured in Figure 7.9 is not unusual, but more often we tend to see situations in which only liberals are mainstreamed. However, if a sufficient number of cases should appear in which mainstreaming "away" from conservative positions could be demonstrated, then Hypothesis 2 would be undercut. We would then need to turn to Hypothesis 3, which suggests that groups furthest from the social-ideo-logical "center of gravity" would demonstrate mainstreaming, regardless of whether they were distributed to the "left" or "right" side of that core position. In cases where the groups furthest from the core position are toward the liberal side, the mainstreaming would be toward the conservative side. On the other hand, in cases where the distance is toward the conservative side, the mainstreaming could well be in the liberal direction.

The work of Gerbner et al. dealt with this issue, though perhaps rather nebulously. The analyses in "Charting the mainstream" were intended to determine the direction in which the cultural mainstream was flowing, and to point out the nature of the currents within which groups of heavy viewers were converging. Gerbner et al. suggested that this mainstream was characterized by traditional values on social issues; conservative currents flowed more strongly into the mainstream. For Gerbner et al., the mainstream was a dynamic constellation of ideas, beliefs, and values, not just a majoritarian collection of individuals. The mainstream emerges as the ideological space where the views and opinions most consonant with the needs and interests of social elites are privileged and cultivated (Shanahan and Jones, 1998).

Still, as consistently seen in many studies and in our meta-analysis, the groups that are most frequently "out" of the mainstream are the liberals, especially the light viewing liberals. In such situations, either Hypothesis 2 or 3 could be correct, because liberals are most distant from the center, and also, by definition, less conservative than the rest of the sample. Thus, when cultivation and mainstreaming occur from a liberal position toward a more traditional, mainstream conservative view, either Hypothesis 2 or 3 can be operant. To show whether Hypothesis 2 or 3 is more plausible, we need to find whether there are cases where groups more conservative than the conservative mainstream will be mainstreamed toward more "liberal" (or even moderate) views.

Hypothesis 4 (that mainstreaming varies by issue) is not completely rejectable at this point, because of the complex nature (and variety) of cultivation data. Undoubtedly, there are more complex interaction patterns going on in each individual variable than we can see in some of the simple specification analyses that have been done thus far (and we will see further complexity in this chapter as well). But while the hypothesis cannot yet be summarily rejected, parsimony suggests that we should investigate the others first. We accept that a "true" model of how television interacts with social beliefs will point toward a very complex social system with many dynamic feedbacks and interactions. But social analysis that moves inexorably toward this complex picture tends to lose its parsimony, as we merely discover that "everything affects everything else." While this may be true, it is also an observation that can be made without much data gathering. For this reason, we argue that cultivation analysis works best at a somewhat simpler and more graspable level.

### Testing the Hypotheses

The preceding conjectures derive from observations of patterns gleaned across many cultivation studies. But mainstreaming has mostly been explored within the confines of the single study. Is there a way to investigate mainstreaming such that we could have more confidence than that provided by a single study? Fortunately, the answer is "yes." Many cultivation studies have used the General Social Survey as a data source. Indeed, over 20 percent of the nearly 6,000 findings in our full meta-analysis inventory come from GSS (NORC) samples; these samples have been extensively used by Gerbner et al., because they provide such a high quality data source. The GSS is based on intensive face-to-face interviews with randomly selected (full probability) national samples. It is also convenient and easily accessible to social researchers. The trade-off is that it is still secondary analysis – others wrote the questions, for a variety of purposes – but because the GSS has consistently presented questions on television exposure and a variety of social beliefs and attitudes, researchers can now look back to the GSS as a twenty-year compendium of cultivation information.

For our immediate purposes, the main advantage is that GSS data provide direct access to the baselines of viewing and attitudes for all respondents. Thus, although the GSS data do not allow for a meta-analysis in the truest sense, the GSS dataset simply has so many data points (over 30,000 potential cases) from so many years (since 1972) that we can do a *mega*-analysis of the accumulated data. This should, in theory, provide results rather similar to the meta-analysis, since each of the nearly yearly databases of about 1,500 people are all independent samples, with the added benefit of providing clear comparisons of trends over time.

The GSS has measured amount of television exposure since 1975, which corresponds to the historical beginnings of cultivation analysis. Its question ("On the average day, about how many hours do you personally watch television?") has been exactly the sort of rough barometer of television viewing needed for cultivation analysis (this question was written for the GSS by the original CI research team). We acknowledge that this measure provides a rougher estimate of television viewing than can be obtained in other ways. However, its consistent availability over the past twenty years makes it especially useful.

The most intriguing mainstreaming processes tend to be political, so we first chose five questions from the ongoing GSS battery of questions related to social and political beliefs (National Opinion Research Center, 1994). Most of these questions were used in earlier studies and, at least at one time, were found to be related to television viewing. However, with fifteen to twenty years having elapsed since some of these analyses were made, it is an open question whether cultivation and mainstreaming work consistently across the years. Our first goal in this chapter is to explore whether cultivation and mainstreaming patterns persist over long time intervals, and whether these make sense with respect to what cultivation theory predicts. Then we look beyond the analyses to see which of the hypotheses we sketched out above emerges as most convincing. The questions were:

"Please tell me whether or not you think it should be possible for a pregnant woman to obtain a legal abortion if she wants it for any reason" (1 = yes/2 = no)?

"Suppose [an] admitted homosexual wanted to make a speech in your community. Should he be allowed to do so" (1 = yes/2 = no)?

"Do you think the use of marijuana should be made legal or not" (1 = yes/2 = no)?

"Do you think there should be laws against marriages between (negroes/blacks) and whites" (1 = yes/2 = no)?

"It is more important for a wife to help her husband's career than have one herself" (1 = strongly agree; 4 = strongly disagree).

Of the many possible variables we could have used, we more or less haphazardly chose these five because they represent a diversity of social topics on which people generally express strong differences of opinion, and because they have been used in previous cultivation analyses.

Generally, previous studies have revealed that television messages tend to cultivate acceptance of the more "conservative" positions associated with these questions (Morgan, 1986). Thus, for instance, heavy viewers would be less likely to accept free speech rights for homosexuals (Gross, 1984). Heavy viewers also have been more likely to discriminate based on race (Gross, 1984), sex (Signorielli, 1989), and to be less "tolerant" on abortion questions (Gerbner et al., 1982).

We analyzed associations between amount of viewing and these questions in much the same way as had been done in earlier studies. However, the novelty in this case was that we were able to use much more data; we treated all the available data as one large sample (generally comprising the years 1975–94, although not all questions were asked every year). For each question, we first analyzed its bivariate relationship with amount of television exposure. This tells us whether any general, overall cultivation relationships show up for the cumulative data. Then, to examine mainstreaming, we looked at responses in political self-identification subgroups (liberal, moderate and conservative).

We used political subgroups as the control variable for two reasons. First, political ideology is a handy way to distinguish people's position rel-

Table 7.1 *Correlations between television exposure and dependent variables*

| Variable | Abortion | Homosexual | Marijuana | Inter-racial marriage | Sex-roles |
|---|---|---|---|---|---|
| Correlation | 0.0338 | 0.0705 | 0.0156 | 0.0860 | 0.0757 |
| N | (12,912) | (9,970) | (11,084) | (11,166) | (11,101) |
| p | < 0.001 | < 0.001 | 0.050 | < 0.001 | < 0.001 |

*Note:*
All variables were coded such that high values reflect more conservative social positions.

ative to the mainstream. Secondly, again, the meta-analytic data in the previous chapter showed that cultivation findings for liberals tended to be stronger, while findings for conservatives and moderates tended to be weaker than average. This pattern strongly suggested mainstreaming.

In each of these analyses, we would expect liberals and conservatives to differ significantly on the questions, and they generally do. If, however, they differ less when they are heavy viewers, there is evidence for mainstreaming, and further, it may be that these mainstreaming patterns help to specify some variance in overall cultivation patterns.

Table 7.1 shows that there are small but significant correlations in the expected (conservative) direction between television exposure and the various dependent variables (although with over 10,000 respondents, almost all associations are highly significant). The average of these five correlations (.056), however, is a little less than those from the meta-analysis (although recall that ideological questions manifested somewhat more modest overall coefficients in the original analysis as well). Again, though, these effect sizes have been commonly observed in cultivation work.

The association for views on interracial marriage, for instance, reflects a difference in support for such laws of about 11 percentage points between heavy and light viewers (heavy viewers, consistent with cultivation theory, are more supportive of the restrictive law proposal). Note also that the weakest correlations correspond to the two areas *least* clearly implicated in television content according to known message system analysis data (i.e., abortion and marijuana use).

As we know, however, small overall effects may mask important subgroup differences, particularly when mainstreaming is at work. More importantly, this masking process may be due to the presence of the "mediator" variable suggested by the meta-analysis, which showed stronger associations among liberals. Thus, in the full, combined, twenty-year GSS dataset, we analyzed differences in association between TV

Table 7.2 *Associations between television exposure and dependent variables, in subgroups defined by political self-identification (GSS samples, 1975–1994)*

| Subgroup | Abortion | | | Homosexuals | | | Marijuana | | | Inter-racial marriage | | | Sex-roles | | |
|---|---|---|---|---|---|---|---|---|---|---|---|---|---|---|---|
| scale values | L | M | H | L | M | H | L | M | H | L | M | H | L | M | H |
| Liberals | 1.41 | 1.48 | 1.55 | 1.15 | 1.20 | 1.27 | 1.57 | 1.64 | 1.69 | 1.11 | 1.17 | 1.25 | 1.84 | 2.01 | 2.14 |
| Moderates | 1.60 | 1.61 | 1.64 | 1.25 | 1.25 | 1.32 | 1.79 | 1.81 | 1.80 | 1.23 | 1.26 | 1.33 | 2.20 | 2.19 | 2.29 |
| Conserv. | 1.70 | 1.66 | 1.69 | 1.32 | 1.31 | 1.36 | 1.85 | 1.84 | 1.84 | 1.24 | 1.27 | 1.35 | 2.26 | 2.30 | 2.39 |
| Regression statistics: | | | | | | | | | | | | | | | |
| $R$ (df) | 0.28(6,11714) | | | 0.37(6,9601) | | | 0.30(6,9947) | | | 0.43(6,10728) | | | 0.43(6,10686) | | |
| (*betas*) | | | | | | | | | | | | | | | |
| education | −0.22*** | | | −0.30*** | | | −0.09*** | | | −0.29*** | | | −0.22*** | | |
| race | 0.03*** | | | 0.03*** | | | 0.02 | | | −0.17*** | | | 0.02 | | |
| sex | 0.01 | | | −0.01 | | | 0.09*** | | | 0.01 | | | −0.07 | | |
| age | 0.01 | | | 0.11*** | | | 0.15*** | | | 0.19*** | | | 0.27*** | | |
| TV viewing | −0.02* | | | 0.00 | | | −0.02 | | | 0.03*** | | | 0.01 | | |
| Political ID | 0.16*** | | | 0.09*** | | | 0.18*** | | | 0.05*** | | | 0.13*** | | |
| TV/pol. interaction | 0.14*** | | | 0.02 | | | 0.18*** | | | 0.01 | | | 0.13*** | | |
| TV/educ. interaction | 0.11*** | | | 0.15*** | | | 0.06 | | | 0.11*** | | | 0.03 | | |

*Note:*
*** $p < 0.001$, ** $p < 0.01$, * $p < 0.05$
All variables were coded such that high values reflect more conservative social positions.

exposure and these dependent variables for liberals, moderates and conservatives, to confirm that those furthest from the television mainstream (liberals) would not only show more dramatic associations with television viewing, but would also converge toward the other groups as heavy viewers.

This full GSS analysis gives us some advantages that are not available either in the traditional narrative review nor in the typical meta-analysis. We can examine baseline responses in subgroups, to determine whether mainstreaming is a phenomenon that makes sense at the broader level, or whether it varies nonsensically across variables, etc.

Table 7.2 shows the scale values of dependent variables in the ideological subgroups, across levels of television viewing (light, medium and heavy). Mainstreaming is suggested when the means of heavy viewers are closer than the means of light viewers across counterpart subgroups; we see this pattern repeatedly here. The table also presents the results of regression analyses that show the size of overall cultivation relationships and reveal the presence of any interaction between television viewing and political self-identification. (The multiplicative interaction terms are kept out of the overall equation to avoid multicollinearity). Interactions were also calculated between television viewing and education level, because controlling for education has also generated mainstreaming patterns in the past (although the scale values for these interactions are not shown in Table 7.2). Together, these coefficients give an idea of the relative contribution of each independent variable, and they indicate whether the interaction effects have an independent contribution to make, controlling for all other variables. If a significant interaction is present, it confirms the suggestion of mainstreaming implied by the means. We used sex, education level, age and race (white/non-white) as demographic controls in each analysis.

The results show that overall television viewing is essentially unrelated to the dependent variables when all control factors are taken into account (consistent with some early critiques of cultivation). In particular, level of education seems to explain much of the shared variance in these analyses. In all cases, the relationships between education and the dependent variables are substantial, while the TV relationships are negligible. Thus, for these issues, amount of television viewing does not explain much overall. That is, the "simple" cultivation hypothesis does not fare well for these data under multiple, simultaneous controls.

However, many of the interactions, particularly with political self-identification, do remain sizeable and significant. For the abortion question, the marijuana question, and the sex-roles question, there are significant interactions reflecting mainstreaming patterns. In all five cases, liberal light viewers are very different from the rest of the sample, but espouse more conservative positions as heavy viewers. The beta weights for these interactions are comparable in magnitude to those for political self-identification's main effect, and are as large as some of the demographic indicators' influence as well. Thus, while overall associations disappear across this multi-year sample, the interactions with political self-identification continue to suggest mainstreaming, even though attitudes have certainly shifted over the years on these questions.

Figure 7.10 shows the mainstreaming patterns for these five questions based on the cumulative twenty-year GSS dataset. The clear pattern is evident in which liberals who are light viewers are very supportive of abortion on demand, yet the heavy-viewing liberals have opinions on the issue much closer to their conservative and moderate counterparts. Even in the two cases where the interaction coefficient is not statistically significant

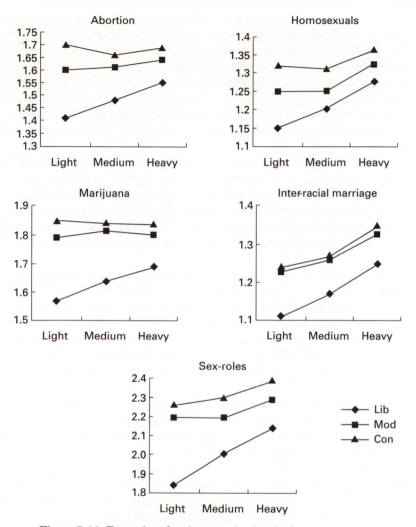

Figure 7.10  Examples of mainstreaming by ideology

(the questions on gays and interracial marriage), the same pattern is still evident. The similarity of the pattern in all the variables is striking. In no case does a contradictory (non-mainstreaming) pattern appear. All the patterns reflect mainstreaming in which more liberal or more educated groups close in upon more conservative positions. Thus, when people differ widely on issues of attitude and opinion, exposure to common messages and stories seems to unite those opinions around a more conservative and traditional view. Still, though, either Hypothesis 2 or 3 could explain these data.

As these examples show, political ideology is a major mediator, perhaps the major mediator, of how television's messages contribute to people's conceptions. Or at least, political ideology is the major mediator of television's ideological repercussions. That is, for these variables, heavy exposure to television clearly represents an important contribution to the worldview of liberals, but it does not make any noticeable difference for conservatives. Why?

The clearest answer lies in the possibility that conservatives are "already close" to the views promulgated by social elites; to change their opinion would be socially counterproductive. Liberals, on the other hand, when they encounter television, apparently encounter a world whose messages and morals differ drastically from what they might naturally perceive in a world without TV. Thus, cultivation can partly be seen as a theory of how media contribute to the beliefs of those who adhere to marginal ideologies. Not only does television outline a view of how to think about outgroups, it may be especially effective at telling us how to think about ourselves if *we* ourselves are in the outgroup.

Those belonging to majority populations can effectively perceive the fact that their own social position is legitimate and valued within society. Those on the margins, however, cannot as easily gain such legitimation. We can speculate that, as heavy viewers of television, outgroup members would be prone to adopt TV messages as a contribution to their worldview; motivated by the desire for social inclusion and acceptance, heavy outgroup viewers might manage themselves into the mainstream as one possible outcome of their viewing.

We can explore these differences further by examining cultivation relationships *only* for liberals, in various conditions. These analyses show that, even where the cultivation relationship is at its strongest (for liberals), other variables still play an important role. For instance, we looked at variation in cultivation among liberals by geographic region, to see how the fact that some regions of the country are "more liberal" would affect the strength of the cultivation relationship for liberals in those regions. The GSS allows for comparisons by region, dividing the country

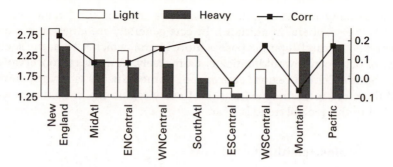

Figure 7.11 Regional variation in cultivation among liberals ("approval" of homosexuality)

*Note*: scale values 1 = "homosexuality always wrong"; 4= "homosexuality not wrong at all." Values on secondary axis are correlation coefficients.

into nine distinct areas, some of which are clearly more liberal than others.

We would expect liberals in more liberal geographical regions (the East and West coasts, for instance) to be mainstreamed more because of the absolute difference of their regional liberalism from the nationally mainstreamed variant. That is, in New England, those who call themselves "liberal" do so in a maximally liberal environment. They are "ultra-liberal" (in relative terms, anyway) and thus rather far from the nationally conservative center of opinion gravity. On the other hand, "liberals" in the East South Central region (Mississippi, Alabama, etc.) are probably less liberal than those in New England. Therefore, they're closer to an "absolute" conservative position and will be mainstreamed less (see also Morgan, 1986).

To explore this, we simply looked at variation across regions on a question about homosexuality. We examined responses to a question on "approval" of homosexuality (different from the free-speech question used above, although the results for both questions are similar). Figure 7.11 shows differences for liberal light and heavy viewers on the variable. The chart also shows (on the secondary axis) the correlation between approval of homosexuality and viewing for liberals in each region, to provide a measure of strength of the relationship (positive correlations reflect support for cultivation theory).

Note that, generally speaking, regions of higher liberalism on homosexuality show stronger correlations between viewing and attitude. Thus, New England liberals are, as hypothesized, "very" liberal, and there is also a stronger relationship between amount of viewing and approval of homosexuality in that region. The same is true for the Pacific region (again, "very" liberal in attitude). Effects generally are larger in regions where the "natural" opinion base is more liberal, which is what the social control perspective would indicate. Conversely, in the very conservative East South Central region, approval of homosexuality is already lower and therefore mainstreamed less. Not every region fits the pattern perfectly, but the general trend is clear.

### Mainstreaming for Whom?

From these data (and many other findings like these spread throughout the cultivation literature), the possibility of a more general theory of mainstreaming emerges in which distance from the conservative social mainstream indicates both greater "need" for and greater possibility of the absorption of the messages of television. In this context, it is worth noting that in the two decades examined here, it has increasingly become the case that to define oneself as "liberal" is to declare oneself to be outside the mainstream *de facto*. Add to this the persistent tendency of television viewing to cultivate "moderate" self-designations (away from both liberal and conservative labels), and we have a fascinating example of television undercutting and blending the categories of a control variable that has generated unmistakable variations in susceptibility to cultivation. The medium seems to weave a tangled web indeed.

Moreover, it is not just about being "liberal" in name (though political views handily denote a major group that is somewhat disenfranchised), but about *being* liberal in way that distinguishes one from the rest of society. Thus, not every group traditionally denoted as liberal may be candidates for mainstreaming. For instance, blacks are generally considered to hold more liberal views than whites (a tendency that is certainly seen in their voting patterns over the years). Given this, one would initially surmise that blacks would be more subject to mainstreaming than whites, particularly black liberals who might be among the most liberal citizens in the country. But self-identifying as liberal does not always accurately predict how particular cultural subgroups respond to issues. For instance, if we again look at the approval of homosexuality item, blacks as a group are actually *more* traditional than whites in their rejection of homosexuality. That is, they are closer to a conservative social position rejecting homosexuality than are whites. Thus, it is not surprising that we find strong associations between TV viewing and attitude for white liberals, but *not* for black liberals, who are actually less tolerant of homosexuality across the board. Thus, being liberal is different than calling oneself liberal, as differential patterns of cultivation reveal.

This helps us to see that is not the absolute mathematical "center" of opinion that drives mainstreaming, but the socio-ideological conservative center of gravity that drives mainstream elite institutions. Thus, the main-streaming tests that are the most provocative are the ones that show the mechanics of how otherwise "liberal" groups are drawn closer to more traditional positions on social issues. Given all of this, it appears that a combination of Hypotheses 2 and 3 best explains the mainstreaming process. That is, *in most cases*, cultivation will be strongest for liberals because of their distance from an essentially conservative cultural "center." However, in cases where self-identified liberal subgroups are not that far from the opinion center, cultivation will be lesser or even absent (consistent with Hypothesis 3). And, in the cases where subgroups find themselves far to the right of the cultural center, cultivation will occur in a "liberal" direction. Umble (1990) provides an example of such a situation. As noted in Chapter 5, she found that heavy viewing Mennonites (overall, a very conservative/traditional group) were more moderate in their views about sexual and moral questions. Consistent with Hypothesis 3, they mainstreamed toward more liberal views on moral issues.

### Crime and Violence

Before fully accepting the implications of Hypotheses 2 and 3, however, it is important to remember that there are analyses where mainstreaming patterns do not appear. In particular, fear of victimization and beliefs about violence seem to be less likely to generate mainstreaming specifications than the more ideological issues we have just considered. In fact, beliefs about crime and violence often provide for a different sort of specification of cultivation, partially because there are different ways to determine which social groups "should" have different outlooks on vio-lence. Race may provide one interesting divide (because blacks might be exposed to more violence than whites and perhaps see the world as more violent). Rural/urban groups also might be expected to differ, since urban subgroups would be more exposed to violence. Gender and, of course, actual experience with crime, leap out as relevant variables. But these are primarily questions of experience more than attitude, and so there may be some qualitative differences for specification with these types of variables.

If cultivation theory is more or less correct on issues of social control, it seems clear that heavy viewers should certainly be more fearful about crime and violence. Data from the combined GSS samples ($N = 10,276$) show that heavy viewers are slightly more likely to answer that there is an area around their home where they would be afraid to walk at night

($r = .06$). Also, heavy viewers are more likely to feel afraid in their own home ($r = .08$); this question, however, was used in only one GSS year (1982) and thus includes far fewer respondents than our overall sample. Again, the correlations are small, but consistent with the predictions of cultivation. However, one can imagine that neighborhood-related fear might be highly related to socio-economic status and other demographic markers, because these would predict the actual "danger" of living in a particular area; they are also likely to be related to television viewing.

As noted earlier, "resonance" was a phenomenon that was explored after Doob and Macdonald (1979) showed that cultivation patterns for violence differed by rural or urban location and local crime rates. As we saw in Chapter 2, Gerbner et al. (1980a) interpreted the stronger association between television viewing and fear of crime among residents of the high-crime urban area by saying that television's messages about violence may be most congruent with the lived worlds of residents of high-crime areas; for them, television's images may "resonate" with everyday reality, producing a "double dose" of complementary messages, and thereby amplifying cultivation.

This again raises the question of the difference between "social" judgments and personal judgments. Note that this particular GSS item about "fear" deals with respondents' perceptions of their local environments, which should be less susceptible to cultivation than more general perceptions of the amount of violence in society. (See also the colloquy about this variable in the original interchanges between Hirsch and Gerbner et al.; see references.) This distinction has been extensively implicated in the discussion on the concept of the "impersonal impact" of mass media information (Tyler and Cook, 1984), which argues that media information influences judgments about general, social risk levels, but does not influence our judgments of our own risk.

Shrum and Darmanin (1998) also point out that social-level judgments are a different breed than estimates about personal likelihood of victimization. They argue that media are more likely to affect perceptions about social phenomena, because "it is likely that direct experience is considered more diagnostic than media reports when people estimate their own risk of crime victimization" (p. 11). But they also realized that interaction patterns have emerged for violence issues in cultivation research and posited that Gerbner's account of resonance could receive support from the notion of the "availability heuristic." That is, individuals who receive more frequent impressions that the world is violent will tend to have such concepts more cognitively available (this is discussed in more detail in the next chapter). Thus, heavy viewers, accessing these available constructs, see the world as more violent. In the resonance case,

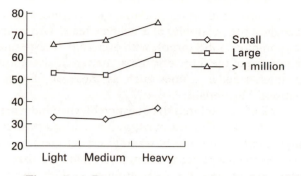

Figure 7.12 Percentage expressing fear in their neighborhood, in small and larger communities

Shrum and Darmanin argue that an additive availability operates, because heavy viewers with direct experience of violence will have even more available constructs of violence with which to judge the world.

In a small survey ($N = 158$), Shrum and Darmanin related people's estimates of crime risk at three levels (in American society at large, in their neighborhood, and in New York City) to television viewing measures (based on "average-day" and "yesterday" reports). They also compared these estimates to personal experience with crime and found that people with more direct experience of violence were, as predicted, more likely to be cultivated by television's violent worldview. Direct cultivation explanations and impersonal impact explanations were reduced to insignificance for all three types of crime risk judgments. This study therefore provided more support for a resonance explanation than either the direct cultivation or the impersonal impact hypothesis.

Shrum and Darmanin's results confirm past research, and also are replicated in the larger GSS dataset. For instance, comparing those from larger and presumably more violent towns to those from smaller areas (using the median city/town size of 22,000 as a cutoff point) we find no mainstreaming. Rather, we see that respondents from smaller cities and towns do not show much relationship between viewing and fear. But for respondents from the more populated areas, we find *greater* fear among heavy viewers. This is resonance (see Figure 7.12).

Figure 7.12 shows that respondents from larger towns and cities express more fear about their neighborhoods than do people from smaller towns, as one would expect. Also, the figure shows that the percentages of people expressing fear are greater at heavier levels of viewing. More interestingly, though, percentage differences between light and heavy viewers are greater in the larger towns, and are especially noticeable in cities with populations of more than 1 million (even though the relatively high fear rates there might suggest the possibility of a ceiling effect). These results, again, are from the combined GSS sample with over 10,000 respondents, so the finding gains some of the force of a meta-analysis; it also confirms the results from much smaller studies such as those of Shrum and Darmanin or Doob and Macdonald.

In the previous section, we explored the question of when mainstreaming could be predicted for various subgroups; we now add another level to that issue by bringing in the question of when to expect mainstreaming and when to expect resonance patterns. First, we should note that mainstreaming has been encountered far more frequently than resonance. Thus, empirically, we should be most concerned with mainstreaming, especially when ideology is the issue. Still, relatively few investigations have examined resonance claims. Apart from Shrum and Darmanin's study, Sparks, Nelson and Campbell (1997) investigated resonance issues for the cultivation of beliefs about "psychic" or "paranormal" phenomena. They suspected that people who had reported experience with psychic phenomena would be more likely to be cultivated by television messages about the prevalence of psychic phenomena in the world. However, they found that television cultivates beliefs about paranormal events precisely for those with *no* previous experience of the paranormal, which is more consistent with a mainstreaming account. Thus, resonance has not been a frequently observed specification pattern, apart from the issue of perceptions of crime, and cultivation researchers have been unable to develop a wider theory of how and when it might work in other contexts.

### What it Means

Based upon the previous analyses and arguments, we can offer the following summaries. Mainstreaming is to be expected primarily for ideological and social issues. Consistent with Hypothesis 2, most mainstreaming will occur for liberals, in a conservative direction. However, in cases where subgroups are located ideologically beyond the mainstream (Mennonites, for instance), cultivation will occur for those subgroups in a liberalizing direction, consistent with Hypothesis 3. Finally, on certain issues, mainstreaming will not occur at all. Violence perceptions seem to be one such issue; this observation is consistent with Hypothesis 4.

The GSS "mega"-analyses hint that mainstreaming/resonance factors (the third variables of the final model presented in Figure 7.4) might well be the variables that explain some of the observed variance from the meta-analysis of Chapter 6. It is rather easy to see how these factors produce variance *within* studies by simply looking at the results we have been presenting in this section. But the fact that mainstreaming is so resilient across large samples suggests that these factors can also influence across-study variance in a number of ways. First, different samples can vary demographically in ways that we didn't measure in the meta-analysis. For instance, city size and urban-rural location were not assessed by sample in non-national datasets, yet we can now see that this variable is extremely important for looking at violence and fear. Further, samples do differ in ideologically absolute terms even when a control variable has been measured. For instance, a sample taken from Baltimore, MD, might be, overall, more or less conservative than a sample taken from Lansing, MI, yet the meta-analysis provides no overall way to assess that at the baseline level. Especially with a variety of findings from different countries, it is by no means assured that samples are equivalent on these demographic variables.

If this is the case, then we can offer a corollary to the basic cultivation hypothesis: for samples that are "further" from mainstream-conservative social positions, cultivation will be more likely to be present or stronger. for samples closer to the conservative mainstream, cultivation will be weaker or absent.

Unfortunately, because few of the studies in our meta-analysis include data on the absolute ideological position of their respondents, we can neither easily nor directly test our hunch that ideological orientation is the missing moderator across studies. Given our suspicions, however, we performed an informal, trial analysis in which we simply guessed about the overall ideological position of given samples from other information that we had coded about them. For instance, for college student samples, we assumed that the respondents would be more liberal than average. On the other hand, we assumed that samples of Asians, Mennonites, etc. would be more conservative than average. And finally, for large random samples such as those obtained from the GSS, we guessed that they would be about in the middle. We then compared average cultivation sizes for these different sample groups, and found that "liberal" samples did manifest higher effect sizes than the moderates or the conservatives (very similar to what we saw in the subgroup mediator analysis of Chapter 6). Across all dependent variables, the twenty-two independent liberal samples averaged about .13 (unweighted); the fifty independent moderate and conservative samples averaged about .085. This analysis is far from conclusive, both because we identified the samples in a very speculative way, and also because this political dimension may not be the key axis on which the samples are differentiated. But we do take the results as suggestive, and as worthy of further investigation in the future.

What our discussion suggests is a functional explanation, consonant with the original formulation of mainstreaming. If social groups are "already" located nearer to the (usually) conservative position represented in the messages of TV, there is little observable evidence of any impact, even though television messages may confirm and strengthen their immersion in the dominant discourse stream. This type of reinforcement would not show up as observable cultivation in the correlational sense, although other measures such as attitude-behavior consistency might get at it (as in Morgan, 1987; Shrum, 1996, also hypothesizes this). For those more out of the mainstream, however, it would show up as cultivation in the traditional sense: that is, heavy viewers would think about things differently than do light viewers. In this model, television viewing plays a subtle maintenance role, normalizing mainstream outlooks and values, even if we are not able to detect any statistical difference between light and heavy viewers of certain subgroups.

### Cultivation and Social Change

The functional argument offered above is, we think, a fairly satisfying explanation of why some social groups manifest cultivation more than some others. But an obvious objection is that, even with huge multi-year datasets, this remains a cross-sectional explanation that says little about the dynamics of this process over time, much less about cause and effect. To get around this complaint somewhat, and for its considerable descriptive value, we think it is worthwhile to explore the operation of cultivation across long time spans, especially to investigate possible answers to the difficult question: does cultivation have anything to do with social change?[2]

Although the content analysis components of Cultural Indicators work have always been treated as an index whose annual variations are of some interest, long-term trends in cultivation relationships have not been analyzed much. A few studies have looked at longitudinal data, but the question of whether general cultivation patterns are stable over longer periods of time has not been examined. There are few prior studies that can help us to be specific about the role played by television viewing in shaping changes and stabilities in widely held perspectives on social issues over time.

How does cultivation relate to the phenomenon of social change? What is the role of television in social movements, and in the progression from one social state to another? Burrowes (1996) notes that functional expla-

---

[2] This section amplifies a discussion begun in Shanahan and Jones (1998).

nations (such as cultivation) have been criticized for their failure to account for social change. Others, however, note that functionalism *can* produce an account of social change, especially if new forms of social organization can be shown to contribute to continued social order and control (Demers, 1996).

One hypothesis is that television's messages may impede or retard social change that is due to social activism and other forces. Consider, for instance, the gradual liberalization of attitudes about proper social roles for women over the past few decades (a change that is not enough for some and too much for others). Television, throughout those years, clearly under-represented women and portrayed them in less-powerful social positions. Has television tended to retard the liberalization process by continuing to cultivate support for traditional gender roles? Gerbner argues (personal communication, 1996), that "positive" social change is generally achieved despite television, which simply seeks to maintain the status quo in favor of social elites. Or did television speed the process by virtue of a few unusual but popular programs that may have been more influential in the public mind? Or, alternately, was television out of the loop on this social movement?

Another idea is that cultivation differences will narrow over time because of the cumulative homogenization process. As more and more people grow up with TV, it is possible that it will become increasingly difficult to discern differences between light and heavy viewers. However, this question has not been addressed.

We do not expect that analysis of social change will find television to be a powerful "causal" variable. Mostly what explains changes in social beliefs over time is education and cohort maturation (Smith, 1993). That is, as people with older value systems die, the social environment changes, allowing new values to enter the mainstream. Education influences this process simply by introducing new ideas to new cohorts, especially as increasingly larger segments of the population obtain higher levels of education. Thus, for instance, the gradual liberalization of attitudes toward women is enhanced and amplified by the introduction of new ideas to new cohorts through education. This is a simplified but common-sense model of social change, and note that it does not include any particular effect for television messages.

We argue that television enters this picture through the role it plays in interpreting, redefining and legitimating social norms. Television can be seen as a marketplace mechanism for evaluating and determining "mainstreamable" ideas. In a marketplace sense, television (selectively) takes thoughts, ideas, values, beliefs and attitudes from the culture and submits them to a marketplace test for social acceptability. Though elites guide this process (by making advertising revenue the standard for judgment) the television marketplace is guaranteed to find a socially acceptable middle position. Of course, some find television's portrayals too restrictive while for others they are too depraved. But if something is portrayed on television, by definition it does not violate mainstream norms. Those outside of the mainstream begin to lose power in such a system, resulting in further strengthening of the hegemonic marketplace mechanism that guides cultural development.

Thus, it is extremely unlikely to expect television messages to be in the vanguard of social change. We expect, conversely, that television will lag behind major social change. However, this does not mean that TV messages might not adopt viewpoints that promote social change after they go through an initial period of volatility, prior to widespread acceptance in the media marketplace. The marketing needs of the medium require it to always appear trendy, on the verge of the next new craze, contemporary and "with it," but in truth it cannot get too far ahead of its audience. Perhaps more importantly, it cannot appear to get too far behind them either; the name of the game is novelty without change.

Let us continue with the example of sex-roles. We know that attitudes about roles for women have liberalized greatly in the past twenty years. The reasons for this are many. More women have chosen or have been forced to enter the workforce, childbearing has decreased, education for women has increased, and older cohorts with traditional attitudes have died off. During this period of change, television has cultivated relatively traditional perceptions about sex-roles for women, as we have seen. Thus, while TV tended to emphasize conventional images of women through under-representation, over-victimization, and restriction to family or romantic contexts, social conditions and attitudes changed (at least somewhat) in favor of liberalized treatment for women. But while change occurred, the frequency of portrayal of women in TV programs did not change; men still dominated the TV demography heavily. This is due to the fact that patriarchal social institutions tend to normalize power differences between men and women.

These facts present us with countervailing forces at work over time. While society liberalizes, TV tends to present more moderating and perhaps even conservatizing images about women. Can these contending forces be seen in real data? If so, what would we expect?

We acknowledge that it is very difficult to formulate simple hypotheses about how cultivation should work over time, in contest with other powerful social forces. Certainly, television's effects should be less pronounced than the influence of cohort and educational variables. In any case, among a potential plethora of possible patterns, a few stand out as reasonable *a priori*.

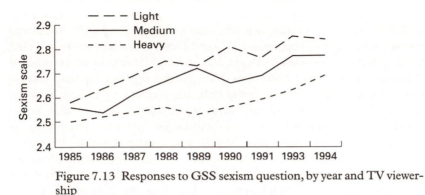

Figure 7.13  Responses to GSS sexism question, by year and TV viewership

First, cultivation could hold up over time, with heavy viewers maintaining traditional views and successive groups of light viewers embracing more progressive perspectives over time. In other words, as the population otherwise becomes more liberal about women's roles, heavy viewers could tenaciously cling to traditional beliefs. In this case, overall cultivation associations would grow *stronger* over time, with the gap between light and heavy viewers widening. Alternately, cultivation could gradually disappear over the years, with even successive groupings of both light and heavy viewers incrementally adopting more progressive views about women over time; in this scenario, the differences between heavy and light viewers would shrink, and everyone would converge toward the more egalitarian position. Third, all groups could be shifting toward generally more liberal views, but the *relative* difference between light and heavy viewers could be stable. In this version, even heavy viewers are swept up by larger social forces, but at a different level than lighter viewers; the changes over time would take the form of parallel lines. There are, again, many other possibilities (including no change for any viewing group over time, or a complete lack of any interpretable pattern, not to mention complex interactions or variations across subgroups), but these three would be among the most interesting for cultivation to observe.

Our analysis looks at responses to a GSS question which gets right to the heart of where people stand on traditional sex-role stereotypes: "It is much better for everyone involved if the man is the achiever outside the home and the woman takes care of the home and family." Responses range from "strongly agree" (1) to "strongly disagree" (4). Men have traditionally been more conservative in their response to this variable than women. Also, heavy viewers of television have been more likely to favor traditional roles. We look at the data on this question in Figure 7.13.

The figure shows how the overall pattern of public opinion has changed over the years. (In this figure, higher scores signify more "liberated" views.) Although the GSS initially asked this question in 1977, it was not until 1985 that the question was regularly included along with concurrent measures of viewing (between 1977 and 1985, there was an overall shift toward more liberal views). Beginning in 1985, it is evident graphically that subsequent heavy viewers of TV changed opinion (upward toward more liberated views) more slowly than did moderate and light viewers. That is, heavy viewers did not begin to respond to the growing social trend until the very late 1980s, while attitudinal shifts were evident for the light and moderate viewers three to four years earlier. Overall, the pace of change is tempered for the heavy viewers as well. The resulting pattern appears consistent with cultivation: heavier viewers were not immune to far-reaching transformations in public discourse, but their rate and level of opinion change appears to have been moderated by their viewing status. In other words, over the past twenty years, television has cultivated resistance to social change, or at least slowed the rate at which it might have otherwise occurred.

But of course this trend pattern does not "prove" that television caused this ostensible slowness of change among heavy viewers. Just as correlations often disappear at the bivariate level, the above data may also conceal more specific patterns. In fact, if the correlation between viewing and support for non-traditional sex-roles disappears under control (as it did when analyzed in Table 7.2), then one can argue that the appearance of a slower opinion change in the trend data is an illusion. One argument, for instance, could be that heavy viewers had other characteristics (lower education, or being older, for instance) that would have predisposed them to "lag" on social change.

But what was true for the cross-sectional examination of cultivation should also be true over time. That is, if effects were particularly strong for those furthest from the conservative opinion pole, then social change should be most altered or affected by TV messages in that same group. In other words, if cultivation works "over time," then mainstreamed groups should also manifest social change differently than non-mainstreamed groups.

To ascertain whether this was happening, we looked at interactions across the same general time span analyzed in Figure 7.13. We wanted to see whether those groups that show mainstreaming in cross-sectional analyses would show any evidence of differential cultivation over time. In this analysis, we summed these three items from the GSS (in this scale, high values denote less sexist attitudes):

"Women should take care of running their homes and leave running the country up to men (agree/disagree)."

"Do you approve or disapprove of a married woman earning money in business or industry if she has a husband capable of supporting her?"

Table 7.3 *Regression equation: relationships between television exposure and support for women in non-traditional roles (GSS sample years 1975–1994; N = 13,242)*

| Regression variable | Relationship with sexism (beta weights) |
|---|---|
| TV exposure | −0.01 |
| Year | −0.13*** |
| Education | −0.32*** |
| Occupation | 0.00 |
| Race | 0.00 |
| Sex | −0.02* |
| Income | −0.06*** |
| Interactions: | |
| TV*sex | 0.087** |
| TV*sex*year | 0.073* |

*Note:*
*** p < 0.001, ** p < 0.01, * p < 0.05

"If your party nominated a woman for president, would you vote for her if she were qualified for the job?"[3]

We began our analysis with a regression equation to assess the overall association between television exposure and the sex-role index. Included in these tests are sex, race (coded white/non-white), occupational prestige, level of education, income (in real 1986 dollars) and year (i.e., year in which the data were collected). The sample year variable gives us a way to measure the impact of the passage of time on the dependent variable. More sophisticated time series analysis procedures such as ARIMA were not used because of the small number of time intervals in the data, and the uneven distribution of time between sample points. Table 7.3 reports the results for these analyses.

Over time, the simple relationship between amount of television viewing and sexism has not varied much, and there has been no consistent decrease or increase in its strength. In each of the years (1975–94), the correlation has fluctuated randomly around an average of .08. However, Table 7.3 shows that, as with our cross-sectional analyses, there are no significant main effects for television viewing when controlling for other variables including sample year. Education and year are the vari-

[3] The alpha for these items is . 57.

ables that explain the most variance in our feminist factor across the years (as found in many GSS reports on social change, cohort and education explain the most variance over time; Smith, 1993). That is, support for women in non-traditional roles has increased overall since 1975, and especially for those with higher education. Other variables contributed only minimally to the power of the equation to explain variance; the fact that even gender itself plays such a small role is striking.

However, as noted earlier, these overall coefficients can obscure meaningful interactions. Because we were dealing with issues relating to women, we thought that gender and television exposure might meaningfully interact, something that has been noted in earlier studies. Thus we tested two interactions. The first was a two-way interaction between gender and television exposure. In our regression equation, we can see that the two-way interaction does contribute explanatory power to the overall equation (note that we kept interaction terms out of the overall equation to avoid multicollinearity). As seen in our first analyses, this type of interaction usually denotes a mainstreaming pattern.[4]

But we also wanted to add the time dimension to this analysis. Thus, we tested a three-way interaction between TV exposure, sex and sample year. We wanted to see if the meaningful interaction between gender and TV exposure changed at all through the sample years. As the equation shows, this interaction was also significant (independently of all other effects included in the equation). This means that the differential conditioning impact of gender on the association between amount of viewing and sex-role stereotypes itself varies over time. What is happening in this complex interaction?

Figure 7.14 shows the pattern. The chart presents moving average values (the moving average, in each case, was calculated as the average from the four previous sample points) on our feminism factor for four groups: light viewing males, light viewing females, heavy viewing males, and heavy viewing females.[5] The figure clearly shows that values on this factor have increased essentially linearly since 1975 for almost everyone. This increase is seen in the regression equation as the relationship between sample year and the dependent variable.

But this does not mean that everything is the same for everyone. The figure also shows that heavy viewers have remained notably more sexist than light viewers despite the clearly rising baselines. Remember, however, that this bivariate relationship disappears in the regression

---

[4] Although not shown in this analysis, there are similar interactions for political self-identification and education.
[5] We used a moving average in this case to help smooth out data fluctuation caused by the smaller $N$ of the subgroups analyzed in each year.

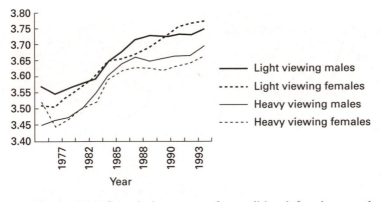

Figure 7.14 Growth in support for traditional female sex-roles, by viewing, year and gender (values on y axis are summative scale, higher values reflect less traditional views)

equation, as other variables (mainly education and year) tend to remove the effect. How, then, is the three-way interaction pictured in these data?

The answer is that the attitudinal "distance" between heavy viewing and light viewing females generally *increases* throughout these sample years, while the distance between heavy and light viewing males remains about the same. These distances are pictured in Figure 7.15. The distance between heavy and light viewing females increases because of the *slower* decline in sexism, across the years, of heavy viewing females. Thus, by 1994, light viewing females were the least sexist of all groups examined, while heavy viewing females were the most (whereas, in 1975, the gap was lesser). This is the key to the three-way interaction, and it solidly supports the concept of mainstreaming.

As seen in the regression equation, this three-way interaction effect (of television viewing, sex and year) is significant. Also, the two-way interaction effect is significant after all other main effects from demographic variables have been removed (showing stronger relationships for females, and indicating mainstreaming), and it clearly becomes larger as the years go by (as witnessed by the three-way interaction).

This analysis is consistent with the notion that mainstreamed groups (in this case the heavy viewing females) will be less likely to follow social change patterns as quickly as other groups. We might call this phenomenon "retardation through mainstreaming." That is, for mainstreamed groups (such as women in this case) heavy viewers should be less likely to match the pace of social change in other sectors and segments.

All this shows that mainstreaming may show up as a phenomenon we

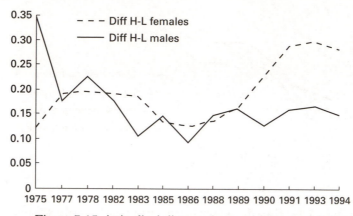

Figure 7.15 Attitudinal distance between heavy and light viewers, by gender and year

can actually observe over time. Still, there are many factors that may tend to obscure such patterns. With data such as these, for instance, the measurement scale is fairly gross. One may wonder whether the correct measurement interval is being used (and in this case, the measurement points are unevenly distributed, creating a further drawback). Furthermore, interpretations such as these tend to be overly abstract; social movements don't always proceed against a universal template. Some issues may show little movement for many years and then undergo cataclysmic change, such as attitudes towards homosexuality, with no simple single explanation for the change. Others may change almost not at all, such as attitudes towards welfare or foreign aid, where public opinion seems extraordinarily divorced from reality or rationality. And on other issues still, such as concern for the environment, discourse and opinions may go through cyclical changes. In some cases, media coverage of a particular event or issue may spur change in a way that would not be detected by cultivation analysis. For all these reasons, other variables may show different patterns than what we observed with only a few variables related to sexism. The time dimension allows many fascinating speculative analyses but it adds an enormous amount of complexity in ways that make any simple conclusion risky. Still, the consistency of cultivation and the interaction over time are interesting findings here.

One final analysis will show that, at the ideological level, television's cultivation of political beliefs remains consistent. Probably the most well-known argument about TV and ideology (Gerbner et al., 1982) is that heavy viewers tend to be much more likely to identify themselves as moderate, when asked to place themselves on a liberal–moderate–conservative

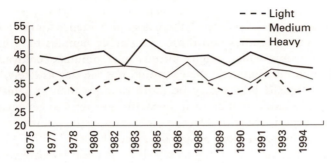

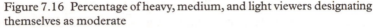

Figure 7.16  Percentage of heavy, medium, and light viewers designating themselves as moderate

spectrum. Typically, about 35 percent of light viewers will call themselves moderate, while 45–50 percent of heavy viewers will choose that designation. This has been seen as a key indicator of television's mainstreaming tendencies, and as Figure 7.16 shows, this light–heavy viewing difference has changed hardly at all over the years. Thus, though many ideological, social and political issues have undergone change through the years, heavy viewers are still more likely to see themselves in the middle of it all. Although the objective ideological location of the "middle" may have changed over the years, TV's heavy viewers continue to see themselves steering their boat directly between the banks of the cultural river.

Thus, it appears that some very important aspects of television's ideological contributions have remained stable. Still, we have to acknowledge that many diverse factors intervene in ways that make it difficult and tenuous to pinpoint television's effect across time. Looking at the meta-analytic data, it is interesting to note that the average size of cultivation coefficients has decreased over the years (Pearson $r = -.15$, p $<$ .001), even though (or perhaps because) television viewing hours have increased on average. Also, the proliferation of critiques, re-analyses and independent investigations has tended to result in reduced sample size since 1975 (the Pearson $r$ between sample year and sample size is $-.18$, p $<$ .001). What effect does this have on observed associations? Meta-analytic theory states that findings with higher $N$'s should be closer to the true mean, as can be seen in a funnel plot, with lower $N$ findings being skewed across a wider spectrum. In our sample, however, the decrease in finding size is not merely an artifact of lower sample size; partial control for sample size does not reduce the negative association between sample year and finding size in our meta-analytic database.

Several possible explanations exist. First, critiques that emerged later in the course of research may simply have been more correct than the earlier studies, showing that cultivation happens to a lesser degree than hypothesized (and at the overall level, there is some evidence for this). Or, perhaps, more recent studies and those with larger samples have used methods or measures which might intrinsically minimize cultivation findings; although meta-analytic theory would not see this as likely, the distribution of Type II errors may be more random than systematic. Another idea, as noted, is that cultivation coefficients tend to get smaller as the culture's experience with television increases to the point of near-total saturation. More and more people have been "raised" with TV; the time when there was no such thing as television is rapidly disappearing from collective memory. This means that the medium's ultimate "success" – ultimate cultivation – may obviate our ability to measure differences between heavy and light viewers at all, both of whom will have been enculturated in a symbolic world dominated by television. But this idea is very difficult to test, for obvious reasons. That is, such across-the-board cultivation would result not in measurable differences but in unmeasurable non-differences. The techniques of traditional social science are twisted beyond recognition in such a scenario.

## Conclusions and Questions

Our data analyses in this chapter have gone beyond what has traditionally been done in cultivation research. Our explorations here yield one firm answer, one promising direction for future research, and a vast host of questions.

The "answer" is that mainstreaming is an extremely durable account of relationships between viewing and attitude. Mainstreaming patterns appear in most cultivation studies (especially the ideologically oriented ones) and in the large GSS datasets examined in this chapter. Further, the appearance of the pattern is consistent with the meta-analytic data from the previous chapter, showing that liberals are far more likely to manifest evidence of cultivation than other groups. Thus, we can firmly conclude that cultivation is especially strong for liberals due to their distance from the conservative social positions desired and promulgated by social elites.

Possible objections to this conclusion include the fact that heavy viewers who call themselves liberal may differ on other (unmeasured) social characteristics, predisposing them toward acceptance of more conservative views. That is possible, though we're not sure exactly what those characteristics would be. The point of the mainstreaming analyses conducted here and throughout the literature is to rule out third variables through control, and most analyses control for the most likely sources of spuriousness. Even controlling for these variables, the interactions between political ideology (and education, often) remain significant. Lacking any clear theory to guide us on further possible sources of spuriousness, our conclusion is that mainstreaming confirms the social control ideas offered in Chapter 1.

Now for the research direction. Further research should assume, other things being equal, that liberals will be more likely to absorb television's messages and demonstrate cultivation. However, this does not mean that there may not be other ways to observe cultivation effects among moderates and conservatives. One idea is that non-liberals may show less *variance* in attitude as heavy viewers, even though average scale responses may remain the same for light and heavy viewers. Also, moderates and conservatives may demonstrate more attitude-behavior consistency, even under conditions of little attitude difference between light and heavy viewers. Thus, there may be other ways to assess cultivation effects that need more attention in the literature. Because the book on the overall cultivation question is in some sense closed, the way to more precisely show the nature of television's contribution to the culture may lie in different "real-world" measurements that can accurately depict how "already-mainstreamed" groups act and think in the ideological world of mainstream America.

The questions raised by this chapter have to do with trends. Admittedly, it is very difficult to form a consistent yet simple theory of cultivation's role in longitudinal terms. Cultivation deals with real social issues, which do not behave straightforwardly. Though we have been able to observe some "slowing down" of social change on some variables, it is more difficult to show how cultivation can be observed uniformly across time intervals. This is due, we feel, largely to the problem of establishing time order and discovering the best intervals at which to measure cultivation effects. Should data be gathered every year? Every month? Every day? This is a tough question, though we expect this area of research to be spurred on by the emergence of secondary datasets that span longer time frames.

However, thinking about trends does again raise the "causal" question. That is, do TV messages in some sense "cause" the effects that we have been observing? And if so, how? We have already suggested some general, conceptual responses to that question, but in the next chapter we turn our attention more fully to the debates that have been carried out on this issue from the "inside." Thus, we next focus on research which seeks to create a blueprint for the cognitive mechanisms by which cultivation may occur.

# 8    How does Cultivation "Work," Anyway?

More than a few researchers have pondered the cognitive "mechanics" of the cultivation process. In this chapter we take a close look at some of the many psychological models that have been offered in order to pinpoint how cultivation takes place within the "black box" of the individual viewer.

The "black box" refers to whatever unobservable cognitive processes underlie the absorption and integration of information (facts, values, assumptions, images, beliefs and so on) from television that results in cultivation. Many different arguments have been proposed about what these processes might be and how they might operate, and the question still excites a good deal of curiosity, speculation and empirical effort. Though no firm or definitive answers have been reached, there is progress being made on this question, as we report in this chapter.

Despite the amount of research activity in this area, cognitive problems have tended to receive short shrift from many of those engaged in cultivation studies. After all, Gerbner et al. did not mean for cultivation to concentrate on the psychology of individuals, nor did they envision a cognitively minded research endeavor; they were focused on macro-social phenomena, and cultivation certainly continues to be best seen as a broad-based attempt to explain the impacts of communication institutions and their outputs on large communities. The theory was conceived, as we have pointed out earlier, to examine "the bucket, not the drops" of television's contribution to the culture. Indeed, we believe that to become sidetracked by the peculiarities of how individuals receive, process, interpret, remember and act on messages can distract attention from the more central questions of cultivation research.

But not everyone agrees with this position, and even the most macro-minded theorists must admit that cultivation, though construed as a societal-level phenomenon, is measured at the individual level. Though most theorists do not see cultivation as simply the sum of what individuals do, this is how they measure it statistically. This opens the door to complex questions about how individuals deal with the TV they watch.

While these questions are legitimate, much of the cultivation-related research on cognitive phenomena has tended to reflect a reductionistic or mechanistic view of the social world. This worldview is not in itself always wrong or bad, but many cultivation theorists, like many sociologically influenced critical functionalists, simply did not and do not adopt it. Thus, they study television at the social level because they see it as a social institution. The position of Gerbner et al. was that knowledge about individual reception mechanics might be interesting, but not in any way vital to cultivation analysis; it was simply assumed (commonsensically, as it were; see proposition 5 in Chapter 1) that people would "internalize" content from a medium with which they spend so much time. To some doing cultivation work, the cognitive questions seemed no more than an irritating can of worms, beside the point, and comparable to wondering how immersion in an ocean might get one wet.

Others, however, have argued that questions about cognition are intrinsically worthwhile and indeed relevant to cultivation analysis. Hawkins, Pingree and Adler (1987), among others, grant that cultivation theory was conceived as a way to think about television in broad social terms (i.e., involving the mass production of cultural symbols consumed by heterogeneous social aggregates over long periods of time), but they contend that it nevertheless raises *psychological* questions about how the symbolic content of television ultimately finds its way into the heads of specific viewers – and out of their mouths in response to survey interviewers (and, presumably, in other contexts as well). In their view, elucidation of the precise cognitive mechanisms that produce cultivation would imbue cultivation theory with a major credibility boost, since the case for its internal validity would be greatly enhanced (Hawkins and Pingree, 1990; Shrum, 1995, also shares this view). That is, if compelling evidence for a specific cognitive principle that provides a satisfactory explanation for how cultivation might occur can be found, then it strengthens the likelihood that associations found in large sample research truly reflect *cultivation* and not statistical artifacts or some other social process. On the other hand, failure to support a specific cognitive model does not in itself cast doubt on cultivation, as Potter (1991c) has claimed; it may simply be that the wrong model is being tested, or that the model has not been tested well, and so on.

Given the rationale put forward by Hawkins et al. (1987), a progression of increasingly complex hypothetical models was developed, seeking to explain the processes by which the various bits of information presented on television are attended to, perceived, interpreted, related to and integrated with other bits, stored in short-term or long-term memory, and then at some point transformed (or not) into general impressions and perceptions that may (or may not) be retrieved, and/or further general-ized, and/or provide a subsequent basis for behavior. Many of these models have been intricate, ambitious and elegant. Some have very strong commonsensical appeal. But for some years, the empirical tests of cogni-tive models pretty much all fizzled out. Thus, Hawkins and Pingree could justifiably comment that isolating "a plausible psychological process for cultivation has proved surprisingly difficult" (1990, p. 36). At first this tended to confirm the suspicion of cultivation theorists that cultivation only "made sense" at the social level. However, as we will see, subsequent cognitive work came to point in more promising directions.

A model first offered by Hawkins and Pingree (1982) inspired most of the early conceptual and empirical work in this area. Their model of how television contributes to conceptions of social reality "within the heads" of individuals broke down the process into two discrete steps, delineated as "learning" and "construction." In the learning (first) phase, viewers "acquire" many different pieces of incidental information from television portrayals (e.g., about gender, age, or racial groups, occupations, violence, social class, lifestyles, etc.); the specific accumulation of this store of learn-ing is held to be influenced by numerous factors such as attention to televi-sion, memory capacity, involvement, focusing strategies, and so on. Later, separately, comes the construction phase, wherein the various pieces of information that were acquired come together in some way to inform the viewer's beliefs about the social world; the extent to which and the ways in which individuals *construct* images of the world from the *learned* (stored) information will be, presumably, influenced by their inference skills, actual experiences, position in family and social structures, and so on.

Studies seeking to confirm the validity of this and related models of "black-box" cognitive processes have often relied on the distinction between "first-order" and "second-order" cultivation measures, about which a few words are needed here. Hawkins and Pingree (1982) first drew attention to the fact that cultivation analysis uses two distinct kinds of dependent variables, which they called "demographic" and "value system" measures. Demographic measures are derived from the observa-tion of persistent differences between "the facts" (based on census or other "official" data) and "the facts as portrayed on television" (as deter-mined by message system analysis). These questions, as we have seen in the earliest cultivation studies, have both a "television answer" and a specifiable "real-world" answer, based on how television distorts the fre-quency of occurrence of some independently verifiable phenomenon (say, the number of people involved in violence, the average age of doctors or scientists, the proportion of married women with children who work outside the home, and so on). Measures based on these "demographic" statistical differences are intended to reveal the extent to which heavy viewers' conceptions of "the facts" are closer to the "real world" or to the world of television. (The forced-error questions used in the early studies are a good example of these "demographic" dependent measures, although other question formats can be used as well.)

More often than not, however, cultivation research uses dependent variables which get at beliefs and outlooks "that are only implied by the manifest content" (Hawkins et al., 1987, p. 561). These are what Hawkins and Pingree called "value system" measures – they tap "the more interesting, general aspects of social reality" (1982, p. 225) – and they include everything from the Mean World syndrome to mistrust of science to sexism to authoritarianism.

Cases of straightforward divergences between symbolic reality and "objective" reality do provide convenient tests of the extent to which heavy viewers take television's versions of "the facts" for granted. But cultivation also implies symbolic transformations – what Gerbner (1990) sees as "the special characteristic of terms of discourse to shift from specific cases to general classes and to be understood symbolically rather than literally" (p. 257). For example, message system data say little directly about either the selfishness or altruism of people, and there are certainly no real-world statistics one can look up about the extent to which people can be trusted; yet, cultivation research finds consistent associations between amount of viewing and the "Mean World" syndrome of apprehension and interpersonal mistrust (a "value system" measure). Such broader beliefs need not be explicitly found in, but may be reasonable responses to, consistent content patterns. Thus, there is no way to assess whether the television world is, in an absolute sense, meaner, more sexist or more authoritarian than the real world (in the same way that one can say that women are outnumbered by men by at least a 2–1 margin), but one can still hypothesize that its messages will cultivate those kinds of general "value systems."

Gerbner et al. (1986) referred to these two dimensions as "first-order" and "second-order" cultivation, respectively. In simplest terms, first-order (demographic) measures can be used to see if television viewing relates to perceptions of (for example) how frequently violence occurs in society, while second-order (value system) measures reflect the extent to which heavy viewers see themselves as likely to be victims of violence, or are fearful for their own personal safety, or are mistrustful of others. The idea is that heavy viewers not only absorb various "facts" about the world from watching television (first-order cultivation) but also that they can also extrapolate from those facts to more general views of reality (second-order cultivation).

As Potter (1991b) notes, Gerbner et al. "treat the two types of measures primarily as a methodological, not a conceptual, feature" (p. 93). Indeed, the labels were offered mainly to categorize and clarify the variety of methodological procedures that have been used in cultivation analysis; there was no theoretical paradigm (grand or otherwise) that posited any necessary relation between them. Nor does the term "first-order" suggest a more direct or "closer" measure of television reality. The terms were introduced simply to make the point that cultivation measures *can* have a specifiable, statistically based, real-world answer, but that cultivation analysis is not limited to such measures. The major distinction between them is that message system analyses provide "facts" about the former (whereby cultivation questions can be devised with specific "television" and "real-world" answers), but there are no clear-cut "real-world" answers to the latter and the "TV answers" are indeed based on the researchers' interpretations – as acknowledged, they may require a "creative leap." Because cultivation research is not solely an investigation of correlations between TV and real-world demography, there must by definition be room for both researchers and audiences to make qualitative as well as quantitative judgments.

Although the original presentation of these terms did suggest that first-order beliefs should provide the basis for subsequent second-order constructions (i.e., the implicit idea was that beliefs about "facts" can provide the basis for more generalized worldviews), the relationship between them (as well as the difference between them) turned out to be more complex than it appeared at first glance. It soon became apparent that, conceptually, second-order cultivation need not simplistically nor automatically follow from first-order. For example, the over-representation of men on television does not mean that heavy viewers ignore daily experience (and common sense) and believe that only a third of the population is female. But under-representation in the world of television means a relatively narrow (and thus more stereotyped) range of roles and activities, and heavy viewers do generally endorse traditional gender stereotypes (we see this in the results from Chapter 6).

There may be, moreover, more than just two "orders" at work here. Using violence as an example, we have seen that there are at least three different potential cultivation dimensions or "realms." First, we have simple perceptions of the amount of violence in society (this is the first-order, or demographic measure). Second, we have the perceived likelihood of *personal* victimization; importantly, this need not be high just because estimates of societal-level violence are high, since so many individual experiential factors come into play. But third, we also have the personal degree of *fear* of being victimized. The latter two may seem similar (and they are presumably both "value system" measures), but they are conceptually and empirically distinct, both from each other (Ogles and Sparks, 1994), and from the first (Sparks and Ogles, 1990). Furthermore, generalized notions of social reality need not be absorbed into *personal* values, aspirations and outlooks. For example, although adolescent girls who watch a lot of television are more likely to believe that *women in general* are happiest staying at home and not working (a general, "second-order," value-system conception of social reality, a belief about what "women" are like), this does not in any way limit their own personal aspirations for education and careers (Morgan and Gross, 1982). The key point is that arrays of societal-level and personal-level conceptions are multidimensional and not necessarily mechanistically built upon or linked with each other.

Realizing that this apparently simple distinction generates distracting complexity (and since the issue is not really central to cultivation theory but is, rather, more germane to problems of cognition and learning in general), Gerbner et al. subsequently decommissioned the terms, leaving others welcome to explore these troublesome issues (and several researchers accepted the invitation). Gerbner (1990) had noted that the very notion of "second-order" cultivation can be misleading, and the group's updated revision of the 1986 article that introduced the terms (Gerbner et al., 1994) dropped all reference to them entirely (and quite intentionally).

### Tests of Cognitive Models

Quite a few tests focusing on "order" distinctions were tried, but no firm, clear or convincing conclusions about cognitive ordering of TV messages emerged from them. Although Gerbner et al. more or less dumped and disowned the scheme of first- and second-order cultivation, the concepts were commonly employed in the early empirical tests of the cognitive processes underlying cultivation. Those path-breaking tests of cognitive processing models also often used various measures of viewers' concep-tions *about television*, despite the fact that Gerbner et al. have always insisted that viewers' conscious interpretations or explicit evaluations of television's messages (including the idea of perceived reality) are irrele-vant to cultivation. (If people were aware of the sources of their con-sciousness, after all, there would be no need for research on the subject.)

In what was apparently the first empirical test of the cognitive compo-nents or "steps" of cultivation, Hawkins et al. (1987) explored whether or not "perceptions of the television world would serve as raw material for construction of beliefs about social reality" (p. 556) – that is, they tested the hypothesis that heavy television viewing leads to *beliefs about television content* which are then generalized to broader beliefs about society. To explore this possibility, telephone interviews were conducted with 100 adults, who were asked four violence-related questions (for example, an average citizen's chances of being involved in violence, the percentage of men who work in law enforcement, and so on). Respondents were also asked the same four questions in specific reference to television characters and the world of TV.

The data failed to validate the hypothesis that beliefs about television constitute an intermediate or intervening step between television exposure and beliefs about social reality. Significant cultivation associations were found between amount of viewing and three of the four social beliefs, even with age, education *and* beliefs about TV held constant; if beliefs about television were indeed intervening, then controlling for them would have eliminated the core cultivation associations. Further, they found a *negative* relationship between amount of viewing and beliefs about the quantity of violence in the TV world, hammering a galvanized nail into the model's coffin. As the authors note, although these results do not clarify how cultivation does occur cognitively, at least "it is clear that beliefs about the demographics of the real world are not constructed from similar estimates about television" (Hawkins et al., 1987, p. 560). Although a test with only 100 respondents should never be taken as a final demonstration of anything, subsequent studies confirmed the muddiness of these waters.

Potter (1988) tested essentially the same hypothesis with a somewhat larger sample, consisting of 252 8th-12th graders. The first step of "learning" in Hawkins and Pingree's model (1982) was again framed as the learning of perceptions *about* television, such as how much violence one thinks is shown on TV; since violence is depicted so often, Potter argued, "the more one watches, the more violence one should perceive on television" (p. 932). Cultivation, however, predicts no such thing; moreover, as we just saw, Hawkins et al. had already found precisely the opposite (and they speculated that this reflected the stereotypes light viewers hold about television). In the "construction" phase in Potter's version, conscious beliefs about the amount of violence shown on television would, once again, shape the amount of violence people perceive in the real world.

Potter contended that testing whether estimates about television intervene between amount of viewing and social conceptions "is, in essence, a test for determining whether the cultivation process is a cognitive one" (1988, p. 932). Yet, he may have realized the logical flaws in this model: after he presents this model by which "TV estimates" allegedly intervene, he surprisingly asserts that he expects "TV estimates" not to have any intervening effect. This is all rather confusing; if his hypothesis was indeed that TV estimates are irrelevant (as Gerbner et al. would indeed argue), and if Hawkins et al. had already shown that these estimates had no impact on cultivation, then it is difficult to see where Potter was taking his replication.

As it turned out, amount of viewing was positively related to TV estimates in his study (contrary to Hawkins et al., who were using adults as opposed to the children in Potter's study), but these estimates *about television content* were thoroughly unrelated to first-order, real-world estimates of violence. Once again a direct exposure → "cognition" → cultivation link could not be supported. TV estimates appeared to be related to second-order victimization measures, but the association changed dramatically (and reversed sign) under different controls. Although neither his nor any other studies had yet provided any support for the two-step subprocess model of learning and construction – and although he had explicitly hypothesized that estimates about TV played no intermediate role – Potter still held out hope, concluding that "it is premature to stop testing the model" (Potter, 1988, p. 938).

Maybe he was correct in this last respect. It could be argued that these studies did not give the model a fair test. For one thing, both were based on fairly small samples, which provides ample opportunity for sample error to emerge. Moreover, the dependent variables that were used might furrow some brows. For example, the "TV estimates" in Potter's study were perceptions of how often "car accidents, murders, robberies, lies and insults" are shown on television in a typical three-hour prime-time block. We know of no message system data on the portrayal of televised car accidents, lies and insults; for all we know, car accidents may even be *less* common on television than in reality! Also, the items intended to tap first-order real-world estimates of violence were based on respondents' perceived chances of being the victim of various unpleasant circumstances (a car accident, a robbery, etc.). But, as we have seen, estimates of *personally* being involved in violence are not the same thing as societal-level perceptions of the prevalence of violence; therefore, since these are not "first-order" measures at all, they cannot be used to test presumed cognitive steps deriving from first-order cultivation.

Finally, there are some discrepancies between Potter's data and his text that generate misleading impressions. For example, as we saw above, the correlation between "TV estimates" and "victimization" (i.e., the alleged "construction" subprocess) changes sign under certain controls (for anomia, locus of control, and IQ). He claims that this shows that these controls are distorter variables, and that "the seemingly positive relationship between amount of television viewing and victimization is only positive" because of the effects of these controls (Potter, 1988, p. 936). But the correlations being discussed are between *TV estimates* and "victimization" – they do not concern "amount of television viewing" at all. Moreover, the crucial distinction between spurious and conditional associations is muddled; after showing that the relationship between amount of viewing and the first-order measure varies sharply and significantly across various subgroups, Potter mistakenly concludes that the relationship is spurious (p. 936).

Still, we tend to think that the failure of these tests to support the model at hand is not due to methodological and analytical problems alone. That is, it is unlikely that any "better test" of the model would support it. Again, the argument that lack of support for the model would create "serious doubt about the overall cultivation process" (Potter, 1991c, p. 84) is flawed. Ultimately, we can neither envision nor invent any reason why perceptions about TV content should have anything to do with cultivation – how or why, and under what conceivable circumstances, would people explicitly "use" their conscious perceptions of dominant patterns in television content *as such* to make inferences about *reality*? – and our assertion is comfortably borne out by these data.

But what about the original formulation, that did not involve the distracting element of estimates about television? Hawkins et al. (1987) also reanalyzed data from three samples of adolescents (two from Australia, one from the USA) to test their proposed model that heavy viewing shapes demographic beliefs about social reality (the first-order, "learning" phase), and that those beliefs then in turn lead to value system beliefs (the second-order, "construction" phase). To the extent possible across the samples, they looked at several different topical areas (including violence, mean world, fear, working women, sexism, women's competence, families and others) for which *both* first- *and* second-order measures were available. So, for example, they used perceptions of the prevalence of violence as a first-order measure, and mean world (mistrust) or fear of going out at night as second-order. This does have some logical appeal; if television viewing indeed cultivates fear of going out at night, it is not inconceivable that this happens by means of first cultivating the assumption that what is "out there" is dangerous.

Two empirical strategies were employed. First, they looked at the correlations between amount of viewing and second-order beliefs, controlling for first-order beliefs (along with grade in school, gender, social class and other relevant controls). If first-order beliefs are intervening – that is, if viewing leads to the acquisition of facts, and if more general impressions are then built upon those acquired facts – then controlling for the first-order beliefs should reduce or eliminate associations between amount of viewing and second-order beliefs. This did not happen; the partial corre-lations were the same as the simple (Hawkins et al., 1987, p. 567), and the cultivation patterns (between amount of viewing and the second-order measures) persisted. The model wherein "TV→learning→construc-tion" just didn't fit the data.

Second, they examined subgroup patterns, looking for conditional associations between amount of viewing and second-order beliefs sepa-rately for those whose first-order beliefs leaned toward television and those whose first-order beliefs leaned toward the real world. Contrary to their expectations (and defying any easy explanation), most of the notable and significant associations between television viewing and second-order beliefs were observed for those whose "demographic" beliefs tended to match those of the real world. Controlling for available measures of cog-nitive skills or academic achievement did not resolve anything, and mainly produced an incoherent scattering of inconsistent patterns, as had been observed earlier (Morgan, 1980).

Overall, they found no evidence that demographic/first-order beliefs in any way intervene in or condition the association between amount of viewing and second-order beliefs, which made them "question not only the proposed implication process, but also the distinction between these two kinds of cultivation beliefs" (Hawkins et al., 1987, p. 573). This ulti-mately supports the conclusion of Gerbner et al., that the whole idea of first- and second-order variables may serve as a handy methodological divider, but it cannot really sustain any further conceptual linkage wherein one or the other is either necessary or sufficient for cultivation.

Nevertheless, we need to mention that, in all three adolescent samples, the first-order measures were made up of forced-error questions with two response options, while the second-order measures were all based on five-point agree–disagree Likert scales. Therefore, it is difficult to know whether any concordances or divergences between them, on their own or in relation to television viewing, reflect their presumed "order" or are simply an artifact of the simple measurement differences between the types of questions. In other words: is the difference one of "order" ("fact" or "generalization") or just one of what kind of response category is used?

Overall, then, it remains fundamentally unclear whether any of these studies are indeed even comparing first- with second-order cultivation processes, as opposed to simply contrasting general estimates with Likert scales. This same problem afflicts Potter's (1991b) more general analysis of the relation between first- and second-order measures, where all first-order measures are based on problematic open-ended percentages; he also applies the terms to specific measures in vague and inconsistent ways, and sometimes provides no information at all about his dependent variables (Potter, 1991a, 1991c). Regardless of what these tests found, we assert again that cultivation is not a test of what heavy viewers think about the TV world, although this is a conceptual glitch that comes up again in some other studies described next.

### Perceived Reality

A few studies have attempted to shed light on black-box cognitive processes by highlighting the concept of the "perceived reality" of television content. The notion usually advanced is that a greater belief in the veracity of television should render one more "susceptible" to cultivation, or even that perceived reality is a necessary precondition for cultivation. The idea has some common-sense appeal to it. Despite a variety of operationalizations, however, it has been difficult to establish any firm or consistent connections between perceived reality and cultivation. Moreover, the concept of perceived reality has been insufficiently explicated in studies that apply it to cultivation.

As a feature of narrative texts and as a criterion by which they may be evaluated, "realism" is admittedly a deceptive and complex concept. Among the questions that one might raise, it is unclear whether perceived reality is a viewer "trait" or a "state"; is it something stable that we carry around with us, or do our judgments of verisimilitude vary from day to day, series to series, or even *during* a given episode? We know about some of the factors that predict it, but it remains unclear whether any of the diverse ways in which perceived reality has been defined and measured have much to do with what actually goes on in viewers' minds while (and after) they watch. Moreover, researchers who use the measure usually assume that each viewer relates to television in isolation from the many elaborate social contexts that influence how texts are experienced and negotiated.

Although perceived reality issues may have some relevance, cultivation has shied from the issue, presuming that the effects are more unconscious, residing in a cognitive location where it would be unlikely for respondents to awarely "get at" them. Thus, perceived reality may be a two-edged sword: it is plausible that those who ascribe the least "realism" to what they watch may be most likely to "let down their guard" and absorb even more of the incidental, background information. At best, self-reports of perceived reality refer to the surface-level, foreground aspects of a narrative; at worst, they merely reflect conventional beliefs about television. Either way, viewers can easily dismiss the surface-level plots and characterizations even as they absorb lessons about the invisible dynamics of human relations, about emotions and motivations, about social, romantic and family relationships, and much more.

Slater and Elliott (1982) first tested the concept of perceived reality in relation to cultivation. Their study of 557 high school students included three groups, differentiated by the nature of their previous experiences with law enforcement. Amount of viewing was based on program check-lists. Eleven dependent variables, dealing with images of law enforcement and perceptions of personal safety, were used (it appears that eight of these neither matched questions used by Gerbner et al. nor had any dis-cernible foundation in message data). Perceived reality was based on ratings (from +2 for very realistic to −2 for very unrealistic) of each of six popular crime programs. (In earlier research, they had found that adoles-cents more often watch shows they rate as realistic.)

In a series of regression analyses, perceived reality was found to be a stronger predictor of the dependent variables than was total program exposure. However, Slater and Elliott never addressed the question of whether cultivation depends on (or, varies according to) the level of realism one ascribes to television – which was, presumably, the central hypothesis guiding the entire project. It would have been useful if they had looked at the associations between television exposure and depen-dent beliefs *within* groups defined by level of perceived reality, in order to see if those who attribute greater "truth" to television show stronger – or weaker – evidence of cultivation. Thus, despite their intentions, Slater and Elliott did not do the sort of study that could shed any light on the question of how perceived reality affects cultivation.

But just that sort of analysis had in fact been done in an exploratory, unpublished examination of data from adolescent surveys in the Cultural Indicators cultivation archives in the early 1980s. It was found that com-paring cultivation patterns at different levels of perceived reality produced inconsistent, seemingly random patterns. Some variables showed stronger associations among those with the lowest levels of perceived reality; others showed the reverse, or no impact of the perceived reality control.

Potter (1986) also found such scattershot, inconsistent patterns when he looked at cultivation associations in separate subgroups defined by three different dimensions of perceived reality. The study was done with two samples: 92 volunteers from undergraduate communication classes (a sample we find to be extremely weak in terms of both size and typical-ity) and 237 adolescents (12–15 years old). Amount of viewing was mea-sured in terms of (once again) weekly hours reported watching each of eight different categories of programs. As in his other studies we have dis-cussed, some of the dependent variables used have no discernible source in message data nor any apparent relevance to cultivation; for example, the college respondents had to estimate the proportion of annual deaths due to pneumonia, cancer and heart disease.

Respondents also estimated the chances in 100,000 that "an average person" (i.e., not *themselves*, personally, as in Potter, 1988) would be a victim of murder, rape, assault, an auto accident, etc. There were huge discrepancies between the two samples in the baselines of these items; adolescent estimates were up to eight times larger. This may reflect age-related developmental differences, or it may signal that many adolescents experience difficulties in estimating the "chances in 100,000" of *anything* occurring. Face validity is cast in further doubt by the surprising consistency in the mean responses across all items; adolescents, for example, thought someone's chances of being a victim of murder (4,250 in 100,000) were just about the same as those of being in a fist-fight (4,180), an auto accident (4,050), and so on.

Respondents were divided according to level of perceived reality along three different dimensions. Within those groups, correlations were examined between amount of viewing and the various dependent variables (the step not taken by Slater and Elliott). Degree of perceived reality did make a difference in the resulting coefficients, but the patterns were strikingly inconsistent across the different kinds of perceived reality, as in the CI unpublished data. Overall, as many associations were significant when perceived reality was low (in some dimensions) as when it was high (in other dimensions). Thus, beyond the measurement problems noted, it is difficult to make any meaningful interpretations from these data because the effects vary so widely, in part perhaps because the low and high perceived reality subgroups are so small (all had between twenty-one and forty-three respondents).

The general failure of cognitive models based on order effects, learning/construction steps, and perceived reality suggested that cognitive processes might never be found to explain cultivation. But researchers continued to adduce additional hypotheses and models, and some of these turned up more conceptually promising results.

## Memory

If "perceived reality" is too murky a construct to help untangle cognitive processes in cultivation, then maybe a sturdier and more reliable concept from the psychological literature might help tighten up the findings somewhat. One strong candidate is "memory." After all, if cultivation means that television images help shape viewers' perceptions of the world, then those mediated images must be stored somewhere, in some way, in the black box. And whether or not they are so "stored," television's representations and messages may mold or color other impressions of the world that *are* stored in memory. Thus, when dealing with beliefs and perspectives that are assumed to have some consistency over time, it seems reasonable to suppose that memory should help clarify some aspects of whatever cognitive dynamics underlie cultivation.

Accordingly, some researchers have begun to focus on the role of memory in the construction of social reality through television viewing (cf. Tapper, 1995). To test ideas about how memory relates to the construction of reality through TV, Shapiro (1991) asked journalism students ($N = 156$) to provide "memory dumps," i.e., to free-recall as many exemplars of crime as they could, and then to categorize those exemplars by communication source (where they first heard about each one: direct experience, TV news, etc.). He found that "event memories" (the number of exemplars and the categorization of those exemplars) were better predictors of beliefs about the frequency of crime than was media exposure. However, the results ran counter to common sense: the *more* crime exemplars people could remember, the *less* dangerous they saw the world. Shapiro argued that this could have been due to the special nature of the sample, though this seems problematic given that direct experience with crime usually leads to seeing the world as more dangerous. Also, asking about television first in this study may have affected both judgments about exemplars and source attributions. In any case, as we will see below, the number of exemplars people may generate is not necessarily related to how *easy* they are to generate; yet, how quickly they come to mind (what has been called "response latency") may have much more to do with cultivation. (Also see Shrum & O'Guinn, 1993, for further comments on Shapiro's study.)

Shapiro and Lang (1991) also proposed a model of television's effect that revolves around various lower-level "responses" to information. For example, "orienting" responses are automatic tendencies to focus more sharply on a stimulus. "Defense" responses occur as automatic reactions to stimuli perceived as threatening. "Startle" responses happen when radically new information enters a person's perceptual sphere. Shapiro and Lang posit that all event memories carry with them contextual information, including information about what sort of responses characterized the phenomenon when first encountered. In this theory, lower-level responses call out higher-order mental processings, but the lower-level responses are retained as contextual information about memory "traces" (units of memory).

Shapiro and Lang then hypothesized that television's role in social reality construction reflects "systematic error" in reality monitoring processes. Because perception of reality is not perfect, and because people can forget contextual information over time, perceptions of reality are influenced by a cumulation of errors in processing television information. In this view, in other words, television can affect reality perceptions because people simply forget that what they see on TV is not real.

Reality-monitoring processes may find television events particularly confusing. . . . Television shares many of the characteristics of the real world (sound, moving images, etc.). Context cues about physiological states may be particularly deceptive in this process. As discussed earlier, television almost certainly produces orienting responses and may elicit startle responses. If such a response is stored as contextual information with a television event memory, that information can be used by a reality monitoring process to determine the relevance of a memory [to perceptions about social reality]. Because these responses are typical of responses to actual events, the reality-monitoring process may be more likely to select such a television memory as relevant to judgments about the real world than memories without contextual information about psychophysiological responses characteristic of actual events. (Shapiro and Lang, 1991, p. 699)

This theory was not devised specifically as an explanation of how cultivation occurs. Nevertheless, since television viewing provides vast opportunities to accrue innumerable individual memory traces (especially for heavy viewers), its implications are clear; if correct, it would provide an important account of how individuals use television-derived memories to construct reality. Yet, Shapiro and Lang did not test this hypothesis. Mares (1996), on the other hand, did conduct a test of the Shapiro/Lang "error" hypothesis. Although she noted that Shapiro's memory-trace argument had not as yet been supported, she expected the tendency to confuse the source of information to play a key role in cultivation.

What if individuals make mistakes about the source of their information? Individuals who tend to misremember events as coming from reliable sources will be more likely to label remembered examples as accurate and hence will be quicker to retrieve a seemingly trustworthy example relevant to the social reality judgment. Individuals who tend to misremember events as coming from a reliable source will be more likely to label examples as unusable and will take longer to find relevant instances. (Mares, 1996, pp. 280–1)

Given these conjectures, Mares examined the relationships between subjects' tendency to confuse sources of information and social judgments. She showed participants (eighty high school seniors and eighty senior citizens) edited versions of a newscast containing a story about a border dispute between Libya and Chad, and a trailer for a movie about conflicts in the Middle East. Respondents were then presented with questions asking them whether various events were shown in the news story or in the trailer (or both, or neither), along with measures of amount of viewing and some standard cultivation dependent variables (violence, mean world, and SES estimates). Thus, respondents could be scored according to their tendencies to manifest both news-to-fiction and fiction-to-news confusions.

She found strong associations between fiction-to-news confusions and social reality estimates; that is, those who tended to confuse fiction for reality saw the world as a meaner, more violent place, and also gave "TV answers" to questions about SES estimates. She also found a clear and significant interaction: amount of viewing was more strongly related to conceptions among those who tended to confuse televised fiction with "real" news. Although Mares acknowledged that this kind of source confusion is not likely to be the only cognitive mechanism producing cultivation effects, her data suggest that source confusions do enhance cultivation.

This model has intuitive, common-sense appeal, and the data seem to support it. People are overwhelmed with so many stimuli from so many complex, ongoing streams (mediated and unmediated) that it is difficult – especially as time passes – for us to accurately note, store and retrieve source information. The more we confuse sources – especially, the more we experience the fiction-to-news variety of source confusion – the more heavy viewing contributes to our conceptions of reality. But one aspect of this model may remain problematic: *the extent to which people even consider the sources of their information at all when making reality judgments.* As Shrum (1997) has noted, Mares' assumption is that people *do* consider the source; they discount it if they perceive it to be false or non-reliable, and they also often tend to make mistakes when attempting to determine just what is the source of their information, but they do evaluate it. This assumption runs counter to a central implication of Shrum's work, which is that people rarely consider the sources of their information when making reality judgments.

There is substantial and persuasive evidence for Shrum's conclusion that sources are seldom considered when making reality judgments. He has carried out a series of studies based on the notion that TV provides a bountiful slate of readily "accessible" images that can be used heuristically by viewers. As described by Mares, "ready accessibility of an example leads to higher estimates of real-world frequencies (the availability heuristic), hence the correlation between viewing and social reality estimates" (Mares, 1996, p. 279). Shrum (and Mares, to some extent) are building on the extensive psychological literature showing that human decisions are often governed by heuristics; these allow for economy of thought when making decisions and forming images (Chaiken, Liberman and Eagly, 1989).

Shrum's basic idea is that, because they see them more often, heavy viewers should have TV-derived images more readily accessible, more likely to spring quickly to mind, and therefore they will be more likely to furnish TV-influenced responses when a situation requires them to formulate a belief – such as when they are asked for their views on surveys. Shrum sees responding to survey questions as a "low involvement task," perfect for eliciting answers derived through heuristic processes. It should be noted that Shrum deals primarily with "first-order" questions (i.e., estimates of frequency). Since these are constructed in real time, he argues that they allow one to observe the process in a more direct way than would be possible with second-order judgments, which are more likely to be already resident in memory. Also, psychological research has provided a good deal of evidence on how people make judgments about the size of things in the world (these are called "set-size judgments"; see Shrum, 1995). Because cultivation proposes that TV influences people's set-size judgments (among other things), Shrum contends that the processes normally used in making such judgments are highly germane to cultivation.

How can we discern whether individuals are using heuristics when responding to questions? Shrum reasons that giving faster responses to questions means that individuals are using concepts which are more heuristically available, whereas respondents who take longer are presumably engaging in more cogitation about the issue. This is not a question of whether or not people can "remember" what they saw on television last month, last week, or even last night; fully congruent with cultivation theory, viewers' conscious awareness of the role of television in their thoughts or their ability to describe what they have seen is irrelevant. A speedy response to a question implies that an answer is more readily accessible, that the general issue is more salient, that the respondent does not have to dig very deeply to come up with an answer.

As a test of these ideas, O'Guinn and Shrum (1997) investigated television's contributions to perceptions about the material world, in an experiment with fifty-one advertising students. They argued that heavy television viewers should have an easier time accessing constructs about material affluence than would light viewers, since these images would have been more frequently stored in memory, due to the greater number of impressions heavy viewers would have received. Unfortunately, as in many other studies, they used open-ended percentage estimates, though this may be less problematic since reaction time is the more important issue in their study. They found that heavy viewers answered the questions about the material world more quickly than did light viewers, suggesting that information relevant to the answers was more readily available. Also, these faster answers corresponded to what cultivation would predict, with about 10 percentage points difference between heavy and light viewers (consistent with earlier cultivation studies showing a similar difference). Importantly, the tendency for heavier viewers to answer more quickly (in this and other studies) held up even controlling for respondents' baseline response speeds, their grade point average, impulsivity, extroversion and other psychologically relevant potential sources of spuriousness.[1]

Shrum (1996) expanded upon on these experimental investigations by looking more precisely at whether construct accessibility "mediates" the relationship between exposure to programs and beliefs about reality. To do so, he examined the impacts of exposure to soap operas on first-order beliefs that might be cultivated specifically by soaps. Using a small sample ($N = 45$), Shrum allowed only heavy (more than five hours a week) and non-soap viewers into the experimental groups. He found enormous relationships between exposure to soaps and beliefs about marital discord, crime and occupations (some betas were above .50). Further, he found that response latency (speed of response) does mediate the cultivation of beliefs by soaps. That is, effects on beliefs were found to work "through" construct accessibility. In general, though, direct relationships between soap viewing and beliefs remained strong and significant, confirming the model shown in Chapter 7 (where direct and indirect relationships are theorized to co-exist).

Of course, much of the methodology of these studies clearly departs from the practices of orthodox cultivation research. They tend to be small-sample, manifestly artificial experiments; some look only at isolated genres (e.g., soap viewing), and all are heavily weighted to measure strong, short-term effects (as in selecting only the heaviest and lightest viewers to participate). But these studies do provide intriguing evidence that cultivation can be explained at a "deeper" psychological level, and they therefore inject the body of survey findings with a potent dose of convergent validity.

In the heuristic processing model, "people do not take the time or make the effort to ascertain the source of the information recalled and thus do not source discount" (Shrum, 1997, p. 350). How can this be reconciled with Mares' (1996) findings about source confusion? Shrum (1997) explains that the design of Mares' study had many attributes (not "flaws") that made it much more likely that participants would actively consider the source – in ways that they don't normally do when making social reality judgments. Moreover, the alleged source confusion mechanism cannot account for his findings about response latency (with heavy viewers responding more quickly). Thus, Shrum demonstrates that

---

[1] The study also includes a content analysis, which they used to generate questions about affluence and wealth, as well as a survey analysis ($N = 785$), which broadly supports the experimental results.

Mares' data are embraced within his heuristic model of cultivation effects.

Further, Shrum, Wyer and O'Guinn (1994) show that experimental respondents, when cued to think about television prior to giving responses, do not manifest cultivation relationships. Shrum argues that this is due to sensitization to TV as a source and to the fact that respondents are cued to think "systematically" rather than heuristically about television and the world. This too tends to bolster Shrum's view that cultivation effects occur through heuristic mechanisms. Although our meta-analytic results differ slightly on this issue, showing that sensitized respondents demonstrated somewhat *higher* cultivation than the non-sensitized group, what's clear is that sensitization can interfere with the stability of cultivation tests.

We have argued that cognitive explanations which stray too far afield from the original spirit of cultivation theory may confuse as much (or more) than they clarify. Yet, Shrum's many innovative investigations (O'Guinn and Shrum, 1997; Shrum, in press; Shrum, 1995; Shrum, 1996; Shrum, 1997; Shrum and O'Guinn, 1993, Shrum, Wyer and O'Guinn, in press; among others) all move toward the notion that viewers whose cognitive world is dominated by television will simply have more TV-derived facts and images ready in memory than will light viewers; plus, they don't usually or often think about the sources of their information when making judgments. This view is eminently consistent with cultivation. Rather than proposing a complex chain of memory events (the stage hypothesis of Pingree and Hawkins, or the lower-order/higher-order explanations of Shapiro), Shrum's cognitive account is both the most parsimonious and the most supportive of cultivation. Heuristic judgments, including those involved with television, are used all the time in thinking about the future, making risk judgments, and simply navigating everyday reality, without much conscious attention to the source of information. This also means that television does not necessarily *change* attitudes (and again, cultivation does not mean attitude change), but that it makes them *stronger*. Given all this, if heuristic logic shows that more exposure to messages = a greater tendency to use those memory images in formulating conceptions of reality (however they are constructed), what else is needed?

## Peeking Inside the Box?

On balance, the early studies on the cognitive implications of cultivation analysis did not tell us very much directly about the micro-processes they set out to illuminate, although they did make it exquisitely clear that certain ways of approaching the question were not going to work. Some of them suffered from extreme methodological flaws, but all research is imperfect and this is not really the main problem with these studies. More importantly, these studies did not stop to consider the question of whether the process of "learning from television" should imply any different or special cognitive mechanisms or functions from those involved in the process of learning from the cultural environment and social experiences in general. Shrum's and Mares' studies begin to get away from this, especially as they deal with dependent variables that were actually used in cultivation research, and with more compelling cognitive models; also, Shrum, in some studies, did content analysis prior to his experiments, whereas some of the early studies relied on untenable assumptions.

Especially given the thrust of Shrum's findings, we are sympathetic to the argument advanced by Hawkins et al. (1987) following the generally unsuccessful tests of most of their cognitive models. They proposed that we all learn the values, norms and stereotypes disseminated by television primarily by growing up and living in this specific culture; heavy viewing, then, does not involve any "new learning" of these beliefs and outlooks, but instead provides "the repeated instantiation of some stereotypes by their exemplars" (p. 575). Shrum demonstrates that these repeated exposures tend to dominate the consciousness of heavy viewers by means of exactly those "mechanisms" proposed by cultivation: repetition, frequency and recency. In effect, both Hawkins et al. and Shrum posit that television might be "reminding" us, over and over, of what we are not supposed to forget. As Shrum contends, it is not that television changes attitudes, but that it makes them stronger. This is, indeed, highly congruent with the notion of cultivation as a process in which selected cultural patterns and lessons are nourished and sustained, and which sees television as the mainstream of the common symbolic environment.

Nevertheless, explanations of the behavior of large systems cannot always be reduced to component parts, despite the arguments (Shrum, 1995) that theories are only adequately understood when the components are adequately described. The cognitive studies can often treat the individuals studied as if they do not exist in a social context. Are there other, additional, "mechanisms" that may be at work which don't ask us to theoretically carve up the process until it is unrecognizable?

## How do Stories Work?

Following Shrum's findings, it would seem that the cultivation of "set-size" judgments of frequency (what some have called first-order conceptions) results partly from heavy exposure to repetitious but disconnected fragments of images, from the common but scattered representations that seep into our impressions and are retrieved when making a judgment. These various bits of "information" coalesce into a coherent "story" (or account of reality) at the time of judgment.

At the same time, these bits of "information" that television presents are usually themselves packaged in the form of stories. But are the stories "made up" out of discrete bits of information, or do the narrative structures of the stories "imbue" the bits with meaning and value? (Or both?) It seems plausible that the overarching structures, outcomes, lessons and morals of stories will to a great extent give sense and relevance to whatever facts occur within those stories. And cultivation, focusing as it does on coherent, large-scale message systems, should be vitally interested in how dominant narratives work. On the other hand, cognitive expeditions into cultivation processes don't always go along with this assumption. Rather, cognitive theorists have often argued "from the bottom up," that all the relevant bits are stored along the way, and then reconstructed at various times as stories that have particular meanings. Still, both camps tend to come together in the agreement that the raw frequency of occurrence of events in the television universe reflects an important fact: that specific observed instances of televised behaviors are relevant to constructing judgments about social reality. Within this problematic, we argue that narrative theory can make a contribution to understanding the cultivation process.

We learn about stories through immersion in a culture, which teaches us what they mean and how to interpret them, at least within certain parameters. Although there is no shortage of implicit assumptions about narrative issues in cultivation theory (and in the Cultural Indicators paradigm broadly), there has been surprisingly little explicit attention to narrative processes, and narrative dimensions have not been operationalized in empirical studies. Here we develop an argument for looking more closely at narrative "mechanisms" as another way to think about explanations for cultivation.

Relevant research on narrative is spread across the humanistic and social scientific disciplines. Certainly, the literary disciplines contribute the bulk of our understanding about how stories move and affect us, though of course most of these accounts hew to non-quantitative types of analysis. Within the human sciences, two disciplines can be looked to for especially relevant theory: rhetoric and science/risk communication. In some ways, findings from the two can combine to give especially interesting new research directions for cultivation.

Rhetoric explores the dimensions and structures of human discourse. Rhetorical work on narrative has centered on the so-called "narrative paradigm," which argues that human ways of thinking are essentially narrative in nature, not logical or rational as in science and philosophy (Fisher, 1984). Essentially, the paradigm argues that humans constantly use stories, images and metaphors to think about the world, more than they use calculation, dialectic or other rational techniques of information management. The paradigm further implies that humans do not exclusively use rational techniques for managing their memory. Rather, they rely on culturally given narrative accounts to structure their view of reality.

Fisher suggests that narrative "integrity" is a key to the way people interpret reality. That is, when examining situations and interpreting them, people are likely to reach conclusions that would be consistent with the story used to present the facts. Further, people's "memory" of these stories is probably likely to focus not simply on the specific facts embedded in the stories but more fundamentally on the outcomes and lessons of the stories.

The narrative view of the world is one highly consistent with cultivation, which depends on the idea that message systems are consistent and formulaic story systems, teaching by virtue of the repetition of a narrative world that itself "hangs together." That is, cultivation is a theory not merely of how people remember facts, but also of how they remember massive numbers of stories and their lessons over time. Most critically, cultivation suggests that a powerful "master narrative" guides the production and reception of most stories.

Where does science/risk communication fit in? It happens that this field is one area where "rational" and "narrative" views of the world come into direct competition. Scientists want to communicate in ways that emphasize facts and logical inquiry. But over and over again, when the media communicate about science, it is found that drama, narrative, images and metaphors "take over" (Shanahan and McComas, 1999). Further, it is found that this is what mass audiences seem to prefer (or at least this is what they have been cultivated to prefer). Thus, even in an area where rational discourse would be favored, the power of narrative is evident. Most especially in media discourse, it is obvious that the narrative paradigm offers an important model for examining how people get facts about the world and remember them. Narratives structure reality.

How do these observations translate to thinking about cultivation? Cultivation obviously deals with how people use stories to make judgments about the world. Just as in "real life," television viewing involves attention to stories to learn about how the world works. Thus, "learning" from television is not that much different from learning from other experiences. In both instances we use stories to absorb facts, make judgments, remember things, and so on. But, perhaps most importantly, the story is the form of communication whose purpose is the assignment and structuration of social meaning. The idea that a story has an "end" or "moral" – that stories structure our perception of time – that stories tell us who are the "good" characters and the "bad" and what happens to each – all of these facts are crucial to the idea that cultivation involves more than just the absorption of discrete facts from a glowing box.

This is one reason why the early cognitive studies proved unsuccessful: they assumed that TV learning would be somehow different or special from learning in some other "real world," but it's not. For better or worse, television *is* the real world, or at least *a* real world. It is therefore not so surprising that people's perceptions "about" television fail to explain cultivation; nor is it so strange that "perceived reality" of television doesn't help much either (cf. Shrum, Wyer and O'Guinn, in press).

What else can a narrative understanding gain us? Apart from understanding why early cognitive studies failed, and why the cultivation body of research tends to be consistent and stable over time, narrative approaches can also help to specify and strengthen our knowledge about cultivation.

The most important research direction would be to move toward an understanding of how specific story *types* are navigated by viewers, and how they are used to structure and give meaning to the discrete bits of information that come from everyday television viewing. Here, the enormous psychological literature on narrative can establish research questions for future cultivation studies (e.g., Gerrig, 1993). Examples of questions that might strengthen knowledge about cultivation include:

"Do more 'realistic' narrative presentations (as defined by popular wisdom) strengthen or weaken cultivation?"

"Do heavy viewers show a greater tendency to use narratives to make judgments and remember facts, as opposed to using rational thought and argument? Does greater exposure to television cultivate a tendency to think using narrative logic and structures?"

"Does narrative 'integrity' (the extent to which television narratives 'hang together') play a role in the extent to which such narratives cultivate conceptions of social reality? Are viewers more likely to remember outcomes that are consistent with the narratives in which they are presented? Conversely, what happens to outcomes that go against the narrative grain? Are these forgotten or do they become memorable exceptions?"

These questions frame cultivation as a process within which viewers construct world-interpreting "meta-narratives" from cumulative television viewing that are consistent with the TV world. As with the cognitive questions, these are examples of inquiries that would help us understand "how" viewers process information, but they are "how" questions that

make sense in a different way for cultivation. That is, if traditional cultivation research presents answers to the "what" question (what is the relationship between viewing and belief?) then an important "how" question
deals with the ways stories carry information to those cultivated by them.
Psychological perspectives on narrative are also relevant here:

Psychologists studying narrative are challenged by the notion that human activity
and experience are filled with 'meaning' and that stories, rather than logical arguments or lawful formulations, are the vehicle by which that meaning is communi-
cated. This dichotomy is expressed by Jerome S. Bruner (1986, 1990, 1991) as
the distinction between 'paradigmatic' and 'narrative' forms of thought which, he
claims, are both fundamental and irreducible one to the other. Sarbin (1986) proposes that 'narrative' becomes a root metaphor for psychology to replace the
mechanistic and organic metaphors which shaped so much theory and research in
the discipline over the past century. (Hevern, 1997)

Especially relevant to cultivation, then, is work on cognitive processing
of narratives, of which an excellent summary is provided by Gerrig
(1993). Gerrig presents a psychological argument that is so compelling
from the point of view of cultivation that it is surprising that the narrative
research he summarizes has not had more impact on cultivation thinking.
Gerrig's argument is that, psychologically and cognitively speaking,
fictional accounts do have "real-world" effects; contrary both to conventional wisdom and to so much theorizing about "perceived reality," there
is essentially no "toggle" used by people to switch between thinking about
fiction and non-fiction. Gerrig summarizes the results of many different
experiments which have shown that the mental processes used for thinking about fiction are about the same as those used for thinking about
reality.

Gerrig further notes that fiction can have real-world effects time after
time, even when we have learned certain stories by rote. The phenomenon of "anomalous suspense" (experiencing suspense even when we
already know the outcome of a given story) shows that stories have
impacts by virtue of their form rather than their content alone. Gerrig distinguishes between two experiences of a story: the veridical and the
schematic: "veridical expectancies are those a listener builds up by
repeated contact with a particular piece of music; schematic expectancies
encode regularities within the overall body of a particular culture's
music" (p. 238). Gerrig claims that in music, stories, films or any text, it is
the schematic expectancies that dominate our understanding, and this
has enormous implications for cultivation. That is, it is repeated experiences with stories that cumulate effects on beliefs, behaviors, attitudes,
etc.

Since narrative reality is little different than real reality, "all a reader must do to be transported to a narrative world is to have in place the repertory of cognitive processes that is otherwise required for everyday experience" (Gerrig, 1993, p. 239). What the cultivation theorist can add to this is that, given the enormous extent to which television disseminates stories, and the extent to which these stories permeate the entire culture, television in effect functions as an important component of social reality, not as something separate and apart. Thus, as cultivation theorists have suggested from the start, fiction and non-fiction blend together; news, drama and comedy are all complementary accounts of human experience, which is fundamentally a narrative experience.

This helps to explain a few other facts we have observed along the way. Why, for instance, is the cultivation effect relatively small? Apart from the many reasons we have already discussed, the plain fact is that virtually everyone is immersed in a narrative universe heavily influenced by TV, even if they themselves don't watch television. Because narrative and real worlds are highly congruent in many respects, to some extent everyone is an "experiencer" of television (if not a viewer) and therefore subject to cultivation of some kind.

This suggests a sort of modified, circuitous N-step flow for television's narrative impact throughout the culture. Heavy viewers should provide the most direct evidence of cultivation (and they do, both cognitively and socially) but the impacts of messages need not end with just the heavy viewers. A hallmark of stories is that they get repeated, reinforced, retold, etc., and through this repetition in family and social contexts they enter the culture where they have their true effect. Admittedly, this culture-level effect is much more difficult to gauge, in the same sense that it is difficult to measure the "impact" of air on our breathing. Indeed, the same can be said of stories. Stories don't necessarily have impacts on beliefs; they *constitute* beliefs.

Our discussions of cognitive cultivation research therefore ironically turn us back to the cultural experience of hearing, learning, repeating and eventually using stories. Peering deeper into the recesses of cognitive mechanisms returns us to the cultural level that cultivation has inhabited all along. The world of television is best understood as a collective social endeavor in which every individual has his or her own chances to extract symbolic meaning individually, but within which the repertoire of lessons, morals, story structures and character behaviors is constrained at any given time by socio-narrative boundaries and material conditions. In this perspective, the "mainstream" cultivated by television may simply be best seen as a story "genre." Viewers of these stories don't necessarily have to believe everything they see in this genre, but the simple (and often repeated) experience of the story-form will teach them a great deal about the world. As we said earlier, Gerbner regularly invokes Fletcher's axiom that one who can tell a nation's stories need not worry about its laws; we can now see that this observation has a cognitive foundation. At this point, then, we might consider adding a corollary to the propositions we developed earlier: social control cannot be effected without narrative control.

The importance of narrative indicates that cultivation researchers in the future need to interact with theories and findings from a wide variety of fields, which could come together in an area that might call itself "narrative studies." Literary scholars, semiologists, cognitive psychologists, psychotherapists, historians, cultural critics, sociologists, anthropologists, and a host of other unnamed researchers can bring needed information to the debate on television's role in culture, just as the cultivation researcher should contribute more to work in these other fields. We see the research clearly heading in this multidisciplinary direction. Now, more then ever, cultivation has a real chance to extend its contribution not just to what we know about TV, but about the wider sphere of human social activity.

But just as we are gaining this foothold, the ground is shifting beneath us. Media forms are rapidly changing, and people are questioning whether TV as we know it will continue to exist. For some, this means the end of cultivation as a relevant research approach. For us, however, it means a new challenge. In the next chapter we will delve into the implications of the changing media environment for cultivation research.

# 9    Cultivation and the New Media

Discussing the advent of something he calls the "teleputer" (a television-computer hybrid), Gilder (1994) says:

Rather than exalting mass culture, the teleputer will enhance individualism. Rather than cultivating passivity, the teleputer will promote creativity. Instead of a master-slave architecture, the teleputer will have an interactive architecture in which every receiver can function as a processor and transmitter of video images and other information. The teleputer will usher in a culture compatible with the immense powers of today's ascendant technology. Perhaps most important, the teleputer will enrich and strengthen democracy and capitalism around the world. (p. 46)

Gilder's pronouncements are characteristic of much media soothsaying today, which looks forward to a new media age in which television's despotism has been vanquished. As Gilder says, "Television is a tool of tyrants. Its overthrow will be a major force for freedom and individuality, culture, and morality. That overthrow is at hand" (p. 49).

Gilder is not alone. Seers of the media future such as Nicholas Negroponte, speaking of video-on-demand (VOD) technologies, say

My point is simple: the broadcast model is what is failing. 'On-demand' is a much bigger concept than not-walking-out-in-the-rain or not-forgetting-a-rented-cassette-under-the-sofa-for-a-month. It's consumer pull versus media push, my time – the receiver's time – versus the transmitter's time. Beyond recalling an existing movie or playing any of today's (or yesterday's) TV around the world (roughly 15,000 concurrent channels), VOD could provide a new life for documentary films, even the dreaded 'infomercial.' The hairs of documentary filmmakers will stand on end when they hear this. But it is possible to have TV agents edit movies on the fly, much like a professor assembling an anthology using chapters from different books. (Negroponte, 1994)

Almost everyone believes that the future will involve a major revamping of the way we watch television. It already has. The amount of anticipation around "new ways to watch" is symptomatic both of the high amount of personal time that we currently invest in television and in the idea that there might be a better way to do it. Thus, it is not surprising that the new media marketplace is looking for ways to meet (and to continue to generate) this demand. Even old fogies like Al Gore have signed on to the bandwagon of a new information infrastructure, in which receiving new media products would be as easy as making a phone call.

But though today's new technologies seem newer, brighter and shinier, the idea of new technologies changing the world is not in itself new. Today's media prophets are of a well-known breed, which we might call the Media Oracle. Their Delphic pronouncements have characterized every age in which new media advancements have confronted established technologies (see Marvin, 1988). In the 1920s, they talked about radio and wondered in awe how the new technology could strengthen democracy, build a nation and inform millions. In the 1950s, TV became the new looking-glass miracle through which social values could be reformed, the poor educated and (again) millions informed. Today, computers and their close relatives are providing the latest grist for this mill, as we face a new century allegedly filled with unlimited potential for expanding global communication, enriching culture, enhancing education and ensuring understanding, prosperity and peace.

Much of the hopeful view of the new media future is driven by self-evident facts. The world's economy is focusing more and more on information, as agriculture and industry are pushed off center stage (Beniger, 1986). The world is becoming "post-industrial" (Bell, 1976). We are moving inexorably into an "information" age (Dizard, 1982). The plain facts, taken together, are indisputable: the world looks much different in the year 2000 and beyond than it did in 1900.

Beyond these facts, however, we enter the realm of technological speculation. In attempting to determine how future technological development will impact sociopolitical reality, there are no firm guidelines except perhaps what has gone before. The tendency of the technological determinist (as represented by today's new media Pollyannas) is to extrapolate from the form of a technology to its social impact. Thus, television is a "one-way" technology with little recourse for democratic interaction within its discourse. By contrast, "interactive" TV is often promoted as contributing to greater democratic development by virtue of the fact that people can "talk back" to their television (and to each other) in a great instantaneous public opinion sampling mechanism.

In our view, predictions of this sort tend to ignore the most important fact, which is the underlying consistency of the content of the messages we consume and the nature of the symbolic environment in which we live. Thus, if "interactive" TV means nothing more than buying or selling your favorite baubles, bangles and beads, it's hard to see how that contributes to democracy. If the new age of the teleputer means that we are meant to interact in a universe largely of the designing of multinational, capitalist entertainment magnates, that probably won't enhance democracy either. Thus, though new media technologies certainly offer new possibilities, the past shows that corporate elites have always succeeded in co-opting new media for their traditional purposes. That this will happen with the new media is already becoming evident.

Schiller (1983) expressed a similar view even before the current crop of electronic marvels were imagined, and his words remain relevant:

The American public, half of which does not bother to vote in national elections, hears the good news that electronic referendums are around the corner. Sitting at home, in front of a domestic information utility, so-called, the happy citizen will be able to exercise innumerable inconsequential choices on an electronic console in the living room. This, we are told, constitutes the most advanced form of democracy. (p. 30)

At the same time, the mass audience, schooled in the ways of the old media, will continue to behave in ways that demand steady doses of mass-produced, mainstream entertainment. Whether the most successful entertainment is delivered through television networks or through video-on-demand through fiber-optic cable, satellites or some other medium may make little difference if the messages don't change. And the Oracles of the new media century have not been able to establish how or why the messages will change.

Indeed, in the past, new technologies tended to adopt message content from previously dominant media. The nascent film industry took its direction from serialized literature, pulp magazines, vaudeville and other antecedent forms of popular entertainment. Radio reified these into specific programming categories, suitable for delivering packaged and packageable audiences. TV simply reframed what radio had done. It stands to reason that the medium which supplants television will follow this trend, perhaps exemplifying McLuhan's dictum that new media reclothe the old in new garb. In this process, the old media don't simply go away (many thought, for instance, that radio would disappear after TV came along). Rather, they create the conditions on which the new are premised.

Of course, we recognize that form and content are inextricably linked: a message delivered by a different medium is a different message. The medium within which a message is structured obviously helps shape and constrain the range of meanings which may be derived from that message. Yet, we have argued that cultivation is a theory of story-telling, not simply a theory of television as a technology or medium. This allows us to de-emphasize (but not deny) the importance of technological form (cf.

Williams, 1975) while focusing primarily on the content and meaning of messages.

On the one hand, we can see that "the same" message cannot be conveyed identically by print media (e.g., a newspaper), sound media (e.g., radio), or visual media (e.g., film or television); as we cross media, the message itself takes on other characteristics. But with most of the new technologies, the media-specific residue is fainter and less dramatic. If we are watching a television program, how much does its message vary according to whether we are watching it over the air (in an analog or digital broadcast), or on a cable network, or on videotape (on whatever tape format), or via satellite, or on a high definition screen in stereo, and so on? The same message ends up being displayed on a screenful of pixels; the only thing that really varies is the delivery system and the packaging.

As should be clear by now, if we are concerned with the broad cultivation of belief systems, then the content of messages is more germane than the technology with which they are delivered. To be sure, television the institution amplifies the power and hold of the messages it delivers by virtue of its technological form, but we do not think that the technology itself "creates" these impacts. Rather, message content is organized by social institutions, and it is by no means clear that these institutions will disappear with eventual and inevitable developments in media technology. Such developments aside, the impacts that concern cultivation research are created by audiences interacting with *messages*. But many have concluded that the new cornucopia of interactive, selective and virtual media opening up on the cultural landscape will mean the end of media hegemony and the demise of media effects as we know them. Indeed, cultivation research has been criticized on these grounds since the 1980s.

### "Old" New Media

Let us review some of the history on this issue. When cultivation was conceived in the late 1960s and 1970s, television absolutely dominated the media environment. Within that landscape, three high mountain ranges loomed over everything. It was absolutely normal for the Big Three television networks to garner an 80–90 percent (or higher) share of the television audience on any given night during prime time, with independent stations sweeping up a few crumbs with network reruns along the way. Clearly, there were few choices, all aimed at the heterogeneous mass market. In this environment, cultivation's arguments about the ideological homogeneity of programming – that the message system could be treated as a single, unified whole – were fairly easy to defend.

From this starting point, cultivation treated "television" as a system in which individual program choices, day-to-day network programming decisions, and cultural fads and trends were less important than the overall thrust of the program message system. Though people disagreed with this (such as Newcomb, 1978), the surface appearance of the media system did not especially contradict what cultivation theorists were saying.

This began to change in the 1980s. Two major technological and institutional developments in the 1980s challenged the supremacy of the television networks. One was the development and widespread adoption of the VCR. Prior to the 1980s, VCRs had been cumbersome devices relegated to TV newsrooms and network control booths. But the competition between the Beta and VHS formats for public acceptance eventually resulted in near-total marketplace adoption of the technology (Secunda, 1990). Court rulings that home taping did not violate copyright law also contributed to the success of the new box.

The diffusion of the VCR was remarkable. In 1980, only 1.1 percent of all TV households owned a VCR. But by the early to mid-1980s, an explosion in VCR adoption was well underway (as seen in Figure 9.1). The average cost of a functional machine dropped into the $250.00 range or lower, and VCR ownership became *de rigueur* for any American household (especially those with children), despite the popular folk wisdom that few people could learn to program them. By the end of the decade VCR penetration was approaching 80 percent, where it still resided in the late 1990s.

The explosion in VCR ownership catalyzed many communication researchers to assume that the VCR would radically change the study of TV. Early on, VCRs were seen as a sensational departure from existing television technology, facilitating taping of programs for later viewing, commercial "zapping," and viewing of rented movies. Viewing and editing of home-made material was secondary. But the mere idea that one could watch shows on one's own schedule seemed revolutionary enough to make some people talk about a new age of viewer "activity" with TV. A standard assumption was that VCRs would increase the amount of control and selection viewers would bring to bear on their TV viewing. It was thought that viewers' new control would qualitatively change the nature of the TV experience, moving it from a passive "couch potato" phenomenon into the realm of a viewer-managed total video experience. Instead of passively and helplessly receiving the predetermined video signal, viewers could freeze frames, rewind favorite portions, or view in slow motion; the vicelike grip of network scheduling was being loosened, and with it the nationwide shared moments of everyone viewing (mostly)

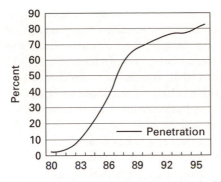

Figure 9.1 VCR penetration in US households (*source*: Motion Picture Association of America)

the same programs at the same time began to wither. This naturally played into the long-running debate on viewer activity that had featured prominently in much communication research, including major critiques of cultivation.

How would such activity be manifested? Rather than being forced to watch *Hawaii Five-O* at its regularly scheduled time, a viewer might opt to tape it and watch it after the *Love Boat*. This simple form, called "time-shifting," is perhaps the lowest amount of increased activity imaginable, because it merely postpones a passive viewing experience to a later time. Renting movies for the home represents a slightly higher level of activity, because it implies viewer choice from a presumably wider array of options. "Zapping" commercials constitutes yet another form of viewer activity, in which viewers edit out the intrusive commercial messages and participate more actively in the flow of the program (perhaps paying even more attention to the commercials in the process). Finally, home taping, editing and viewing implies the highest level of viewer activity.

From the perspective of the 1990s, any description of the VCR as providing for meaningfully increased viewer activity seems rather foolish. Yet Secunda (1990) argued that VCRs changed American media drastically, principally by threatening network dominance and contributing to the rise of video rentals. He also thought that the era of "watching TV by the clock" was ended by VCRs. But does that square with our current understanding of the VCR as an important but subservient accoutrement to the standard TV? Why did people predict that it would change the TV environment so radically?

Part of the reason had to do with the tendency to construct viewer activity as a key variable within communication research, regardless of whether actual social practices warranted it. In fact, communication researchers were highly attuned to viewer activity issues long before the arrival of the VCR. Though viewer activity can mean many things, the resuscitation and maintenance of an "active" or "obstinate" audience notion has been a key feature of communication research since the 1950s, often in the context of the notion that media have limited effects. Researchers accepting this notion might also be predisposed to think that VCRs would represent a significant enhancement of an already-existing tendency for high viewer activity. In such a view, the link of the VCR to the enhancement of participatory democracy seems obvious.

Audience activity studies were often carried out within the "uses-and-gratifications" paradigm, which assumes that such activity is a crucial variable in understanding media effects. That is, audiences are seen as gratifying specific needs at specific times. This can be contrasted with cultivation's assumption that people watch ritualistically. Early studies focusing on time-shifting were by definition documenting "novelty" uses of the VCR, as video rental eventually outstripped other uses of the technology by the late 1980s (see Lin, 1990, for review of many studies). VCRs did challenge the network domination of program distribution, but it turned out that most viewers (especially heavy viewers) were primarily interested in using VCRs to watch what they had been watching all along: fictional entertainment. The VCR offered Hollywood studios a direct route into the viewers' homes (without mediation by TV networks; they were separate industries in those days), but the idea that VCRs were increasing viewer "activity," even at the minimal level of time-shifting, was open to argument.

As VCRs subtracted somewhat from the overall three-network share, this began to suggest that cultivation's message system assumptions might lose validity as more program producers got access to the living room. In distinction to this view, cultivation theorists saw VCRs as new "delivery vehicles" for the same mass-produced content that had been present on the network airwaves. It was not assumed that viewers would stampede toward high-brow cultural, international, minority-produced, or otherwise alternative programs simply because the VCR made it possible (though undoubtedly some small market segments have taken this path). Cultivation, rather, saw VCRs as an extension or strengthening of the existing marketplace mechanisms and content patterns.

These assumptions were tested several times, in different ways. Morgan, Shanahan and Harris (1990) looked at the impact of VCR ownership and use from a cultivation perspective. They found that VCRs amplified cultivation tendencies on a variety of dependent variables. They concluded that "the similarities between television and other like technologies are more pronounced than their differences" (p. 121). Morgan et

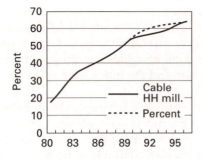

Figure 9.2 Growth in US cable households (*source*: Motion Picture Association of America)

al. (1990) also examined the role of VCRs in family life over time, concluding that the effects of VCRs were highly intertwined with television's impacts.

It now appears obvious that, throughout the 1980s, people incorporated the VCR into their existing patterns of television use; it was not adopted as a separate tool for liberation from the corporate media machine. This became even more apparent as Mom 'n' Pop video rental outlets were swallowed up by large national chains, themselves part of giant media conglomerates, tying the links between production and distribution tighter still.

Most tellingly, Dobrow (1990) addressed this question in her study of whether people used VCRs to concentrate network viewing or to diversify their choices. She did not find that VCRs open new windows to alternative content. Rather, she found that heavy TV viewers used VCRs to extend their network viewing, while light viewers (who by definition tend to be more selective) were able to vary their viewing even further. Given all this, we can say that the VCR revolution made it more convenient to watch your favorite programs *when* and *as often as* you wanted to watch them. And network share (and the shared simultaneity of viewing) did begin to decline slightly because of the VCR. But in the first wave of "new technologies" that were supposed to create a brave new world of individually controlled media, the VCR for most viewers did not in any meaningful way alter the *content* of the media environment, nor did the audience's experience of that content change very drastically.

The other significant change in the media world came pretty much concurrently with the arrival of VCRs: cable TV. Arguably, cable originally represented and still continues to represent a more menacing threat to network dominance (and to the coherency of the common message system) than that embodied by VCRs.

As Figure 9.2 shows, cable growth has been strong ever since the early 1980s. Cable started from a stronger base than VCRs, since CATV installations had existed since the 1950s to serve rural audiences. But it was not until the 1980s with the emergent strength of cable-only programming channels that the networks really began to feel the pinch in terms of lost audience share.

With the emergence of dozens of national cable networks, the number of channels available to the home viewer has increased markedly. Channel proliferation is all but certain to accelerate in the future; developments such as digital compression allow many more channels to be squeezed into high bandwidth fiber-optic cable, and the inauguration of digital broadcasting bestows the possibility of up to six additional channels upon all current license holders in the short term. But what has this shift to greater channel availability meant in terms of actual viewer choice, and what are the implications for cultivation? Does the segmentation of channels mean the end of the dominance of certain types of stories, so long a feature of the mass media market?

Gerbner summarizes the cultivation view about cable in an interview with the *Capital Times* in September of 1997. Gerbner was asked:

Q: There was some hope in the early days of cable that with more channels we would get more diversity of selection. That doesn't seem to have worked.

A: No, and it never will. There is no technological fix to basically a social-caused problem. Technology is a tool that is used by those who have the most power and ability to use it.

The fact is there are more channels but fewer owners. That means that the same kind of programming can be programmed across many more channels.

Time Warner today can commission a book, then commission a movie made on the book, then commission a movie made on the making of the movie about the book.

Now Seagrams [has] bought Universal Studios. It no longer has to place advertising. It no longer has to place drinking scenes. Now they can just produce movies on their own, and programs of their own, in which their product is more frequently represented as a part of life than if it were owned by a tobacco company. If it is owned by a tobacco company, then you have the stars smoking.

It is a new and insidious development. Advertising is not the prime mover anymore of marketing. It is not so much the commercials but it is what the advertisers and those who own and finance productions want to express and build into the program and the motion pictures themselves.

Gerbner's point is that the mere availability of more channels does not fundamentally change the socio-economic dynamics that drive the production and distribution of programs. On the contrary, that dynamic is intensified by increased concentration of ownership and control and by the dissolution of the traditional barriers between and among networks, station owners, production studios, syndicators, MSOs, cable networks and advertisers.

Even given these changes, viewers have not changed their behavior as dramatically as might have been expected – except for steadily spending even more time with their televisions. But this is not to say that nothing has changed. In the good old days of network dominance, each network would have split up an 80–90 percent nightly share, gaining on average a 25–30 share for their prime-time programs. Now fallen from their lofty perch, in the late 1990s the old big three networks together attract only about half of the viewing audience. So what has happened to the millions of other viewers who have turned their attention away from the standard-fare offerings of the three large networks?

Quite a few are watching the *new* broadcast networks (UPN, the WB and especially FOX); indeed, the *six* broadcast networks combined attract around 65–70 percent of the viewing audience. Some of them are watching independent stations, which mostly show sports, movies, off-network syndicated shows and other network-type fare. Of course, some small slices of the audience may be watching PBS, and a variety of religious, infomercial and shopping channels also make their presence felt. Clearly, however, the decline of the big three networks has not been matched by an equal decline in exposure to *network-type* programming.

Clearly, due largely to cable, far more diversity is both potential and available than has ever been the case. In addition to the broadcast networks, a typical cable system now offers a daunting lineup of channels, most of which are devoted exclusively to a single type of program. Thus, there are channels featuring nothing but news, or regional news; weather reports and forecasts; sports, or sports news; children's programs and cartoons; current movies; older movies; "classic" television genres (e.g., science fiction, comedy, nostalgic reruns from the 1950s and 1960s); music of various popular genres (such as rock or country); business information (and business news); politics and public affairs; courtroom trials; "high" culture, opera, theatre, international arts; entertainment news and celebrity gossip; health and fitness advice; demonstrations of outdoor activities; home, cooking and gardening information; religion; soft-core adult programs; travel guidance; "educational," documentary, and history-oriented programs; and many more. And there are channels offering mixed programming for specialized audiences (e. g., Black Entertainment Television, Telemundo, Univision, the International Channel), and, of course, many home shopping channels.

Given these many options, what is perhaps most surprising is that the networks have not lost *more* of their viewers. Yet, few of these channels attract even 2 percent of the audience on a regular basis. More importantly, the few that attract any significant, sustained viewing time rarely provide programming that differs substantially from what the broadcast networks offer(ed). All told, the picture of centrally produced entertainment's domination of the airwaves and wires of the nation has not changed drastically from what it used to be, except perhaps on the surface. Mostly, people are still using their free time to view televised entertainment. The steep erosion in broadcast network share has simply not meant much of a reduction in our overall exposure to typical mainstream entertainment programs. As McKibben (1992) pointed out, the sheer quantity of information available in the typical large cable system really doesn't change the nature of the television experience, and may even enhance the drone of its most oft-repeated messages.

The big networks have lost share in areas that they traditionally did not give much attention to during prime-time. One of the greatest cable successes has been Nickelodeon, which dominates the upper reaches of the listing of top cable shows; in 1997, it garnered almost 60 percent of children's weekly viewing. But it does so by programming representational realism for kids (cartoons, scary stories, action shows and maybe one or two "educational" shows). No real threat to the dominant media order here, even though Nickelodeon was originally conceived to be commercial-free (and of course let's not forget that it is part of MTV networks, owned by Viacom, itself a media giant). Sporting events also attract significant audiences on cable, but again this involves no real increase in programming diversity. Cable's most notable and trumpeted success story (CNN) relies more on a global audience and does not compete seriously with network share.

As all this shows, most of the lost network share is simply going to channels that provide more extended, exclusive versions of what broadcast stations and networks used to do in specific dayparts. So, for instance, the less than 1 percent share that tunes into a typical cable presentation of a Hollywood movie is seeing something that probably would have made it to a regular network in the 1960s and 1970s (except that pay cable channels, unconstrained by advertisers' restrictions, allow for more explicit sex and graphic violence). Neither do the large number of movies churned out for the home video market add any qualitative diversity to the media mix. Further, those watching cable sports, or weather, or news, or even documentaries, are watching programming not unlike that available on the networks; there's simply more of it, available any time. In fact, very little of the programming offered on cable can be seriously seen as offering greater or more "liberating" options.

To be sure, channels such as C-SPAN do offer some greater access to the process of democracy (without the usual commercial constraints or anchor distractions), but in the "national entertainment state" (Miller, 1996) almost no one cares. Channels such as Bravo do make an attempt to offer more serious cultural fare (of course, with tiny audiences), while other cable arts ventures have fallen by the wayside (as in the case of an earlier CBS venture) or turned to less highbrow cultural fare (such as A&E). A network such as CNN or the Fox News Channel provides technically greater opportunity for free and open dialogue (by offering 24-hour "news"), but sensational feeding frenzies, such as the cases of O. J. Simpson, Princess Diana and many others, when all programming obsesses on a single compelling story, show that even cable news channels thrive on the mass market ratings-premise that drives the networks.

Offerings as varied as the Travel Channel, the Discovery Channel, Country Music Television, the Home and Garden Channel, Outdoor Life, the History Channel, the TV Food Network, and so on, may give the impression that television is now at long last the video equivalent of the magazine stand, with its hundreds and hundreds of titles targeted to vastly different audiences. Yet, in terms of what any sizeable number of viewers – especially *heavy* viewers – actually watch, much of cable's content is simply an intensification of the offering of what networks used to provide. In the old days, networks presented Hollywood movies after their feature runs: this function is now amplified by specialized cable movie channels. Networks also provided sports programming, which is now amplified by the sports channels. And many cable channels have survived simply by programming older network reruns: the Family Channel, Nick at Nite, USA Network, Lifetime, and some others do little new programming of their own, providing yet another mass market archive for network-type programming that won't go away. Thus, many of the viewers lost by the networks are simply watching stuff that networks would have shown anyway – or actually *did* show – in the old days.

From the perspective of cultivation, it matters little whether viewers do their viewing on traditional networks or on new cable networks; they are still watching mass-produced programming made by a still-concentrating mass media industry. Moreover, the advent of cable actually increased and amplified some of the negative tendencies of the old network-dominated media system. For instance, cable premium channels have much higher levels of violence than what any television network shows. Thus, one effect of the cable "liberation" has been an increase in overall violence, without any noticeable increase in political representation or access. Nor is there any evidence that more channels has meant more diversity in voice.

All this points to the fact that the mass market model introduced by the three networks has not changed qualitatively. Rather, viewers have turned to cable as a delivery vehicle for a great deal of "more of the same" program offerings. The old days when cable was talked about as a way to provide advertising-free TV can now be remembered nostalgically. Though viewers were promised a tradeoff of paying for TV but getting no commercials in the bargain, they rapidly found themselves *both* paying and receiving commercials. The cable alternative to TV turns out to be like choosing between Burger King and McDonald's. We conclude that the dominant commercial interests of the institution of mass communication ate cable alive much as it did VCR, TV and radio before it. And the same thing is poised to happen to the new computer technologies.

Thus, as with VCRs, cultivation treated cable as a new delivery vehicle for more of the same type of content. Early studies included Morgan and Rothschild's (1983) investigation of cable's influences on sex-role perceptions. They found that cultivation of traditional sex-role perceptions was greatly strengthened in cable-owning households. They also concluded that "The economic structure of the cable industry, the cost of producing programming, and the track record so far all suggest that cable will follow the course of other media institutions. A small handful of companies will produce and distribute the bulk of what most people watch most often" (p. 48). Since that time, cultivation theorists have not seen cable viewing as meaningfully distinct from "television viewing" in general.

All the arguments we have presented so far in this chapter can be summarized, fairly succinctly, as follows. Cultivation theory was formulated in the 1960s and 1970s, when most viewers watched nothing but three broadcast networks. Those networks have lost nearly half of their audience since those years, and they now have to compete with multitudinous alternatives. But this does not render the idea of cultivation obsolete. Most of all, it is clear that the steep declines in network share do not imply a parallel reduction in exposure to "network-type" programming. For one thing, the networks have hardly disappeared; inasmuch as the networks remain the most reliable conduit to the largest audiences reachable at one time, network advertising revenues continue to rise yearly into the late 1990s. Even more importantly, many of the "new" channels have ended up offering mostly more of the same types of programs. Therefore, the developments that have reduced exposure to the three broadcast networks have not reduced exposure to the types of messages they disseminate. And as we shall see below, the number of channels available is only a small part of the story.

### More Channels, Fewer Voices

Even with the multiplication and diversification of channel options, the new media environment is characterized by something more important from the perspective of cultivation: concentration of ownership and production. Thus, while channel options are increasing numerically, a key detail from the perspective of the propositions developed in Chapter 1 is that the number of owners is shrinking. Though different analysts offer different estimates, the number of media conglomerates controlling television and other media outlets has greatly decreased in the past twenty years. Especially since the revision of media ownership regulations in 1996, it is now possible for larger and larger conglomerates to own more and more stations, essentially restricting the diversity of viewpoints that can be expressed. Cultivation's propositions imply that concentration of ownership is more important than surface diversification of programming options. Thus, though there may be many dozens of cable channels (162, as of 1996) they are owned for the most part by several huge companies (with Disney, TCI, Time-Warner, Cablevision, and Viacom leading the pack). Indeed, by the late 1990s, the six largest multiple operators controlled fully 70 percent of the national cable market.

Further, TV outlets are now more directly tied to multinational conglomerates than ever before. All three major networks are subsidiaries of or have subsumed larger corporate concerns (GE, Westinghouse, and Disney), which raises issues about the willingness of TV broadcasters to disseminate views contrary to corporate elite interests. Simultaneously, greater centralization of programming control increases the pervasiveness of standardized messages, diminishing the visibility of local variations and further marginalizing non-mainstream styles, voices and interests. All this is enhanced by the growth of alternatives for the single corporation to disseminate its messages across new and old technologies, as GE, for instance, can do with NBC, CNBC, MSNBC and so on.

The implications of this trend have been evident for years (e.g., Bagdikian, 1997), but the most recent developments are more relevant than ever to cultivation theory. As Miller (1996) points out:

This new order started to get obvious in the spring of 1995, when the F.C.C. summarily let Rupert Murdoch off the hook for having fudged the actual foreign ownership of his concern (an Australian outfit, which Murdoch had not made clear to the busy regulators). The summer then saw ABC sucked into Disney, CBS sucked into Westinghouse, and Ted Turner's mini-empire slated for ingestion by Time Warner: a grand consolidation that the press, the White House, Congress and the F.C.C. have failed to question . . .

With the mergers came some hints of how the new proprietors would henceforth use their journalists: Disney's ABC News apologizing to Philip Morris – a major TV advertiser, through Kraft Foods – for having told the truth, on a broadcast of Day One, about P.M.'s manipulation of nicotine levels in its cigarettes; and CBS's in-house counsel ordering the old newshounds at 60 Minutes to bury an explosive interview with whistleblower Jeffrey Wigand about the addictive practices of Brown & Williamson.

Such moves portend the death of broadcast journalism, as does the radical cost-cutting now being dictated by the networks' owners. And yet some good seems also to have come out of this *annus horribilis* of big waivers, big mergers, big layoffs and big lies. Suddenly, the risks of media monopoly are now apparent not just to the usual uptight minority of activists and scholars but, more and more, to everyone. People want to know what's going on, and what to do about it.

Miller's analysis was correct in most regards, but he may have been somewhat optimistic in hoping that the wider public would become interested in media ownership concentration. Precisely because the conglomerates could control the product that was of the most interest to the wider market (entertainment) they could reduce the likelihood that compromised journalistic integrity would raise any serious ruckus. Indeed, since 1996 when Miller wrote, the press and public have paid little attention to this issue, perhaps evidence of television cultivating perceptions of itself. As McChesney (1997) put it:

The preponderance of U.S. mass communication is controlled by less than two dozen enormous profit-maximizing corporations, which receive much of their income from advertising placed largely by other huge corporations. But the extent of this media ownership and control goes generally unremarked in the media and intellectual culture, and there appears to be little sense of concern about its dimensions among the citizenry as a whole pp. 6–7.

McChesney goes on to point out the political ramifications of the concentration of market-driven entertainment:

The corporate media are carpet-bombing people with advertising and commercialism, whether they like it or not. Moreover, the present course is one where much of the world's entertainment and journalism will be provided by a handful of enormous firms, with invariably pro-profit and pro-global market political positions on the central issues of our times. The implications for political democracy, by any standard, are troubling. (p. 23)

These implications will not be solved by technological advances that bring more and more channels in the absence of institutional or structural changes. Audience fragmentation can serve advertisers' purposes and intensify commercial control. Again McChesney:

Media firms solicit the capital and input of advertising firms as they prepare programming. 'Networks are happy to cater to advertisers who want a bigger role,' one report stated [fn 42]. A U.S. advertising executive expects advertisers everywhere to demand similar arrangements. 'This is just a forerunner of what we are going to see as we get to 500 [television] channels. Every client will have their own programming tailored to their own needs, based on their ad campaign' [fn 43]. (p. 29)

As ownership concentrates, cultivation's assumptions are strengthened, even as programming channels increase in number. Very simply, more channels provide an intensified opportunity for cultivation, not a vitiation of the conditions under which cultivation occurs.

### "New" New Media

Cable and VCRs have certainly changed media structures and network ratings, but not the conditions under which cultivation occurs, especially because public access to these media remains scant. But the development of more radically new technologies offers a different array of questions. The Internet, online services, computer games, video games and a host of other user-interactive information services present a different kind of challenge to the hegemony of the existing media structure. Although cable and VCRs may have ultimately entrenched the power and reach of the prevailing media dynasty, there are many who think that the age of traditional, one-way mass communication is now over, to be replaced by a highly interactive world in which users not only select their programming but interact with it – a world in which all users are both senders and receivers. In such a case, where audiences truly become interactive participants, what happens to cultivation? Can individuals in fact become their own programmers in this new world of decentralized message production? If they do, and if the mass audience no longer exists, wouldn't any cultivation simply be the outcome of a democratic competition for viewpoints to be heard?

It is obviously too early to answer this question. Computers are present only in about 40 percent of American homes (as of 1998). In these homes, television is viewed less, but that appears to be more a function of social class than of the effect of the computer. As of 1998, Nielsen reported that only about a quarter of the US/Canadian market was using the Internet for any purpose; despite the fact that "dotcom" URLs are plastered across the media landscape in national and local advertising for an extraordinary range of goods and services, only 17 percent of US adults were using the World Wide Web. Moreover, only a tiny minority of all users access the Internet for viewing video or listening to audio programs as an alternative to dominant message providers. Despite widespread hopes (and fears) that the Internet will make possible a new information highway that may replace standard mass media, there are no popular Internet or web-based programs that yet threaten the network–cable alliance. At most, the most popular online services such as AOL gain audience share comparable to that of CNN or MTV, which is a rather small and specialized audience.

However, even if there are no "programs" on the Internet that are gaining widespread audience share, it is possible that the simple act of using computers in the home is taking time away from TV, which might threaten some of the assumptions of cultivation. But, there is evidence that Internet use does not replace traditional media use. Rather, the emerging evidence indicates that audience members *add* online time on to other previously existing media use patterns, extending (not redistributing) the overall amount of time spent with media. This is a question of overall time use, which has been extensively studied in the sociological literature.

Cultivation theorists have always proceeded under the assumption that TV is "the dominant feature of Americans' free time" (Robinson and Godbey, 1997). Robinson and Godbey's diary-based studies of time use show that TV dominates available free time even for those groups that watch it proportionately less. As they note, the continuing attraction of television is that it "requires no advance planning, costs next to nothing, requires no physical effort, seldom shocks or surprises, and can be done in the comfort of one's home" (p. 149). Small wonder then that even in a universe of expanding entertainment options, television remains king. When free time is available, television is Americans' first choice, bar none. Robinson and Godbey also found that, even when people's available free time increases, that free time is taken up by television viewing, "even though Americans rate it as their least favorite form of leisure" (Tierney, 1997, p. 47). Though we may not like TV much, we can't help watching.

So far, available data suggest that home computer use does not markedly detract from television viewing. Robinson and Godbey found, not surprisingly, that computer use was most prevalent among higher socio-economic classes, where TV viewing was already lower. They detected no negative correlation between viewing and home computer use. They also found positive correlations between home computer use and other "informational" media such as newspapers, magazines and books, which again were due to the fact that higher social classes were more likely to use such media. Thus, although home computer use may have widened ease of access to certain kinds of information among the more privileged classes in particular, it has not challenged TV viewing very much in its stronghold, the lower reaches of the socio-economic spectrum.

The question becomes, will home computer and online use spread to the lower classes where it could seriously threaten the consumption of television entertainment as the nation's true pastime? And if it does spread how will it change to become more attractive to the wider market? One troubling thing about the development of the world online is that it has been a phenomenon that exacerbates the "information gap." The cost of computers remains out of reach of the poorer classes, while TV tech-

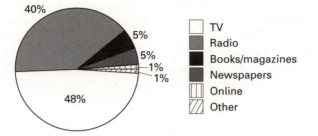

Figure 9.3  Share of various media for personal leisure time

nology is easily accessible for all, even those beneath the poverty line. Internet access, at levels where the technology can be really useful, remains an up-market item. The Internet may change the way people book their airline tickets, write term papers, keep in contact with their friends, or discover pornography; it is not likely to dislodge television from its position as our chief provider of *stories*.

To put things in perspective: according to the *Statistical Abstracts of the US*, in 1995 adults 18 and over spent a total of 1,575 hours per person watching television (836 of those hours, or 53.1 percent, were spent watching *network* television); this is to be compared to a total of 7 hours per person using online or Internet services. Looking to the year 2000, forecasts presented by the Census in 1997 projected overall television viewing to increase to 1,650 hours (with network viewing dropping to 775 hours, or 47 percent) per person. Internet access time should zoom to a full 28 hours per person per year. In proportional terms, this is a major burst, on the order of 400 percent; but it will continue to be dwarfed by television.

Stated otherwise, if these projections are correct, those of us over 18 will collectively be spending 3,540 hours per person per year on all media in the year 2000. Altogether, television viewing will get about 47 percent of those total person hours (22 percent of the total for network stations, 16 percent for basic cable); 30 percent of the media time pie will go to radio, 5.3 percent to consumer books and magazines, and 4.5 percent to daily newspapers. By contrast, only 0.8 percent of our total collective media time will be spent online (see Figure 9.3).

Further, though cost curves for computers now show a downward trend, computers still represent a sizeable investment. VCRs became affordable to even the lower classes by the late 1980s; they became a commodity, found in over 80 percent of all US households by 1995. It is uncertain whether computers will show the same pattern. Even as computers do become markedly more affordable and easy to use, it may be that the skills required for their use will prevent further widespread adoption. Mindful of how precarious it can be to predict the future, it is difficult to imagine that personal computers will penetrate virtually every home as extensively as TV; to imagine a future in which computers are being used for over seven hours a day in the average home is nearly impossible.

### "InterTV"

A more intelligent and useful question is to ask how TV will interact and "converge" with computers in the future, as will undoubtedly happen. One possibility is that the Internet will actually strengthen the appeal and dominance of traditional television. Given that in the future over-the-air television may be supplanted, this does not mean that the corporate forces that have guided television won't have a role to play in the new environment. Thus, NBC, CBS and ABC (or their corporate parents) will all probably play a major role in developing programs, producing them and even distributing them. Certainly, they have all invested resources in developing websites which promote and supplement their programs and stars.

Moreover, although pay-per-view options will probably increase through cable/Internet convergences (threatening video rental operations), it seems virtually certain that most programming will still be developed under an advertising model. American culture is trained in advertising; it prefers advertising-supported media to that which we pay for personally. Thus, even though an Internet-TV hybrid could make possible a future in which we personally select our TV at personally paid-for rates, most consumers would be willing to take a deal in which they paid less or nothing up front for services supported by advertising.

That means that advertisers would still desire programming which could attract specific audiences. In many cases, advertisers would be looking for relatively cheap access to undifferentiated mass audiences; in other cases highly specific segments would be targeted. The advertisers looking for the mass audience would therefore need to find programs attracting large general audiences, even if those audiences were not being served through an all-at-once over-the-air mechanism. With these forces in place, a mass audience would coalesce out of the many individual sender-channel-receiver possibilities made real in an interTV or video-on-demand universe.

In some ways, this type of system enhances possibilities for cultivation. Advertisers, for instance, could more accurately track the reception and impact of the programs they buy time in, allowing program material to be tailored more directly to their needs. Suppose, for instance, that some interTV viewers agreed to make themselves available as data subjects for program producers, in return for which they receive programs at lower or no cost. The program producer would then have access to the recipients' interTV data which could then be sold to advertisers who may wish to have access to that client or to that type of client. Within a market filled with individual interests, desires and the channels to serve them, such a data-gathering enterprise would still allow advertisers to assemble mass audiences from the fragmented media system.

Hitching the TV to the computer would give advertisers a level of information that has previously been very difficult to gather. Even TV ratings would become a relatively simple proposition if all programs were delivered through addressable computer video or cable modems. Thus, advertisers might accrue a degree of control over the activities not previously imagined in the old three-network environment. But beyond changing the world for the TV advertiser, there would be important implications for cultivation.

Greater control over advertising data implies a higher level of ability to manipulate viewers through programs. Nothing sinister is implied here; mass advertising in its current form is simply a grosser form of manipulation of mass audiences. The interTV would make possible manipulation at a finer level. But the greater level of manipulation also implies that viewers would be more likely to be cultivated, because programs could be more tightly tailored to the qualities that mass audiences would find interesting and compelling. Control over knowledge of viewer qualities and behaviors, in our opinion, would enhance cultivation. Thus, the greater level of channel selection and receiver targeting is not necessarily a liberating force, particularly if the new system is harnessed to a commercial model.

One can already see the tendency of commercialism to dominate the new media. For instance, the latest release of Microsoft system software links desktop operation to web use, and links both of them to "channels" where content is provided by traditional media players like Disney, the Wall Street Journal, Time-Warner's CNN, etc. The early days when web-geeks defended their precious bandwidth from commercial hacks are long gone. Now the game is in establishing whether the web of the future will be entertainment- or information-driven and especially in making the software that allows one to control the gateway. Thus, new information technologies, though potentially liberating, are controlled even more strongly by monopolistic forces than the supposedly mass-media broadcasting form is.

Also, we should differentiate between computer-based developments ("getting TV on the computer") and TV-based developments (especially with cable modems, "getting the Internet on TV"). It seems clear that "the web" (which is computer-based) will primarily be informational and commercial in the near future. Also, it clearly does provide new space for a enormous range of noncommercial, non-profit voices (as well as hundreds of pages devoted to TV programs and stars and commercial pop culture). Still and all, it is not likely to supplant TV as the culture's main *story-teller*. But we should also differentiate this from the imminent (in 1998) arrival of cable modems, which may bring not only the Internet to TV, but also provide the main gateway for the multi-channel video-on-demand we have been discussing. How these two subsystems will interact remains to be seen, as cable, television, computer and telephone interests continue to strategize about who will control the pipeline that finally emerges as dominant.

### Cultivation Research with the New Media

The new media – past, present and future – do present measurement challenges for cultivation research. The primary challenge is to determine how best to measure media "exposure" when that exposure comes in widely different forms. This problem has not yet been severe because simple TV use still dominates people's time. But in the near future when people get their stories from a variety of different machines (some on TV, some on CD, some on the computer, etc.) cultivation researchers will need to spend more time looking at ways to capture all these uses. Undoubtedly, the simple question that asks, "how much TV do you watch?" will lose some of its effectiveness.

But, the likelihood is that cultivation researchers will be able to tap into the same technology used by the advertisers. As viewing habits are coded into computer data with greater frequency, it is likely that cultivation researchers will be able to combine these data with opinion and belief questions to assess cultivation more quickly and with greater accuracy.

A new future of computer-aided cultivation research holds many possibilities. The idea of tracking relationships between exposure and beliefs, in a real-time environment, may finally provide the realistic longitudinal data that have been lacking in cultivation. Rather than tracking cultivation at yearly intervals, researchers could access data on a regular, frequent basis, to chart and track how opinions shape, form and coalesce as a function of viewing over time. It would be particularly important to do this research with children and adolescents, to see how viewing shapes opinions and beliefs in their more formative stages. It should be clear that the flexibility of cultivation research under such an environment would be strengthened.

## Conclusion

As the scene changes, the story remains the same. No matter what new media develop, under current policies and institutional conditions we cannot envision an environment in which story resources are not controlled by a relatively small number of elite institutions. The essential propositions of cultivation do not become false in such a new media environment; rather, in many respects they are strengthened. This rather grim prognostication is born out of a sense of history, from looking at new technologies with the same glasses we use to look at the old ones.

Of course, social change does happen. The Berlin Wall came down, after all. But social institutions are relatively hardened to change, and it is important to remember that cultivation investigates two institutions tightly connected: story-telling and advertising. As Gerbner so often points out, now stories are told by people with something to sell rather than something to tell. The new media will change this only in very small ways: the total number of stories out there may increase along with number of technologies by which they may be consumed, but membership in the story-tellers' club will remain highly restricted.

# 10    Test Pattern

And what is honoured is cultivated, and that
which has no honour is neglected.          Plato, *Republic*

## Cultivation's Narrative

Throughout this book, we have attempted to explicate and assess cultivation research as even-handedly as possible. Obviously, we're biased because we *do* cultivation research, but we have tried to be fair (as far as possible) about both its flaws and achievements. Certainly, the cultivation paradigm is not perfect, but we have tried to demonstrate that it has a great deal to commend it, and that it offers a valuable, practicable and critical lens through which to view the complex dynamics of media, culture and society. It tells us some important things about how we perceive the world in which we live (and which we construct), as well as about the consequences of our cultural policies. As we have offered rebuttals both to some familiar critiques and to some others that have been floating around unanswered for years, we have tried to defend cultivation analysis vigorously in these pages, without (we hope) being overly defensive.

In any case, most accounts that admit to bias sooner or later structure themselves as stories. Though it is perhaps unusual for the academic monograph to conclude with a narrative recounting of a field of research, that is what we propose to do here. As usual, most of the good stories have already been taken, so we hope that we don't raise too many hackles if we adopt and adapt from some classics to help make our point. When our story is done we'll look at some future directions and new possibilities that may help tell the new stories.

It look'd a wild uncultivated shore;
But, whether humankind, or beasts alone
Possess'd the new-found region, was unknown.

Virgil, *Aeneid*

In Chapter 1, we argued that cultivation, though dressed up as a social scientific enterprise, is really about common sense: it is simply the examination of the role played by the most important story-teller in the culture:

television. All of the data, the survey design issues, the criticism and colloquy, and all the other in-depth techniques, won't make much sense if one
does not accept the common-sense idea that stories (a) contribute to our
beliefs about reality and (b) are themselves "real."

We like to believe in stories too, and that is why we have adopted a narrative format throughout much of the book, showing how the research got
started, what troubles it met along the way (so far), and how it was able to
overcome them (at least more or less). As such, cultivation has followed a
mini-epic of its own (complete with heroes and hubris, tragedies and trav-
esties, risks and rivals, duels and dilemmas, and sundry confrontations
with the research gods) going through a twenty-plus-year journey to
hopefully arrive back home with something to say for itself. Let us
recount the journey:

As we show in the early pages of the book, the research began with an
attempt to win a battle: the battle over the question of TV violence.
Gerbner's Violence Index and content analysis was much like a Trojan
horse (though not quite in the same sense as Gross, 1977, cast television
itself). It entered the policy debate in a way that tended to disguise its real
nature: though outwardly characterized and received as dealing with the
issue of violence on TV, once in the arena the horse opened to reveal cultivation, whose true purposes were other than simply counting stabbings,
punches and murders.

At first, the research soldiers who sprang from the horse found fertile
ground for their activities. They won some research victories, establishing
important ideas like the "cultivation differential" in the research dialogue. These early gains were motivated by intellectual curiosity and ideological commitment, especially to some propositions about "social
control" (as reviewed in Chapter 1), but most everyone saw the early
studies as an isolated struggle to establish a research position on violence,
without much idea of the extended contest that was to follow.

We recounted in Chapter 2 the general principles that accompanied the
early studies. But as with any story, this one wouldn't be very interesting
without challenge, complication or conflict. Leaving Troy with modest
booty, cultivation researchers thought to return home to a prosperous
career advancing their new idea. As we have seen, though, the research
gods decreed a different course.

Heart, be still, you had worse than this to bear on the day when the terrible
Cyclops ate your brave companions; yet you bore it in silence till your cunning got
you safe out of the cave, though you made sure of being killed. (*Homer, Odyssey*)

In Chapter 3, we told the story of the various Lestrygonians, Sirens,
Cyclops and other dangers that seemed to beset cultivation research
throughout its formative stages. To be sure, many of the attacks on

cultivation contained legitimate arguments that helped advance the debate and sharpen both theory and method. But as we saw in Chapter 3, some of this was done with what seemed with an excess of personal stridency, for what might have been a modest academic tempest in a teapot; methodological debate over statistical details evolved into a fierce ideological and epistemological struggle. The very nature of the scientific enterprise was at issue. By the end of Chapter 3, we saw that many people had written off cultivation as a valid research form.

Only in Chapter 4 did we begin to see the nature of the response that cultivation developed. Here, navigating between the Scylla of methodological obscurantism and the Charybdis of ideological stubbornness, cultivation seized on the idea of the "mainstream" and refined it to full advantage. Tied to the mast for the duration, cultivation sought to ride out the storms of criticism without diluting its own original contribution too much. After the storms subsided, mainstreaming remained as a key theoretical and analytical contribution to be made by cultivation. Further progress against the goal is described in Chapter 5, where we learned how later work extended cultivation's achievements across a wider ideological field, widening, broadening and deepening the variety of topics dealt with in cultivation.

They took me over the sea while I was fast asleep, and landed me in Ithaca, after giving me many presents in bronze, gold, and raiment. (Homer, *Odyssey*)

Returning home from the battles, weary yet invigorated, it remained to consolidate the gains won in the early work. Our data analyses in Chapters 6 and 7 review the entirety of the journey to date, and re-tell the story as a whole, perhaps for the first time with the entire cast. And with completion in narrative comes the possibility to think about a moral for the future. In Chapter 8, we learned of new ways to link cognitive thinking with cultivation's work. And in Chapter 9, we learned that the suitors still may eat us out of house and home, if cultivation can't meet the challenge of thinking about the new media environment.

### Does the Story End?

Our task in this book has been to examine the achievements of cultivation research, and to look at where it may go in the future. Now, we can step back and take a look at some of the wider issues of the contribution of television *as an institution* to society, in light of what we have learned from cultivation research. Most importantly, we need to think about how to make contributions to solving the problems identified by cultivation research. Some of the cognitive work being done may suggest that viewers can be taught to be aware of, and hence resist, cognitive habits that allow social judgments to be shaped by television imagery. This work, along with individual-based media literacy efforts in general, may be highly effective and useful, but it should not deflect attention away from systemic, institutional problems. Although the larger and more ineffable systemic problems cultivation implicates are not amenable to easy solutions, we next discuss some steps that are currently being taken to "liberate" the cultural environment.

Few knew in the late 1960s that Gerbner's research would spawn a social and cultural discussion whose consequences are still being felt today. Certainly, Gerbner's contributions to research continued. In the mid-1990s, for instance, Gerbner elaborated ongoing basic content research by establishing the PROD ("Proportional Representation of Diversity" index), which is intended to monitor the cultural diversity of mainstream entertainment.

The first index covered broadcast network programming and major Hollywood movies in 1995–96. The point of the index was to look at the extent of distortion in representation across the demography of the media landscape. The idea was to provide viewers with another way to examine media products from a cultural perspective. "Far from being 'quotas' to be imposed on creative people," Gerbner said, "the Index reflects the limitations on creative freedom in the television and motion picture industries. This is a 'report card' of industry performance. We look forward to steady improvement in the diversity and equity of the cultural environment into which our children are born and in which they come to define themselves and others" (Press release, Gerbner, 1997).

Almost every group examined in the index (see Figure 10.1)[1] is proportionately misrepresented, and the index as a whole (calculated as summed index of proportional representation for all examined groups) reflects the homogeneity of media demography. In the figure, any group whose index is less than 100 is being proportionately misrepresented, and virtually every group portrayed is well under the mark. Even groups that have made significant strides toward greater civil liberties (blacks, women, gays, etc.) continue to be under-represented. The index is merely another indicator of how media industries continue to work in ways reflecting the needs and desire of dominant groups.

## The Cultural Environment Movement

Building on the continuing research program, Gerbner has also turned his attention more directly to matters of policy and social action. In 1995,

---

[1] Note that Native Americans appear to be exceedingly well-represented. This is due, presumably, to their relatively small population proportion.

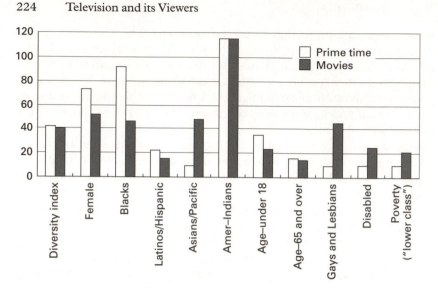

Figure 10.1  Gerbner's diversity index

after almost four decades in the academic trenches of communication research, Gerbner decided to take Cultural Indicators research directly into the political sphere. In March of that year, Gerbner assembled the founding convention of the "Cultural Environment Movement." This meeting, held at Webster University in St. Louis, was a unique gathering; participants ranged from research-oriented academics to people concerned with single issues (violence, sex, race, etc.) to well-known writers on cultural problems to disenchanted former media professionals.

Gerbner gathered them together to admonish them with a phrase that he has uttered with increasing frequency: "Don't agonize, organize." The purpose of the meeting in St. Louis was to create a new coalition which would take on, in a direct and active fashion, the problems whose effects had been identified by cultivation research throughout the years (among others). Gerbner was thinking that a social and political movement analogous to the environmental movement was needed. Surely if so much activism and passion could be mustered to defend natural resources, couldn't a similar movement be catalyzed to defend our cultural resources as well?

To be sure, CEM joined a variety of other organizations that had sprung up over the years to deal with problems associated with media's impact on society. Organizations such as FAIR (Fairness and Accuracy in Reporting) address problems of media accuracy on journalism issues. Groups such as the Media Literacy Foundation or the Media Education Foundation work for better citizen understanding of media processes and images (along with others such as the Union for Democratic Communication, Media and Democracy project, etc.). And also, we shouldn't forget the very active media lobbyists who work from the conservative side of the fence, such as Accuracy in Media, an organization that argues that the media are dominated by those with a liberal, anti-business perspective; even more extreme groups imagine a powerful leftist conspiracy committed to the destruction of traditional family values and morality. The diversity of voices speaking out on media issues shows the importance that the civil society has assigned to the issue in recent years, making it a key battleground for all points across the political spectrum.

But CEM sought to do more than add another voice to the cacophony. CEM sought to unite people with varying but complementary concerns, not just traditional single-issue concerns about violence or sex. Most importantly, the point was not to promote more restrictions or censorship, as is so often the case among media activist groups. Rather, the problem from CEM's view is that we have far too much censorship *now*; rather than add even more, the media need to be liberated as much as possible from the restrictive and repressive yoke of commercial control. As it has become increasingly clear that factionalized efforts to confront the cultural Leviathan have not been very successful, CEM sought to further the view that media policy should promote "organized diversity, whether it pleases or not" (c.f., Morgan, 1995). For the most part, an oppositional critique to elite media dominance is heard only as a still-small voice.

Gerbner certainly recognized the difficulties any such movement would face. He began the meeting by quoting a toast often used by dissidents in the most desperate days of the Soviet Union: "Let us drink to the success of our hopeless endeavor." The spirit of confrontation against powerful odds ran high at the founding convention. Some of the attendees felt that a new front could be established against cultural domination; others suggested rearguard actions. But they all united behind the central idea of a broadly focused social dialogue moving toward a more liberated view of the cultural environment.

CEM's founding meeting thus brought together people with a wide variety of opinions about media problems; there was some healthy disagreement as well as recognition of a shared problem. CEM has since tried to bring everything into greater harmony through its focus on a few simple objectives that stress the movement toward a liberation of the cultural environment away from socio-economic elites. Not all of the dissonant notes have been harmoniously resolved, and CEM continues to debate the best strategy for achieving a more liberated cultural environment.

CEM began with first principles, as expressed in its "Viewers' Bill of Rights," which enunciates the negative repercussions of commercial control and offers ideas for change (the document can be viewed at http://www.cemnet.org/viewer.html). The document "challenges us to mobilize as citizens as effectively as commercials mobilize us as consumers." At a broader level, CEM also is a signatory to the "People's Communication Charter," which is a document created and endorsed by organizations such as the Third World Network (Penang, Malaysia), the Centre for Communication & Human Rights (Amsterdam, the Netherlands), and the AMARC-World Association of Community Radio Broadcasters (Peru/Canada). The development of the Charter began in the early 1990s, prior to the founding of CEM, but CEM picked up the themes of the charter from the beginning.

There are several main ideas addressed in the charter, which reads something like a communication bill of rights. There are also similarities with documents produced by UNESCO in the "New World Information and Communication Order" debate of the 1970s and 1980s. In this section we review some of the proposals of the charter, and comment on how cultivation research is relevant to the issues addressed. First, the text:

We, the Signatories of this Charter, recognize that:

Communication is basic to the life of all individuals and their communities. All people are entitled to participate in communication, and in making decisions about communication within and between societies. The majority of the world's peoples lack minimal technological resources for survival and communication. Over half of them have not yet made a single telephone call. Commercialization of media and concentration of media ownership erode the public sphere and fail to provide for cultural and information needs, including the plurality of opinions and the diversity of cultural expressions and languages necessary for democracy. Massive and pervasive media violence polarizes societies, exacerbates conflict, and cultivates fear and mistrust, making people vulnerable and dependent. Stereotypical portrayals misrepresent all of us and stigmatize those who are the most vulnerable. Therefore, we ratify this Charter defining communication rights and responsibilities to be observed in democratic countries and in international law.

### Article 1 **Respect**

All people are entitled to be treated with respect, according to the basic human rights standards of dignity, integrity, identity, and non-discrimination.

### Article 2 **Freedom**

All people have the right of access to communication channels independent of governmental or commercial control.

*Article 3* **Access**

In order to exercise their rights, people should have fair and equitable access to local and global resources and facilities for conventional and advanced channels of communication; to receive opinions, information and ideas in a language they normally use and understand; to receive a range of cultural products designed for a wide variety of tastes and interests; and to have easy access to facts about ownership of media and sources of information.

Restrictions on access to information should be permissible only for good and compelling reason, as when prescribed by international human rights standards or necessary for the protection of a democratic society or the basic rights of others.

*Article 4* **Independence**

The realization of people's right to participate in, contribute to and benefit from the development of self-reliant communication structures requires international assistance to the development of independent media; training programmes for professional mediaworkers; the establishment of independent, representative associations, syndicates or trade unions of journalists and associations of editors and publishers; and the adoption of international standards.

*Article 5* **Literacy**

All people have the right to acquire information and skills necessary to participate fully in public deliberation and communication. This requires facility in reading, writing, and storytelling; critical media awareness; computer literacy; and education about the role of communication in society.

*Article 6* **Protection of journalists**

Journalists must be accorded full protection of the law, including international humanitarian law, especially in areas of armed conflict. They must have safe, unrestricted access to sources of information, and must be able to seek remedy, when required, through an international body.

*Article 7* **Right of reply and redress**

All people have the right of reply and to demand penalties for damage from media misinformation. Individuals concerned should have an opportunity to correct, without undue delay, statements relating to them which they have a justified interest in having corrected.

Such corrections should be given the same prominence as the original expression. States should impose penalties for proven damage, or require corrections, where a court of law has determined that an information provider has wilfully disseminated inaccurate or misleading and damaging information, or has facilitated the dissemination of such information.

*Article 8* **Cultural identity**

All people have the right to protect their cultural identity. This includes the respect for people's pursuit of their cultural development and the right to free expression in languages they understand. People's right to the protection of their cultural space and heritage should not violate other human rights or provisions of this Charter.

*Article 9* **Diversity of languages**

All people have the right to a diversity of languages. This includes the right to express themselves and have access to information in their own language, the right to use their own languages in educational institutions funded by the state, and the right to have adequate provisions created for the use of minority languages where needed.

*Article 10* **Participation in policy-making**

All people have the right to participate in public decision-making about the provision of information; the development and utilization of knowledge; the preservation, protection and development of culture; the choice and application of communication technologies; and the structure and policies of media industries.

*Article 11* **Children's rights**

Children have the right to mass media products that are designed to meet their needs and interests and foster their healthy physical, mental and emotional development. They should be protected from harmful media products and from commercial and other exploitation at home, in school and at places of play, work, or business. Nations should take steps to produce and distribute widely high quality cultural and entertainment materials created for children in their own languages.

*Article 12* **Cyberspace**

All people have a right to universal access to and equitable use of cyberspace. Their rights to free and open communities in cyberspace, their freedom of electronic expression, and their freedom from electronic surveillance and intrusion, should be protected.

*Article 13* **Privacy**

All people have the right to be protected from the publication of allegations irrelevant to the public interest, or of private photographs or other private communication without authorization, or of personal information given or received in confidence. Databases derived from personal or workplace communications or transactions should not be used for unauthorized commercial or general surveillance purposes. However, nations should take care that the protection of privacy does not unduly interfere with the freedom of expression or the administration of justice.

*Article 14* **Harm**

People have the right to demand that media actively counter incitement to hate, prejudice, violence, and war. Violence should not be presented as normal, "manly," or entertaining, and true consequences of and alternatives to violence should be shown. Other violations of human dignity and integrity to be avoided include stereotypic images that distort the realities and complexities of people's lives. Media should not ridicule, stigmatize, or demonize people on the basis of gender, race, class, ethnicity, language, sexual orientation, and physical or mental condition.

*Article 15* **Justice**

People have the right to demand that media respect standards of due process in the coverage of trials. This implies that the media should not presume guilt before a verdict of guilt, invade the privacy of defendants, and should not televise criminal trials in real time, while the trial is in progress.

*Article 16* **Consumption**

People have the right to useful and factual consumer information and to be protected against misleading and distorted information. Media should avoid and, if necessary, expose promotion disguised as news and entertainment (infomercials, product placement, children's programmes that use franchised characters and toys, etc), and the creation of wasteful, unnecessary, harmful or ecologically damaging needs, wants, products and activities. Advertising directed at children should receive special scrutiny.

*Article 17* **Accountability**

People have the right to hold media accountable to the general public and their adherence to the standards established in this Charter. For that purpose, media should establish mechanisms, including self-regulatory bodies, that monitor and account for measures taken to achieve compliance.

*Article 18* **Implementation**

In consultation with the Signatories, national and international mechanisms will be organized to publicize this Charter; to implement it in as many countries as possible and in international law; monitor and assess the performance of countries and media in light of these Standards; receive complaints about violations; advise on adequate remedial measures; and to establish procedures for periodic review, development and modification of this Charter.

This text from: http://www.web.apc.org/amarc/charteng.htm

Now let us examine some of the proposals in the light of what has been learned in the *œuvre* of cultivation. Article 1 deals with respect, which has been a key issue for cultivation, especially in the demographics of media portrayals. Though Article 1 does not address communication issues specifically, it sets the groundwork for establishing an ethics of communication in which a diverse world can better represent and express itself. A major conclusion of cultivation is that this has not been possible under current cultural policy.

Articles 2 and 3 deal with freedom and access, key issues from the perspective of cultivation. As we have seen throughout, cultivation can be seen as a documentation of the fact that mass communication resources have been controlled by social elites. If that control could be loosened somewhat, it seems obvious that broader and more balanced cultural benefits would accrue. In much the same way that the civil rights movement slowly but surely brought new freedoms to millions of people, the Charter proposes to identify a new right, which goes above and beyond the right to speak freely. Rather, the right to speak freely in a context in which that speech *can be heard* is proposed. Thus, the Charter proclaims that free speech is not a meaningful right if it is effectively circumscribed and controlled by commercial, private interests, as documented by cultivation research.

Article 4 recognizes that these changes will not come easily, that specific policy decisions are required to help create and transform the institutions that will expand the diversity and pluralism of the world communication system. As we saw in Chapter 9, the new media developments seem to be taking us even further into a world dominated by capital communication. To reverse this trend will require an awakened and aware vision by the world's policy-makers and an active voice from the audiences of those policies. It is not easy to be optimistic about this.

Article 5 deals with literacy, and more broadly with the issue of media literacy. Though media have been very powerful forces in our lives, our experience with them does not help us to become literate in terms of how to decode their messages, nor does it instruct us as to how programs are produced, funded, etc. We do not learn a lot about the economics or politics of the media system simply through repeated exposure. Article 5 is intended to support the nascent efforts to improve understanding of the institutional structures of international media; we also hope this book contributes to that enterprise.

Articles 6 and 7 deal with concerns more pertinent to journalism, and we will not address them here. Articles 8 and 9, however, address an issue very relevant to cultivation. They propose that cultural diversity and language diversity be explicitly recognized in the media sphere. As cultivation has shown, current mass communication practices tend to restrict and homogenize cultural diversity and to keep social change in check. Since it is a presupposition of the charter that cultures fundamentally deserve protection, media-induced homogenization is seen as a trend that needs counteracting. We agree with that call.

Article 10 also addresses a key cultivation issue: people simply do not have much say in the making of information policy. Government policy-making bodies often tend to be in the service of powerful industry players, as the history of communications legislation in the USA repeatedly shows, with the 1996 Telecommunications Act only among the more recent, and blatant, examples (McChesney, 1997). The situation is exacerbated at the international level, where widespread globalization and privatization is eradicating public service-oriented media structures.

The rest of the document deals with specific issues that we will not address in detail (children's rights, advertising, cyberspace issues, etc.), although all of the provisions in the document are highly congruent with the findings of cultivation work. More importantly, the entire document dovetails with the critical spirit embodied in cultivation research. Too often this essence has been lost in methodological debate, but it should be clear by now that the real implications of cultivation research will be found at the level of social action.

### Old Wine, New Bottles

Thus, over the years, cultivation results have contributed heavily to a variety of debates on how to "fix" the problems of the cultural landscape. We have already discussed cultivation's role in the early debates on violence. To reiterate, cultivation proposed that imitation or instigation of violence should not be the only, or even the major, concern; rather, the effect on broad social beliefs about violence were highlighted as the key social effect and the more significant policy issue.

But despite thousands of pages of rhetoric, data, pleading, diatribes and argument, decades of social debates on media violence have produced scant effect. Though we think that cultivation research made an enormous contribution to the literature, the problems continue unabated, and in some senses have become worse.

In the mid-1990s, for instance, the entire discussion of the "V-Chip" showed that policy-makers had not gained a much clearer understanding of the dynamics of cultivation. The V-Chip provides a sort of technological Band-Aid that is guaranteed to fail, even if it allows posturing lawmakers to proclaim a moral victory. As Krcmar and Cantor (1997) have shown, in fact, strategies such as the V-Chip or program ratings are just as likely to attract viewer attention to depictions of violence as they are to "protect" viewers from those depictions. Thus, cultivation researchers saw the V-Chip as a flawed way to deal with the more basic questions raised by the amount and nature of violence in the symbolic environment.

Not surprisingly, even though the television industry found the V-Chip distasteful, they were willing to accept it in tradeoff for massive revision of federal rules that had limited concentration of ownership and in order to get new digital channels for free, with little-to-no additional public service obligations. This highly imbalanced tradeoff, with massive gains for the industry and dubious payoffs for the audience, was a prelude to hefty increases in the stock prices of many media companies, especially in the radio and TV broadcast sector, where massive mergers and buyouts swept the country. Ironically, the press failed to cover this at all, as media concentration easily won Project Censored's annual under-reported stories contest in 1995. If anyone doubted the tight connection between media industries and social elites (see proposition 1, Chapter 1), developments in 1995 left little doubt:

The most troubling aspect of the bill allows easing – and outright elimination – of current anti-trust regulations. In what the *New York Times* described as "a dazzling display of political influence," the nation's broadcast networks scored big in the House version of the bill by successfully getting the limits on ownership eased so that any individual company can control television stations serving up to 50 percent of the country. The Senate version of the bill provides for a more modest 35 percent coverage. (Project Censored, 1996)

Since the passage of the 1996 Telecommunications Act, broadcasters have reaped unprecedented rewards as a result of increased merger and concentration activity. All of this is highly consistent with the cultivation notion that communication policy is directed by the industries that represent elite positions. The near-subservience of the FCC to these industries is but one case in point. In the USA, the stage is set not for more diversity and freer information flow (the great hope of the new media future) but for increased homogenization of program material. Even greater concentration of control therefore also means even greater possibility of cultivation, despite the fact that sharply targeted marketing techniques and channel explosion appear to be fragmenting the audience into tinier and tinier slivers.

To return to the question of social action, cultivation's results obviously imply that systemic deficiencies must be attacked at the level of production and control; that is, media access and ownership must be made more open and diverse. The Telecomm legislation of 1996 represents a major defeat for that idea, though it was not unexpected.

The most obvious observation is that the cultural environment is resistant to change. Idealistic and broad-based movements such as CEM (among many others) may be able to make some progress, although not a lot has been achieved to date. As critical scholars we participate in and support the activities of groups such as CEM. But does the continuance of the cultivation research project help to shape the problems it examines?

Along the way, there have been important contributions, piecemeal though they may be. Cultivation research has managed, even in a fairly hostile media environment, to convey widespread knowledge about the level of violence in our media products. Through the Violence Index and now through other CI products such as PROD, Cultural Indicators work has certainly attracted its own share of attention for a critical perspective on media issue. Also, cultivation has helped, sometimes, to steer the violence debates away from the detrimental themes of imitation and toward a broader cultural dialogue about the roles and rules of TV violence. Whether these discussions will have lasting influence remains to be seen.

Where all critical voices, including cultivation and CEM, have been less successful is in creating a political-ideological debate on the structure of our media system. However, attention can successfully be drawn to content issues. For instance, as mentioned in Chapter 3, during the Persian Gulf War, Lewis et al. (1991) published a widely reported study that showed the propaganda effects of the media for American audiences. Titling the study, "The More You Watch, the Less You Know," they found that viewing actually cultivated misinformation about the war (showing, for instance, that more heavy viewers thought Kuwait had been a democracy before its invasion by Iraq, and that Iraq "had been warned" not to invade Kuwait). More relevant to cultivation research, it was found that heavy viewers were strikingly more approving of the employment of force against Iraq, which ran parallel to cultivation findings in the USA and elsewhere that heavy viewers are more open to the use of violence "for a good reason." Obviously, the study did not change the huge success of American propaganda in the war, but it did at least catalyze some small debate on the issue.

However, even when the atmosphere is less ideologically charged than it was during the Gulf War, certain questions resist discussion. While CEM, Cultural Indicators, or other media critics can easily gain wide agreement about problems with specific media portrayals – violence, sex, sensationalism, etc. – it has been almost impossible to put media structure and ownership on the national agenda. To argue that commercial control is not necessarily more "natural" or more "democratic" – and that the government is not the only threat to freedom of speech – is difficult for the public to recognize. This, of course, is highly congruent with the arguments we have advanced throughout the book. Social and commercial control is precisely the feature of the media system that resists debate.

## Cultivation in 2010, and Beyond?

After we completed our initial meta-analysis of cultivation results, we wondered whether there was need for any further cultivation studies.

Feeling that our results had conclusively demonstrated the presumed relationship, we thought that the time for continued replication of cultivation work might have come to an end. But while critics would applaud this view, in the end we decided that further cultivation research will be both necessary and valuable. In this section we develop our ideas on where we'd like to see cultivation go in the future.

If it is true, as we predict, that new media developments will not change the fundamental dynamics of cultivation, then certainly cultivation research should continue simply to monitor and track the continued impact of media on society. At that level, cultivation will continue to perform its role as a "cultural indicator"; there will probably always be a need and place for such research, on "traditional" dependent variables such as violence and sex-roles, on the wider slate that developed (including political orientations, health beliefs, images of science, family values, environmentalism, and others), and also on new and novel dependent variables not yet explored. All of these demand continued assessment as new technologies develop and social values evolve.

Beyond that, though, cultivation needs to push back some theoretical frontiers. These boundaries have two effects: they limit our understanding of the dynamics of the cultivation process, and they limit our ability to devise ways to counteract the process. What are these boundaries? First is the general lack of understanding about the relationship between mental processes and cultivation. Having examined this issue in detail in Chapter 8, we can deal here with some wider issues and possible directions.

As we have argued, cultivation is a narrative process. At the same time, the best cognitive work on cultivation has suggested that people learn from television in the same way that they learn from everything else; they don't generally make significant distinctions between fact, fiction, reality, etc. when making judgments about the world. We see those observations as fitting together very nicely, and as pointing the way toward the idea that a better understanding of cultivation will most likely be a narrative understanding.

Where can we glean more information about how people use narratives to view the world? The ironic answer is: "almost anywhere." In fact, it may well be that developments in cultivation, which is a very particular discipline in a small field, resemble those around the social sciences, where perhaps one may speak of a "narrative turn" toward more story-based understandings of human meaning. What is the "narrative turn"? Like the linguistic turn in twentieth-century philosophy, the narrative turn is a discipline-crossing realization that narratives have broad application to understanding how the world is pictured and understood. Further, like the linguistic turn, the narrative turn represents a reaction to something, in this case the idea the cognitions, facts and rationality are the primary phenomena which structure perception of the human world. As Brown et al. argue:

We take the expression 'narrative turn' to denote the recent attention given by many social science scholars to the way human conduct can be seen as the expression and enactment of different kinds of stories. It is increasingly argued in this body of work that understanding how we organise accounts of both nature itself and our own activity into meaningful, logically organised stories is crucial in making sense of our world. (1995, p. 1569)

Where does cultivation fit in the narrative turn? Certainly it is not the only paradigm for communication theory and research that emphasizes narrative issues (cultural criticism has been doing this for years). But it may be one of the few that shows in numerically concrete ways how stories construct consciousness. In that sense, cultivation helps to estimate the importance of the problem without overstating it. Because narratives themselves resist quantification, the idea that exposure to narratives and their consequences can be measured at all is an important task that can be carried on by cultivation. But are there other tasks in this turn toward narrative issues?

Another is to make cultivation more sophisticated through further development of the types of dependent variables used in cultivation. That is, we need to rethink how effects are measured in cultivation research. Typically, we have used very basic attitude and opinion measures (even though their topics vary widely), and on balance we have been successful with these. But attitudes and opinions are not fundamentally narrative constructs, they are in fact products of the social science against which the narrative turn is reacting. Attitudes and opinions are in many respects measured as rational reactions (or estimations of reactions) to factual-seeming belief statements about the real world. As such, they may not get at narrative mental processes.

We would argue that one new approach would be to use reactions to *stories* as dependent variables in cultivation research. Or more radically, we may use stories themselves as dependent variables. This is not just a methodological issue. Rather than asking people how violent they think the real world is, for instance, we might ask them to read stories involving violence and comment upon different outcomes of the story. Suppose, for example, that we asked people to read a story about a violent black football star who had killed his wife. Would heavy viewers be more likely to think that such a person should get the death penalty? By comparison, suppose we had asked people to read a story about some policeman who had beaten and killed a black man in the course of making, say, a traffic arrest? Would heavy viewers be more likely to recommend capital punishment in that case? Although heavy viewers as a rule prefer capital punishment, in this case we think they would actually be less likely to suggest it because that would counter the standard television narrative in which police use force with justice on their side, usually against dangerous minorities. In this way, reactions to specific narratives as dependent variables might provide more exact measurement of cultivation on specific issues. This scenario could be played out in many ways, whether the topic is dangerous dictators, lurking minorities, mysterious scientists, etc. In the end we might ask, what *stories* do stories cultivate?

Apart from the narrative issue, cultivation will probably need to measure its independent variable in some different ways. As the phenomenon of "watching television" comes to include exposure to more and more content outside the purview of what most concerns cultivation, empirical relationships will be increasingly under-estimated. (Indeed, this may in part account for the apparent decline in the magnitude of cultivation associations over time.) As we saw in Chapter 9, by the year 2010 it seems virtually certain that people will have many different options for getting access to mass produced narratives, including television. We think that more automated and precise tracking of viewer behavior will become possible in such an environment, and this will ultimately benefit the precision with which cultivation can examine viewer impacts. The important thing will be to find ways to assess exposure to narrative systems without getting lost in the forest of the many new media options.

We began this book by making the simple argument that watching a great deal of television, over many months and years, might reasonably be expected to have some consequences for how people see the world. We can now accept this basic proposition with a great deal of confidence, while recognizing that it is not nearly so simple as it may appear at first glance. The link between what we watch and what we believe is sometimes strong, sometimes fragile, and sometimes does not exist at all; it is forged in highly complex, dynamic processes. It is affected by age, sex, race, class, education and a host of other family, social and demographic factors. It is also affected by attention, memory, interpretation, distraction, repetition, frequency and myriad cognitive variables and mechanisms, many of which remain to be hypothesized. And it is affected by social networks, daily interaction and other mediated and unmediated experiences. And all of these are ongoing and *interacting*; through them, television cultivates beliefs, perspectives and practices that reproduce specific patterns of culture and power.

Gerbner and Gross worked with the first generation of researchers at

Penn, who themselves trained a next generation. Now, more than twenty years later, the research tradition has carried on. We have dozens of studies in our meta-analytic database, and every year conferences feature papers by new graduate students who are fascinated with the simple but elegant hypothesis proposed by cultivation. Research is now even going on outside of the communication field, as other scholars become aware of the immense amount of data that has been gathered by cultivation which is relevant to a variety of fields. We expect this trend to continue, as political scientists, sociologists, consumer behavior experts and others become attuned to the history and findings of research in this area.

Yet some major changes lie ahead for cultivation research, in terms of both theory and method. These changes are necessary and healthy; cultivation research in the twenty-first century will look very different from cultivation research in the 1970s, as it should. We look forward to the paradigm's continuing evolution as a vital, data-based and critical research tradition with significant policy implications.

So, stay tuned. We return you now to your regular programming...

# Methodological Appendix

This Appendix[1] provides methodological details for the analyses discussed in Chapters 6 and 7. "Meta-analysis generally refers to the statistical integration of the results of independent studies," according to Mullen (1989, p. 1). As simple as this sounds, in the present case it involved literally hundreds of decisions about the coding of thousands of findings to produce a dataset that reflects Mullen's definition. This Appendix describes the process and the decisions.

Prior to our article in *Communication Yearbook 20*, no one had undertaken a systematic meta-analysis of the body of cultivation data, although several reviews had appeared along the way. Despite the widespread and growing interest in meta-analysis in the communication field, some serious difficulties were awaiting anyone who chose to undertake a meta-analysis of cultivation results. One problem is that *so many* individual cultivation studies have been done. Another problem has to do with the fact that many cultivation studies report many different results using different techniques of data analysis; although from a meta-analytic perspective, "the more, the merrier" (since accumulating larger samples of results helps differentiate random from systematic error), the problem is that cultivation data have been reported in many inconsistent and often incompatible forms. Moreover, unlike some other areas of research in which results are reported in fairly simple terms, the essence of cultivation work within a given study or sample could not always be easily "boiled down" to a single coefficient. Yet in some ways all these studies can be seen as distinct investigations of related issues. How then to treat them?

To be sure, some meta-analyses have come close to an overall study of cultivation results. Herrett-Skjellum and Allen (1996) performed a meta-analysis of television and sex-role perceptions that included some of the same studies meta-analyzed here. Their results were quite close to what our study showed, but they only covered about a quarter of the total

[1] This appendix is based largely on the methodological discussion of Morgan and Shanahan (1997).

number of studies we examined. Thus, our analysis (first reported in 1996 and extended here) can claim to be the most complete meta-analysis of cultivation, even though significant gaps in this analysis remain, as we report below.

In Chapter 6, we give a brief description of the meta-analytic procedures we used. Here we offer a more detailed description. As noted, in meta-analysis, each observed result is assumed to come from an overall distribution whose mean represents the "true" effect. Each individual study or independent sample, when all taken together, contributes to an analysis that, in theory, gives a better estimate of that true effect. (In what follows, we use the term "effect" strictly in a statistical sense, and we stress that cultivation does not imply "effects" in the sense of stimulus-response causality.) But even meta-analysis, though more resistant to random variation and noise, can be influenced by factors that may influence how the results "come out." One such issue is that there are no predefined procedures for selecting studies to be included in the meta-analysis. If the researchers do a good job of selecting studies, the meta-analysis certainly is better than a single study. On the other hand, if the researchers allow significant bias to creep into the study selection process, the meta-analysis may be misleading. These biases can slither in when selecting studies, when cumulating data, or when coding data. After these stages are completed, however, the analysis is *relatively* cut-and-dried, and more resistant to misuse and misrepresentation than the usual statistical techniques.

### Study Selection

We began with the regularly updated, comprehensive bibliography of cultivation studies that have been published since 1976. This is available from online databases such as Comserve and various communication-related world wide web pages. Further computer and bibliographic searches turned up no additional citations, though continuing research since 1997 has added some studies to the *œuvre* (we cut off our search for the analyses in this book at 1997). From our initial list of over 300 publications, we compiled a database of studies that: (1) tested a relationship between amount of exposure to television (however measured) and a dependent variable which could be thought of as providing a "television answer," and (2) specifically adduced or criticized cultivation theory as an explanation of the results.

There are many dozens of studies published every year on some aspect of media effects, most of them dealing with television. For obvious reasons, we wanted to limit our project to those that specifically took a cultivation approach, or sought to critique cultivation, even though many studies with titles like "Television's influence on . . ." could have been relevant. Our choice was necessary to keep the study theoretically coherent. This is not to claim that "non-cultivation" studies are never relevant to cultivation questions; we merely sought to maintain a clean conceptual focus for what could have otherwise been a much more diffuse dataset. Also, we simply needed to manage the size of the dataset, which became very large.

Some studies that met our selection criteria could not be included for other reasons. A few studies that are highly supportive of cultivation were excluded because they did not use the individual respondent as the unit of analysis, and therefore they provided no comparable estimate of "effect size" that could be coded. For example, Morgan (1983) found that subgroups more victimized on television showed stronger evidence of cultivation, Rothschild (1984) used the "peer group" as the unit of analysis, and Morgan (1986) observed mainstreaming in an erosion of diversity across regions of the USA. Although these studies all provided data that strongly supported cultivation hypotheses, it was not possible to compare them to ones that reported data for individuals.

Also, we could not code data that were implied or summarized but not explicitly presented. For example, Gerbner et al. (1981b) provided a table summarizing 90 simple correlations, 580 1st-order partials within subgroups, and 90 7th-order partials, across 5 variables tapping perceptions of danger. The vast majority (715 out of 760, or 94 percent) of these correlations were positive (consistent with cultivation) and most (615, or 81 percent) were statistically significant. Only 5 of the 760 correlations were negative and significant. Similarly, Morgan (1984) looked at relationships between amount of viewing and four "quality of life" indices in a variety of different subgroups; the text describes the general pattern of results of 272 correlations (68 for each index). And Morgan and Shanahan (1992b) note that 415 of 462 separate subgroup comparisons (90 percent) fit their cultivation-based expectations about viewing and voting behavior, and that 274 (66 percent) of these were significant. Despite these strongly supportive patterns, almost 1,500 findings from these three studies alone are *not* included in our meta-analytic database; since the actual coefficients were not given in these cases, nothing was (or could have been) coded.

In some cases, authors note something along the lines of, "The data in Table X look very similar when control Y is applied," or "The results shown in the table are comparable to those for the other dependent variables (not shown)." In these cases when no data are explicitly presented, nothing could be coded.

Some studies touched on relevant issues but did not present any data about amount of television exposure and beliefs that could be coded in our meta-analytic framework. As one example, Reep and Dambrot (1989) raised intriguing issues about the relative import of (a) pervasive but non-prominent stereotypes and (b) non-typical but highly popular portrayals that are counter-stereotypical. This question is certainly relevant to cultivation. Their study, however, investigates how viewers' evaluations of selected characters vary according to gender, exposure to certain shows, and so on; the actual data presented are irrelevant to cultivation and could not possibly fit within our data format, so the study was not coded. So, studies such as this, where cultivation theory was discussed but no actual relevant results about the "effect size" of cultivation were presented, were not included.

Research design was another factor in the selection process. Cultivation studies are by and large survey-based. There are some experimental tests of cultivation relationships or experimental manipulations of cognitive variables (many of the most important are discussed in Chapter 8), but most of these deal with short-term phenomena in artificial contexts and hence they do not estimate the magnitude of cultivation relationships in the field. This decision excluded studies both supportive of cultivation (those of Shrum, for instance) and others that are more critical. Thus, we included only survey-type cultivation studies, which are by far the most common, and ignored the small handful of relevant experiments (for some examples, see Bryant et al., 1981; Shapiro, 1991; Wakshlag, Vial and Tamborini, 1983; Zillmann andWakshlag, 1985).

In some studies there was no way to theoretically determine what the "television answer" would be. We included all studies where it was possible to make some reasonable connection to cultivation theory without straining credulity beyond the breaking point. This was a close judgment call in some cases; in general, we erred as much as possible on the liberal side, to favor inclusiveness. But in some cases, no plausible expectations whatsoever for cultivation relationships could be inferred. For example, Gunter and Wober (1983a) examined associations between amount of viewing and perceptions of personal risk from such events as lightning, flooding, heart disease, nuclear attack, road accidents and food poisoning, without providing any evidence (empirical or otherwise) that television represents these dangers in any particular way. Similarly, Potter (1986) looked at associations between amount of viewing and estimates of the percentages of deaths due to accidents, cancers, pneumonia and heart disease, but with no evidence that television tends to over- or under-represent these dangers. The absence of any relevant message data (or extrapolations based thereon) means that it was impossible to code the results according to whether or not they fit what cultivation would predict. Therefore, we simply didn't include them in the dataset.

Other studies were excluded because they were judged to be essentially irrelevant to cultivation, regardless of how the author(s) may have framed their research. For example, Newhagen and Lewenstein (1992) delved into the cognitive "learning" process that may (or may not) underlie cultivation (cf. Chapter 8; also Hawkins, Pingree and Adler, 1987; Potter, 1988); they tried to explain cultivation in terms of cognitive cataloging and memory connections, based on the notion of exemplars "fading" from "episodic memory." Four weeks after the Loma Prieta earthquake, ten "trained interviewers rode the commuter trains between Palo Alto and San Francisco" (Newhagen and Lewenstein, 1992, p. 51) searching for respondents; 179 were obtained. Respondents indicated – a month after the fact – how soon after the earthquake they started watching television, and how much they watched during the first thirty-six hours of coverage. The primary dependent variables were retrospective reports of fear and the number of images of the disaster they articulated. The results offered some interesting insights into what we recall of media images in situations of crisis, but the notion that thirty-six hours of earthquake coverage might have "cultivated" *anything* is so far removed from cultivation theory that this study was not included in our database. (In any case, the data presented could not have been coded according to our instrument.)

Another important selection criterion was that only *published* studies were included, thereby excluding data from many unpublished conference papers, dissertations and other research reports. It might be argued that this favors studies with stronger results, since non-significant findings often go unpublished in some fields (this is known as the "file drawer" problem in meta-analysis). In the case of cultivation, however, this seems extremely unlikely, since journals have shown no apparent reluctance to publish studies that claim to debunk cultivation. This also keeps our analysis more even-handed. That is, we had access to many unpublished reports that Gerbner et al. have produced (Violence Profile technical reports, grant reports, and others). These contain large amounts of data that demonstrate cultivation (literally, thousands of correlations), but we have no way to balance these with any comparable amount of unpublished data from other sources that may (or may not) be contrary. We might even argue, given the peculiar controversies that have swirled around cultivation research, that restricting the data analysis solely to published studies might actually diminish the strength of our accumulated results. In any case, data from studies that were not "published" (in the conventional sense of the term) were not included. At the very least, this decision facilitates the replicability of our meta-analysis.

On the other hand, no studies were eliminated simply because we judged them to be methodologically "weak," or because of the way the key independent variable of TV exposure was measured. This variable has taken many diverse forms, including self-reports of viewing hours (per day, per week, "yesterday," or for different times of the day), frequency of viewing specific programs or types, number of programs of various types seen, diary measures, and many others (see Potter, 1994, for a discussion of the range of techniques that have been employed). It would be inappropriate to exclude studies based upon their measurement of the independent variable, since that disagreement itself represents an important part of the cultivation literature. Thus, we included (and coded) any remotely relevant operationalization of viewing, in order to determine meta-analytically if measuring television exposure in different ways has any consequences. (The meta-analysis showed us a forest of relatively little variation in this regard, despite all the quibbling about the trees.)

## Data Cumulation

In meta-analysis, the individual study is normally treated as the unit of analysis, with each independent study (or independent dataset) contributing a single finding – i.e., a single estimate of effect size – to the cumulative data set that is then meta-analyzed. But many studies (especially cultivation studies) present multiple findings from a given sample – for example, they may analyze several measures or indices of a single construct –which means that the tests are not independent. In these cases, meta-analysts sometimes choose one finding to "represent" a particular study; in other cases they average all the correlations presented, so that each datum in the meta-analysis constitutes an "independent" test.

Independence simply means that each sample represented in the dataset is distinct from all other samples. Each sample represented in the meta-analysis dataset should appear once and only once, otherwise too much weight can be given to results from a particular study. For instance, if a study with ten different findings were "counted" ten different times in the meta-analysis, that would violate the assumption of independence and grant the particular study ten times more importance than it should have. Thus, ideally, every study should be represented once and only once in a meta-analysis.

However, there are some reasons for violating the requirement of independence. In cases where an enormous number of disparate findings would need to be combined to present one, single independent finding from a given sample, one gets the feeling that apples, oranges and golf balls are being compared. This is a particular problem with cultivation, because cultivation studies have been known to present *hundreds* of findings. Some may deal with very different issues (violence, ideology, sex-roles, etc.). Arguably, an averaging of these different types of findings (in this example, across qualitatively distinct dependent areas) is not warranted. The problem is further magnified in cultivation studies that report extensive "subsidiary" findings. Particularly, findings that have been controlled for other variables present valuable information, but can't be included in the normal meta-analysis. Thus, in some of our analyses, especially those of a descriptive nature, we purposely ignored the requirement of independence, being careful to note exactly when we did so. Fortunately, violation of the assumption of independence does not generally affect the estimate of the effect size, but it does affect both the observed variance of effects and the estimate of variance expected by sampling error (Hunter and Schmidt, 1990, p. 480).

After selecting studies, we essentially coded every relevant finding. In some cases, this meant that we had to code literally hundreds of findings. Our basic intention was to average and compile them later on, but we felt it would be best to retain the data in disaggregated form. Yet, cultivation research raises the problem of multiple findings to an extreme. Cultivation studies almost never report a single "effect" (e.g., an F-test or a correlation); it is usual to find many dozens of correlations, or gammas, or ANOVA means tests, etc. in a single paper. All told, our very inclusive selection criteria yielded a set of 87 published studies (indicated by asterisks in the References), and these contained a total of 5,799 different findings that we coded. This very high number of multiple (and non-independent) findings is due to three factors, which required three different solutions in order to achieve a meaningful independent cumulation across studies.

First, some studies contain multiple measures of dependent variables. For example, some studies combine a set of variables into an index of some sort (e.g., the three-item "Mean World Index"), but sometimes the individual items are analyzed separately. When the different dependent variables were intended to be measures of a single underlying dimension or factor, we simply averaged the results and counted them as one finding. This is the least problematic situation, although because of lessened reliability, the estimate of effect size derived from this average is smaller than would be obtained from the same variables if they were combined in index form (Hunter and Schmidt, 1990, p. 456).

Second, many studies present numerous partial correlations; almost 40 percent of 5,799 findings we coded are partials (partial correlations and regression coefficients are used to see if relationships between television exposure and independent variables are spurious as a function of third variables). In some studies, for example, partial correlations between amount of viewing and some dependent variable or index are presented controlling for sex, education, income, age, other media use, and more – first singly and then simultaneously. These are obviously not independent tests, but averaging them is not an appropriate or satisfying way to handle the problem. Meta-analysis typically needs to be done on zero-order effect estimations; it is not advisable to use partial correlations or beta coefficients, because the different estimates of effect size then become non-comparable (Hunter and Schmidt, 1990, p. 502). Therefore, for the meta-analyses, we did not cumulate *any* partials (or betas), and instead analyzed only simple associations. But in some cases we found it useful to analyze partials and other more complex data, ignoring the independence issue when we did so.

This raises a problem in cultivation research, however, given the persistent concerns with spuriousness. This problem is partly ameliorated by addressing the third reason for the high number of non-independent findings, which is that cultivation data are so often analyzed separately within various subgroups. That is, associations are typically presented for males and females, younger and older respondents, and so on. This has been an important technique, for instance, in the analysis of mainstreaming. But since these are overlapping groups (i.e., the same people can count in more than one subgroup), the tests are not independent. It would not make any sense to average all these separate subgroups, since the result would then be equal to the overall data for the sample as a whole.

Therefore, we conducted meta-analyses not only for overall samples, but also separately within key demographic subgroups. That is, after we cumulated and analyzed the data for entire independent samples as a whole, we also carried out separate meta-analyses for males, females, more and less educated respondents, those of different age groups, and so on. As detailed in Chapter 6, these are not independent tests across subgroups (e.g., females versus people with high education), but they are independent between each exclusive demographic division (e.g., male versus female). This is not standard meta-analytic procedure, and Hunter and Schmidt (1990) do argue against subgroup meta-analysis in general (since subgroup analyses reduce degrees of freedom, raise the likelihood of chance relationships, and diminish power), *unless* there's a good theoretical reason to conduct such analyses. Yet, it is difficult to conjure up a body of research with a better theoretical reason to examine subgroups than cultivation. Subgroup meta-analysis thus seemed both highly justifiable and reasonable given the nature of cultivation data and the pressing need to examine subgroup variations in ways other than as moderator variables. About 30 percent of the findings in our sample were from overall samples, the rest dealt with various subgroups, with gender being the most frequent variable used to create subgroups (about 10 percent of the findings are broken down by gender). For simplicity, findings coded as applying to "sub-subgroups" (as in "younger females") were dropped from the final analysis.

## Further Reductions and Modifications

As should be clear, cultivation research presents a bewildering variety of data about widely divergent issues, obtained using very different methods and measures, from many distinct samples, subjected to diverse statistical procedures, and with little consistency in the kinds of information reported that meta-analysis should ideally have (e.g., reliability estimates, standard deviations, etc.). Some studies report findings from several different data sets; some papers report results of more than one distinct study. And some datasets are used in numerous publications. All this means that further modification and paring down was required before meta-analysis could be done.

As is typical in meta-analysis, we compiled findings that were expressed as correlations. Thus, if a given study had reported a finding of $r = .10$ for a relationship between exposure to TV and some variable, that was the most relevant information to be coded (along with the $N$ of that finding). We chose correlations as the standard metric, because they are the most common across the literature. For our database, we coded 676 simple correlations (along with another 2,363 *partial* correlations which, as we've noted, could not be part of the meta-analysis proper).

But correlations are not always available. For instance, some cultivation studies have used ANOVA to examine mean differences on some dependent variable across light, medium and heavy viewers. Formulas do exist to transform these kinds of data to an equivalent $r$ coefficient, but unfortunately the published studies rarely contain the variance information necessary to do this. Therefore, no findings based on mean differences across viewing groups were included; this excludes 250 findings that we coded.

Fortunately, however, many other findings could be transformed to an $r$ metric. In particular, cultivation research often uses gamma coefficients – about 30 percent of the 5,799 total findings are gammas. Gammas are roughly conceptually comparable to Pearson correlations although they are based on ordinal data (for a discussion of some computational advantages of gamma, see Nelson, 1986). Extensive searching and consulting provided no guidance on how to transform a gamma to an $r$, so we developed our own formula through a modified Monte Carlo simulation. We calculated both $r$'s and gammas of TV viewing with 100 randomly selected variables from the 1994 NORC General Social Survey. The $r$'s were all based on continuous (interval-level) data, and the gammas were computed with the variables collapsed into ordinal scales. Gamma and $r$ were highly correlated ($r = .946$, adjusted $R^2 = .895$). A variety of linear, nonlinear and polynomial regression equations were calculated, and in *every* case it turned out that gamma alone accounted for over 90 percent of the variance in $r$; no other transformation or variable added more than .0014 percent to the explained variance. Thus, we used the obtained regression formula ($r = .6024 *$ gamma $- .0032$) to achieve an approximate but satisfactory transformation of gamma to $r$. At the end of coding, we were able to transform over 1,700 gammas (a very large chunk of the findings) to a correlational metric.

## Instrument

In most meta-analyses, the data-gathering instrument is not of paramount importance, since only a few discrete bits of information are recorded for each study. In our study, however, we were ambitious about the sorts of information we wished to collect, and our instrument was therefore fairly extensive. Much information was coded on each of the findings (although our central analysis focused mainly on the independent, cumulated data).

For each study, we recorded relevant identifying information (author, year of publication and journal) and we noted the date(s) when the data were collected (some studies report data gathered over multiple years). Next, we coded how television viewing was measured in each study (almost two-thirds of the findings were self-reports of daily viewing hours; the next most common was the constructed week, accounting for 14 percent of the results). We also coded how the data were collected (over 60 percent are from questionnaires, and about 30 percent are from personal interviews). Also coded were the dependent and the independent variable (over 75 percent reflected overall viewing, although many others such as specific genres, foreign programs, etc. were coded), and the subgroup (if any) to which the result applied.

For each finding we recorded the degrees of freedom and/or the $N$ of the finding. (Sample sizes for the studies ranged from $N = 63$ to $N = 14,405$; for individual findings, $N$'s ranged from 11 to 9,125). In many cases we were forced to estimate these, due to inconsistencies in data reporting. Where we could make a justifiable estimate (from other information in the study) we did so. In some cases, there was not enough information to make these estimates. We also recorded the significance of each finding (although Hunter and Schmidt, 1990, do not think that significance is very important), often only estimating significance *level* (such as .05 or less) based on asterisks or other codes presented in summary tables.

Also, we coded the sample's country of origin and the general nature of the sample. This allowed us to differentiate between, for example, convenience samples of undergraduates and national probability samples of adults, and indicates the comprehensiveness and age focus of the sample from which the data emerged. Although over three-quarters of the findings are from the USA, over a dozen countries are represented; 550 findings, nearly 10 percent, are from Argentina. About a third of the findings are from adolescents, and another third from national adult samples; the remainder are divided among college student samples, adult convenience samples, and others.

As we extracted the findings from each included study and further condensed the database during cumulation, we interacted continuously to insure quality of data entry. Independent coders were not used, due to the highly specialized nature of interpreting cultivation findings. While this may have left some possibilities for coding bias, we feel it helped insure a more accurate dataset. It is important to note that, once informed judgments were made, this was more of a transcribing process than a data coding exercise. Moreover, as Hunter and Schmidt remind us, it is "well known that meta-analysts do not make errors" (1990, p. 262).

### Notes on the GSS

Some of the analyses we used rely on the General Social Survey (GSS). Results from the GSS have played a crucially important role in cultivation research. Approximately 28 percent of the results that we gathered together in our meta-analysis came originally from the GSS. GSS results also played a key role in the early debates about cultivation, as reanalyses by Hirsch, Hughes and others opened up a variety of questions. Because GSS results play such a central role, we offer some brief notes about the data.

Literally hundreds of studies have been conducted with GSS data, across a wide variety of fields of inquiry. For cultivation purposes, the data from the GSS provide unquestionably the best source of data, outside of our own meta-analysis. The reason is that the GSS is the only data source that has been gathered virtually yearly since 1972, and is certainly the only data source in that span with so many questions of real interest to cultivation analysts.

Of course, the most important thing is that questions on television viewing have been asked every year. The question (wording) is probably not quite as specific and exact as all might like, but this is offset by the availability of TV viewing data in almost very year of the GSS.

Combined with that, the GSS questions on social and political beliefs really facilitated the growth of cultivation into diverse substantive areas. Measures of political orientation, support for abortion, federal spending, beliefs about sex-roles, attitudes about race, fear of crime, institutional confidence, and a host of others are all regularly included in the GSS, and all of these can be easily correlated to television viewing. Many cultivation articles published by Gerbner et al. used this data source.

Approximately every year, the GSS is conducted through face-to-face personal interviews with a national sample of non-institutionalized adults aged 18 and greater. Details of the sampling procedures can be found in Smith (1993). Each time the GSS is conducted a sample of roughly 1,500 individuals is gathered, though recently the GSS has moved toward larger samples conducted bi-yearly. The quality of the samples is very high (again, these are personal interviews with national samples), much higher than many of the convenience or non-probability sampling methods used in social research.

In compiling the data for meta-analysis, and especially in the process of "boiling down" the full dataset of all findings into a dataset of *independent* findings only, the GSS data presented some special challenges. For example, one study might present data from the 1993 survey, another might use the 1994 survey, and a third might analyze the two years combined into a single dataset; although the 1993 and 1994 surveys are completely independent, neither is independent from the combined 1993–94 samples. Published cultivation work presented data from sixteen independent (i.e., yearly) GSS samples, but data for another nineteen *combination* samples were also published. Fortunately, in most cases, when these samples were sorted by the dependent variable analyzed, the overlaps disappeared; thus, we could analyze findings that were independent *for a specific dependent variable*. When data were presented for both individual years and combined years, only the individual year data were retained for analysis.

In this book, we used a cumulative GSS sample encompassing the years 1975–94 for our "mega" analysis in Chapter 7. The total sample size of this cumulative sample is over 30,000. However, due to some particularities of the sampling process, most of our analyses use about 10–12,000 of these sampled individuals. This is mostly due to the fact that GSS uses sample "ballots" to reduce the burden of having to ask all the questions of all the respondents. Thus, when television exposure is measured on a separate ballot from dependent variables for some respondents, the usable base is thereby reduced. For regression analyses with many variables, the sample size is normally reduced by two-thirds from the total. Still, a national sample of 10–12,000 individuals that spans ten or twenty years, and drawn with probability sampling techniques, is obviously a highly desirable and valuable dataset.

## Final Note

This Appendix, we hope, conveys at least a hint of the extent to which this meta-analysis of cultivation research posed a daunting challenge of ingenuity and endurance. Especially endurance. We also hope it convinces the reader of the extent to which we strove to be as meticulous as possible over the four years during which we coded and meta-analyzed thousands of cultivation findings. Nevertheless, this Appendix only presents a brief summary of our methodological travails. There were many decisions about coding, cumulation, analysis, collapsing, etc. which allowed for subjectivity to creep in along the way. Alas, even meta-analysis cannot be perfectly objective. Fortunately (or not), we have retained copious notes and extensive documentation of the hundreds of coding decisions we made along the way. Although these are far too technical and detailed to warrant publication, we shall gladly share them with any interested researcher or archaeologist.

# References

References marked with an asterisk indicate studies in our meta-analysis.

Allen, M., Emmers, T., Gebhardt, L. and Giery, M. (1995). Exposure to pornography and acceptance of rape myths. *Journal of Communication*, 45(1), 5–26.

Altemeyer, R. (1988). *Enemies of freedom: understanding right-wing authoritarianism*. San Francisco: Jossey-Bass Publishers.

Altheide, D. (1985). *Media power*. Beverly Hills: Sage.

*Armstrong, B. and Neuendorf, K. (1992). TV entertainment, news and racial perceptions of college students. *Journal of Communication*, 42(3), 153–76.

Aukney, R., Heilman, P. and Kolff, J. (1996). Newspaper coverage of the coronary artery bypass grafting report. *Science Communication*, 18(2):153–64.

Bagdikian, B. (1997). *The media monopoly*. Boston: Beacon Press, 1997.

Baker, R. K. and Ball, S. J. (eds.) (1969). *Violence in the media*. Staff Report to the National Commission on the Causes and Prevention of Violence. Washington, DC: US Government Printing Office.

Bandura, A. (1965). Influence of models' reinforcement contingencies on acquisition of imitative responses. *Journal of Personality and Social Psychology*, 63, 589–95.

Barnouw, E. (1978). *The sponsor*. New York: Oxford University Press.

Basalla, G. (1976). Pop science: the depiction of science in popular culture. In G. Holton and W. Blanpied (eds), *Science and its public* (pp. 261–78). Boston, MA: Beacon.

Bell, D. (1976). *The coming of post-industrial society: a venture in social forecasting*. New York: Basic Books.

Beniger, J. (1986). *The control revolution: technological and economic origins of the information society*. Cambridge, MA: Harvard University Press, 1986.

*Berman, D. and Stookey, J. (1980). Adolescents, TV and support for government. *Public Opinion Quarterly*, 44, 330–40.

Blank, D. (1977a). The Gerbner Violence Profile. *Journal of Broadcasting*, 21(3), 273–9.

(1977b). Final comments on the Violence Profile. *Journal of Broadcasting*, 21(3), 287–96.

Bogart, L. (1972). *The age of television: a study of viewing habits and the impact of television on American life*. New York: Ungar.

*Bosompra, K. (1993). TV, sexual behavior and attitudes towards AIDS: a study in cultivation analysis. *Africa Media Review*, 7(3), 35–62.

*Bouwman, H. (1984). Cultivation analysis: the Dutch case. In G. Melischek, K. Rosengren and J. Stappers (eds.), *Cultural indicators: an international symposium* (pp. 407–22). Vienna: Verlag der Osterreichischen Akademie der Wissenschaften.

Brown, N., Crawford, P. and Lewis, A. (1995). Interaction, language and the narrative turn in psychology and psychiatry. *Social Science and Medicine*, 43(11), 569–1578.

Bruner, J. S. (1986). *Actual minds, possible worlds.* Cambridge, MA: Harvard University Press.

(1990). *Acts of meaning.* Cambridge, MA: Harvard University Press.

(1991). The narrative construction of reality. *Critical Inquiry*, 18, 1–21.

Bryant, J. (1986). The road most traveled: yet another cultivation critique. *Journal of Broadcasting & Electronic Media*, 30, 231–5.

Bryant, J., Carveth, R. and Brown, D. (1981). Television viewing and anxiety: an experimental examination. *Journal of Communication*, 31(1), 106–19.

*Buerkel-Rothfuss, N. and Mayes, S. (1981). Soap opera viewing: The cultivation effect. *Journal of Communication*, 31(3), 108–15.

Burrowes, C. (1996). From functionalism to cultural studies: manifest ruptures and latent continuities. *Communication Theory*, 6(1), 88–103.

Campbell, D. (1950). The indirect assessment of social attitudes. *Psychological Bulletin*, 47, 15–38.

*Carlson, J. (1985). *Prime time law enforcement: crime show viewing and attitudes toward the criminal justice system.* New York: Praeger.

*(1993). Television viewing: cultivating perceptions of affluence and support for capitalist values. *Political Communication*, 10, 243–57.

*Carveth, R. and Alexander, A. (1985). Soap opera viewing motivations and the cultivation process. *Journal of Broadcasting & Electronic Media*, 29, 259–73.

Centerwall, B. (1993). Television and violent crime. *Public Interest*, 111, 56–71.

Chaiken, S., Liberman, A. and Eagly, A. (1989). Heuristic and systematic processing within and beyond the persuasion context. In J. Uleman and J. Bargh (eds.), *Unintended thought* (pp. 212–52). New York: Guilford.

*Choi, J. and Tamborini, R. (1988). Communication-acculturation and the cultivation hypothesis: a comparative study between two Korean communities in the US. *Howard Journal of Communication*, 1(1), 57–74.

Coffin, T. and Tuchman, S. (1972–73a). Rating television programs for violence: a comparison of five surveys. *Journal of Broadcasting*, 17(1), 3–20.

(1972–73b). A question of validity. Some comments on 'apples, oranges, and the kitchen sink'. *Journal of Broadcasting*, 17(1), 31–3.

Cook, T., Kendzierski, D. and Thomas, S. (1983). The implicit assumptions of television research: an analysis of the 1982 NIMH report on television and behavior. *Public Opinion Quarterly*, 47, 161–201.

Cook, S. and Sellitz, S. (1964). A multiple-indicator approach to attitude measurement. *Psychological Bulletin*, 62, 36–55.

Dahlgren, P. (1995). *Television and the public sphere.* London: Sage.

Davis, R. (1963). Scientists and engineers: the public's image. Paper presented at the American Society for Engineering Education Annual Meeting, Philadelphia, PA.

References                                                              253

Demers, D. (1996). *The menace of the corporate newspaper: fact or fiction?* Ames: Iowa State University Press, 1996.

Dizard, W. (1982). *The coming information age: an overview of technology, economics, and politics.* New York: Longman.

Dobrow, J. (1990). Patterns of viewing and VCR use. In N. Signorielli and M. Morgan (eds.) *Cultivation analysis.* Newbury Park, CA: Sage.

*Doob, A. and Macdonald, G. (1979). Television viewing and fear of victimization: is the relationship causal? *Journal of Personality and Social Psychology,* 37(2), 170–9.

Dornan, C. (1990). Some problems in conceptualizing the issue of "science in the media". *Critical Studies in Mass Communication,* 7(1), 48–71.

Eastman, S. and Newton, G. (1995). Delineating grazing: observations of remote control use. *Journal of Communication,* 45(1), 77–95.

Eleey, M., Gerbner, G. and (Tedesco) Signorielli, N. (1972–73a). Apples, oranges, and the kitchen sink: an analysis and guide to the comparison of "Violence Ratings." *Journal of Broadcasting,* 17(1), 21–31.

(1972–73b). Validity indeed! *Journal of Broadcasting,* 17(1), 34–35.

Fisher, W. (1984). Narration as a human communication paradigm: the case of public moral argument. *Communication Mongraphs,* 51.

*Fox, W. and Philliber, W. (1978). Television viewing and the perception of affluence. *Sociological Quarterly,* 19(1), 103–12.

Gerbner, G. (1958). On content analysis and critical research in mass communication. *AV Communication Review,* 6, 85–108.

(1959). Education and challenge of mass culture. *Audio-Visual Communication Review,* 7(4), 264–78.

(1969). Toward 'Cultural Indicators': the analysis of mass mediated message systems. *AV Communication Review,* 17, 137–48.

(1970). Cultural Indicators: the case of violence in television drama. *The Annals of the American Academy of Political and Social Science,* 388, 69–81.

(1972). Communication and social environment. *Scientific American,* 227(3), 152–60.

(1973). Cultural Indicators: the third voice. In G. Gerbner, L. Gross and W. Melody (eds.), *Communications technology and social policy* (pp. 555–73). New York: John Wiley and Sons.

(1977). Television: the new state religion? *et cetera,* 34(2), 145–50.

(1978). The dynamics of cultural resistance. In G. Tuchman, A. Daniels and J. Benet (eds.), *Hearth and home: images of women in the mass media* (pp. 46–50). New York: Oxford University Press.

(1986). The symbolic context of action and communication. In R. Rosnow and M. Georgoudi (eds.), *Contextualism and understanding in behavioral science.* New York: Praeger, 1986.

(1990). Epilogue: advancing on the path of righteousness (maybe). In N. Signorielli and M. Morgan (eds.), *Cultivation analysis: new directions in media effects research* (pp. 249–62). Newbury Park: Sage.

(1997). PROD press release.

*Gerbner, G. and Gross, L. (1976). Living with television: The Violence Profile. *Journal of Communication,* 26(2), 173–99.

(1979). Editorial response: a reply to Newcomb's 'humanistic critique.' *Communication Research*, 6, 223–30.

*Gerbner, G., Gross, L., Eleey, M., Jackson-Beeck, M., Jeffries-Fox, S. and Signorielli, N. (1977). TV Violence Profile No. 8: the highlights. *Journal of Communication*, 27(2), 171–80.

Gerbner, G., Gross, L., Hoover, S., Morgan, M., Signorielli, N., Cotugno, H. and Wuthnow, R. (1984). Religion and television. Philadelphia: The Annenberg School of Communications, University of Pennsylvania.

Gerbner, G., Gross, L. Eleey, M., Jackson-Beeck, Jeffries-Fox, S. and Signorielli, N. (1977a). The Gerbner Violence Profile – an analysis of the CBS report. *Journal of Broadcasting*, 21(3), 280–286.

(1977b). One more time: an analysis of the CBS 'Final Comments of the Violence Profile.' *Journal of Broadcasting*, 21(3), 297–303.

*Gerbner, G., Gross, L., Jackson-Beeck, M., Jeffries-Fox, S. and Signorielli, N. (1978). Cultural Indicators: Violence Profile No. 9. *Journal of Communication*, 28(3), 176–207.

*Gerbner, G., Gross, L., Morgan, M. and Signorielli, N. (1980a). The "mainstreaming" of America: Violence Profile No. 11. *Journal of Communication*, 30(3), 10–29.

(1980b) Violence Profile No. 11: trends in network television drama and viewer conceptions of social reality 1967–1979. Philadelphia: The Annenberg School of Communications, University of Pennsylvania.

(1980c). Some additional comments on cultivation analysis. *Public Opinion Quarterly*, 44, 408–10.

(1981a). On the limits of "The limits of advocacy research": response to Hirsch. *Public Opinion Quarterly*, 45, 116–18.

*(1981b). A curious journey into the scary world of Paul Hirsch. *Communication Research*, 8, 39–72.

(1981c). Final reply to Hirsch. *Communication Research*, 8, 259–80.

*(1981d). Scientists on the TV screen. *Society*, May/June, 41–4.

(1982). Charting the mainstream: television's contributions to political orientations. *Journal of Communication*, 32(2), 100–27.

*(1984). The political correlates of television viewing. *Public Opinion Quarterly*, 48, 283–300.

(1985). Television entertainment and viewer's conceptions of science. Research report to the National Science Foundation, the Annenberg School of Communications, University of Pennsylvania.

*(1986). Living with television: the dynamics of the cultivation process. In J. Bryant and D. Zillman (eds.), *Perspectives on media effects* (pp. 17–40). New Jersey: Lawrence Erlbaum.

*(1994). Growing up with television: the cultivation perspective. In J. Bryant and D. Zillman (eds.), *Media effects: advances in theory and research* (pp. 17–41). New Jersey: Lawrence Erlbaum.

*Gerbner, G., Gross, L., Signorielli, N. and Morgan, M. (1980). Aging with television: images on television drama and conceptions of social reality. *Journal of Communication*, 30(1), 37–47.

Gerbner, G., Gross, L., Signorielli, N. Morgan, M. and Jackson-Beeck, M. (1979)

The Demonstration of Power: Violence Profile No. 10. *Journal of Communication*, 29(3), 177–196.

*Gerbner, G., Morgan, M. and Signorielli, N. (1982). Programming health portrayals: what viewers see, say and do. In D. Pearl, L. Bouthilet and J. Lazar (eds.), *Television and behavior: ten years of scientific progress and implications for the 80's, Vol. II, technical reviews* (pp. 291–307). Rockville, MD: NIMH.

Gerbner, G. and Signorielli, N. (1978). The world of television news. In W. Adams and F. Schriebman (eds.), *Television news archives: issues in content research* (pp. 189–96). Washington, DC: George Washington University.

Gerrig, R. (1993). *Experiencing narrative worlds.* New Haven, CT: Yale University Press.

Gilder, G. (1994). *Life after television.* New York: Norton.

Gitlin, T. (1982). Media sociology: the dominant paradigm. In *Mass Communication Review Yearbook*, 1981. Beverly Hills, CA: Sage, pp. 50–73.

Glynn, E. (1956). Television and the American character: a psychiatrist looks at television. In W. Elliot (ed.), *Television's impact on American culture* (pp. 175–82). East Lansing: Michigan State University Press.

Goethals, G. (1981). *The TV ritual: worship at the video altar.* Boston: Beacon Press.

Goldman, S. (1989). Images of technology in popular films: discussion and filmography. *Science, Technology, and Human Values*, 14(3), 275–301.

Goodell, R. (1977). *The visible scientists.* Boston: Little Brown.

Gramsci, A. (1971). *Selections from the prison notebooks.* New York: International Publishers.

Gross, L. (1977). Television as a Trojan horse. *School Media Quarterly*, 5(3), 175–80.

*(1984). The cultivation of intolerance: TV, blacks and gays. In G. Melischek, K. Rosengren and J. Stappers (eds.), *Cultural indicators: an international symposium* (pp. 345–63). Vienna: Verlag der Osterreichischen Akademie der Wissenschaften.

*Gross, L. and Jeffries-Fox, S. (1978). What do you want to be when you grow up, little girl? In G. Tuchman, A. Daniels and J. Benet (eds.), *Hearth and home: images of women in the mass media* (pp. 240–65). New York: Oxford University Press.

*Gross, L. and Morgan, M. (1985). Television and enculturation. In J. Dominick and J. Fletcher (eds.), *Broadcasting research methods* (pp. 221–34). Boston: Allyn and Bacon.

Gunter, B. and Wober, M. (1983a). Television viewing and public perceptions of hazards to life. *Journal of Environmental Psychology*, 3, 325–35.

*(1983b). Television viewing and public trust. *British Journal of Social Psychology*, 22, 174–6.

Hammond, K. (1948). Measuring attitude by error choice: an indirect method. *Journal of Abnormal and Social Psychology*, 43, 38–48.

Haney, C. and Manzolati, J. (1981). Television criminology: network illusions of criminal justice realities. In E. Aronson (ed.), *Readings about the social animal* (pp. 125–36). San Francisco: Freeman.

*Hawkins, R. and Pingree, S. (1980). Some processes in the cultivation effect. *Communication Research*, 7, 193–226.

  *(1981). Uniform content and habitual viewing: unnecessary assumptions in social reality effects. *Human Communication Research*, 7, 291–301.

  (1982) Television's influence on social reality. In D. Pearl, L. Bouthilet and J. Lazar (eds.), *Television and behavior: ten years of scientific progress and implications for the 80's, Vol. II, technical reviews* (pp. 224–7). Rockville, MD: NIMH.

  (1990). Divergent psychological processes in constructing social reality from mass media content. In N. Signorielli and M. Morgan (eds.), *Cultivation analysis: new directions in media effects research* (pp. 35–50). Newbury Park: Sage.

*Hawkins, R., Pingree, S. and Adler, I. (1987). Searching for cognitive processes in the cultivation effect. *Human Communication Research*, 13, 553–77.

Herman, E. and Chomsky, N. (1988). *Manufacturing consent*. New York: Pantheon.

Herrett-Skjellum, J. and Allen, M. (1996). Television programming and sex stereotyping: a meta-analysis. In B. R. Burleson (ed.), *Communication yearbook 19* (pp. 157–85). Thousand Oaks, CA: Sage.

Hevern, V. (1997). Narrative psychology: Internet and resource guide. Syracuse, NY: http://maple.lemoyne.edu/~hevern/narpsych.html.

Hilgartner, S. (1990). The dominant view of popularization: conceptual problems, political uses. *Social Studies of Science*, 20(3), 519–39.

Himmelweit, H., Oppenheim, A. and Vince, P. (1958). *Television and the child: an empirical study of the effect of television on the young*. New York: Oxford University Press.

*Hirsch, P. (1980). The 'scary world' of the nonviewer and other anomalies: a reanalysis of Gerbner et al.'s findings on cultivation analysis. *Communication Research*, 7, 403–56.

  (1981a). On not learning from one's own mistakes: a reanalysis of Gerbner et al.'s findings on cultivation analysis, pt. II. *Communication Research*, 8, 3–37.

  (1981b). Distinguishing good speculation from bad theory: rejoinder to Gerbner et al. *Communication Research*, 8, 73–95.

*Hoover, S. (1990). Television, religion and religious television: purposes and cross purposes. In N. Signorielli and M. Morgan (eds.), *Cultivation analysis: new directions in media effects research* (pp. 123–40). Newbury Park, CA: Sage.

Hornig, S. (1990). Television's 'nova' and the construction of scientific truth. *Critical Studies in Mass Communication*, 7, 11–23.

Huesmann, L. and Eron, L. (eds.) (1986). *Television and the aggressive child: a cross-national comparison*. Hillsdale, NJ: Erlbaum.

*Hughes, M. (1980). The fruits of cultivation analysis: a re-examination of the effects of television watching on fear of victimization, alienation, and the approval of violence. *Public Opinion Quarterly*, 44, 287–302.

Hunter, J. and Schmidt, F. (1990). *Methods of meta-analysis: correcting error and bias in research findings*. Newbury Park: Sage.

Jackson-Beeck, M. (1977). The non-viewers: Who are they? *Journal of Communication*, 27(3), 65–72.

  (1979). Interpersonal and mass communication in children's political socialization. *Journalism Quarterly*, 56(1), 48–53.

Jeffries-Fox, S. and Signorielli, N. (1979). Television and children's conceptions about occupations. In H. S. Dordick (ed.), *Proceedings of the Sixth Annual Telecommunication Policy Research Conference* (pp. 21–38). Lexington, MA: Lexington Books.

Jhally, S. and Lewis, J. (1992). *Enlightened racism: the Cosby show, audiences, and the myth of the American dream.* Boulder: Westview Press.

Jhally, S. and Livant, B. (1986). Watching as working: the valorization of audience consciousness. *Journal of Communication*, 36(3), 124–43.

*Kang, J. and Morgan, M. (1988). Culture clash: US TV programs in Korea. *Journalism Quarterly*, 65, 431–8.

Katz, E. and Lazarsfeld, P. (1955). *Personal influence: the part played by people in the flow of mass communications.* New York: Free Press.

*Kiecolt, J. and Sayles, M. (1988). TV and the cultivation of attitudes toward subordinate groups. *Sociological Spectrum*, 8, 19–33.

Kim, M. and Hunter, J. (1993). Attitude-behavior relations: a meta-analysis of attitude relevance and topic. *Journal of Communication*, 43(1), 101–42.

Kincaid, H. (1994). Assessing functional explanation in the social sciences. In M. Martin and L. McIntyre (eds.) *Readings in the philosophy of social science* (pp. 414–28). Cambridge, MA: MIT Press.

Klapper, J. (1960). *The effects of mass communication.* Glencoe, IL: Free Press.

Krcmar, M. and Cantor, M. (1997). The role of television advisories and ratings in parent-child discussion of television viewing choices. *Journal of Broadcasting & Electronic Media*, 41, (3) 393–411.

Lazarsfeld, P. and R. Merton. (1948). Mass communication, popular taste, and organized social action. In S. Bryson (ed.), *The communication of ideas* (pp. 95–118). New York: Harper.

Lent, J. (ed.) (1995). *A different road taken: profiles in critical communication.* Boulder: Westview.

Lewenstein, B. (1989). Magazine publishing and popular science after World War II. *American Journalism* 6(4), 218–34.

Lewis, J. (1991). *The ideological octopus: an exploration of television and its audience.* New York: Routledge.

Lewis, J., Jhally, S. and Morgan, M. (1991). The Gulf War: a study of the media, public opinion, and public knowledge. Unpublished Research Report, Center for the Study of Communication, University of Massachusetts.

Liebert, R. (1982). Review of television, imagination, and aggression: a study of preschoolers. *Contemporary Psychology*, 27(11): 896–7.

Lin, C. (1990). Audience activity and VCR use. In J. Dobrow (ed.), *Social and cultural aspects of VCR use.* Hillsdale, NJ: Erlbaum.

Lippman, W. (1922). *Public opinion.* London: Transaction.

Long, M. and Steinke, J. (1996). The thrill of everyday science: images of science and scientists on children's educational science shows in the United States. *Public Understanding of Science*, 5(2), 101–20.

Mander, G. (1991). *In the absence of the sacred.* San Francisco: Sierra Club.

Mares, M. (1996). The role of source confusions in television's cultivation of social reality judgements. *Human Communication Research*, 23, 278–97.

Marvin, C. (1988). *When old technologies were new: thinking about electric communication in the late nineteenth century.* New York: Oxford University Press.

*Matabane, P. (1988). Television and the black audience: cultivating moderate perspectives on racial integration. *Journal of Communication*, 38(4), 21–31.

McChesney, R. (1993). *Telecommunications, mass media, and democracy: the battle for the control of US broadcasting, 1928–1935.* New York: Oxford University Press.

    (1997). *Corporate media and the threat to democracy.* New York: Seven Stories Press.

McCombs, M. (1994). News influence on our pictures of the world. In J. Bryant and D. Zillman (eds.), *Media Effects* (pp. 1–16). Hillsdale, NJ: Lawrence Erlbaum.

McKibben, B. (1992). *The age of missing information.* New York: Random House.

    (1994). *The comforting whirlwind.* Grand Rapids, MI: Eerdmans.

McLeod, J., Atkin, C. and Chaffee, S. (1972a). Adolescents, parents, and television use: adolescent self-report measures from Maryland and Wisconsin samples. In G. A. Comstock and E. A. Rubinstein (eds.), *Television and social behavior (Vol. III). Television and adolescent aggressiveness* (pp. 173–238). Washington: Government Printing Office.

    (1972b). Adolescents, parents, and television use: self-report and other-report measures from the Wisconsin samples. In G. A. Comstock and E. A. Rubinstein (eds.), *Television and social behavior (Vol. III). Television and adolescent aggressiveness* (pp. 239–313). Washington: Government Printing Office.

Mead, M. and Metraux, R. (1957). Image of the scientist among high school students. *Science*, 126, 384–90.

Mediascope. (1996). *National television violence study.* http://www.mediascope.org/ntvs1.htm

Milavsky, J., Kessler, R., Stipp, H. and Rubens, W. (1982). *Television and aggression: a panel study.* New York: Academic Press.

Miller, M. (1996). Free the media. *The Nation*, 6 June.

Morgan, M. (1980). Television viewing and reading: does more equal better? *Journal of Communication*, 30(1), 159–65.

    *(1982). Television and adolescents' sex-role stereotypes: a longitudinal study. *Journal of Personality and Social Psychology*, 43, 947–55.

    (1983). Symbolic victimization and real-world fear. *Human Communication Research*, 9, 146–57.

    *(1984). Heavy television viewing and perceived quality of life. *Journalism Quarterly*, 61, 499–504.

    (1986). Television and the erosion of regional diversity. *Journal of Broadcasting & Electronic Media*, 30, 123–39.

    *(1987). Television, sex-role attitudes and sex-role behavior. *Journal of Early Adolescence*, 7, 269–82.

    *(1990). International cultivation analysis. In N. Signorielli and M. Morgan (eds.), *Cultivation analysis: new directions in media effects research* (pp. 225–48). Newbury Park: Sage.

    (1995). The critical contribution of George Gerbner. In J. Lent (ed.), *A different road taken: profiles in critical communication* (pp. 99–117). Boulder: Westview.

Morgan M., Alexander, A., Shanahan, J. and Harris, C. (1990). Adolescents, VCRs, and the family environment. *Communication Research*, 17(1), 83–106.

Morgan, M. and Gross, L. (1982). Television and educational achievement and aspiration. In D. Pearl, L. Bouthilet and J. Lazar (eds.), *Television and behav-*

*ior: ten years of scientific progress and implications for the 80's, Vol. II, technical reviews* (pp. 78–90). Rockville, MD: NIMH.

*Morgan, M. and Rothschild, N. (1983). Impact of the new TV technology: cable TV, peers and sex-role cultivation in the electronic environment. *Youth and Society*, 15, 33–50.

*Morgan, M. and Shanahan, J. (1991a). Do VCR's change the TV picture?: VCR's and the cultivation process. *American Behavioral Scientist*, 35, 122–35.

*(1991b). Television and the cultivation of political attitudes in Argentina. *Journal of Communication*, 41(1), 88–103.

*(1992a). Comparative cultivation analysis: television and adolescents in Argentina and Taiwan. In F. Korzenny and S. Ting-Toomey (eds.), *Mass media effects across cultures* (pp. 173–97). Newbury Park: Sage.

*(1992b). Television viewing and voting, 1975–1989. *Electoral Studies*, 11, 3–20.

*(1995). *Democracy tango: television, adolescents, and authoritarian tensions in Argentina*. Cresskill, NJ: Hampton Press.

(1997). *Two decades of cultivation research: an appraisal and a meta-analysis*. In B. Burleson (ed.), *Communication Yearbook 20* (pp. 1–45). Thousand Oaks: Sage.

*Morgan, M., Shanahan, J. and Harris, C. (1990). VCRs and the effects of television: new diversity or more of the same? In J. Dobrow (ed.), *Social and cultural aspects of VCR use* (pp. 107–23). Hillsdale, NJ: Erlbaum.

Morgan, M. and Signorielli, N. (1990). Cultivation analysis: conceptualization and methodology. In N. Signorielli and M. Morgan (eds.), *Cultivation analysis: new directions in media effects research* (pp. 13–34). Newbury Park: Sage.

Mullen, B. (1989). *Advanced BASIC meta-analysis*. Hillsdale, NJ: Erlbaum.

National Opinion Research Center. (1994). *General Social Surveys: cumulative codebook*. Chicago: University of Chicago.

National Science Board. (1991). Public science literacy and attitudes towards science and technology. In National Science Board (ed.), *Science and engineering indicators – 1991*. Washington, D.C.: US Government Printing Office.

Negroponte, N. (1994). Prime time is my time: the blockbuster myth. *Wired*, 1 August.

Nelkin, D. (1990). Selling science. *Physics Today*, 43, 41–46.

Nelson, T. (1986). Basic programs for computation of the Goodman-Kruskal gamma coefficient. *Bulletin of the Psychonomic Society*, 24, 281–3.

Neville, T. (1980). *Television viewing and the expression of interpersonal mistrust*. Unpublished doctoral dissertation. Princeton, NJ: Princeton University.

Newcomb, H. (1978). Assessing the Violence Profile of Gerbner and Gross: a humanistic critique and suggestion. *Communication Research*, 5, 264–82.

Newhagen, J. and Lewenstein, M. (1992). Cultivation and exposure to television following the 1989 Loma Prieta earthquake. *Mass Comm Review*, 18, 49–56.

Noelle-Neumann, E. (1993). *The spiral of silence: public opinion, our social skin*. Chicago: University of Chicago Press.

Novak, M. (1986). Television shapes the soul. In G. Gumpert and R. Cathcart (eds.), *Inter/Media: Interpersonal Communication in a Media World* (pp. 583–96). New York: Oxford University Press.

O'Guinn, T. and Shrum, L. (1997). The role of television in the construction of consumer social reality, *Journal of Consumer Research*, 23(4), 278–94.

*O'Keefe, G. (1984). Public views on crime: TV exposure and media credibility. In R. Bostrom (ed.), *Communication Yearbook 8* (pp. 514–35). Newbury Park: Sage.

O'Keefe, G. and Figge, M. (1997). A guilt-based explanation of door-in-the-face influence strategy. *Human Communication Research*, 24(1), 64–81.

Ogles, R. (1987). Cultivation analysis: theory, methodology, and current research on television-influenced constructions of social reality. *Mass Comm Review*, 14, 43–53.

*Ogles, R. and Sparks, G. (1994). Question specificity and perceived probability of criminal victimization. *Mass Comm Review*, 20, 51–61.

*Passuth, P. and Cook, F. (1985). Effects of TV viewing on knowledge and attitudes about older adults: a critical reexamination. *The Gerontologist*, 25, 69–77.

Pearl, D., Bouthilet, L. and Lazar, J. (eds.) (1982). *Television and behavior: ten years of scientific progress and implications for the 80's. Vol. II: technical reviews.* Rockville, MD: NIMH.

Perse, E. (1986). Soap opera viewing patterns of college students and cultivation. *Journal of Broadcasting & Electronic Media*, 30(2), 175–93.

*(1990). Cultivation and involvement with local television news. In N. Signorielli and M. Morgan (eds.), *Cultivation analysis: new directions in media effects research* (pp. 51–70). Newbury Park: Sage.

*Perse, E., Ferguson, D. and McLeod, D. (1994). Cultivation in the newer media environment. *Communication Research*, 21, 79–104.

*Pfau, M., Mullen, L., Diedrich, T. and Garrow, K. (1995). Television viewing and public perceptions of attorneys. *Human Communication Research*, 21, 307–30.

Phekoo, C., Driscoll, P. and Salwen, M. (1996). US television viewing in Trinidad: cultural consequences on adolescents. *Gazette*, 57(2), 97–111.

*Piepe, A., Charlton, P. and Morey, J. (1990). Politics and television viewing in England: hegemony or pluralism? *Journal of Communication*, 40(1), 24–35.

*Pingree, S. (1983). Children's cognitive processes in constructing social reality. *Journalism Quarterly*, 60, 415–22.

*Pingree, S. and Hawkins, R. (1981). US programs on Australian television: the cultivation effect. *Journal of Communication*, 31(1), 97–105.

*Potter, J. (1986). Perceived reality and the cultivation hypothesis. *Journal of Broadcasting & Electronic Media*, 30, 159–74.

*(1988). Three strategies for elaborating the cultivation hypothesis. *Journalism Quarterly*, 65, 930–9.

*(1991a). The linearity assumption in cultivation research. *Human Communication Research*, 17, 562–83.

(1991b). The relationship between first- and second-order measures of cultivation. *Human Communication Research*, 18, 92–113.

*(1991c). Examining cultivation from a psychological perspective: component subprocesses. *Communication Research*, 18, 77–102.

(1993). Cultivation theory and research: a conceptual critique. *Human Communication Research, 19*, 564–601.

(1994). Cultivation theory and research: a methodological critique. *Journalism Monographs*, 1–35.

Potter, J. and Chang, I. (1990). Television exposure measures and the cultivation hypothesis. *Journal of Broadcasting & Electronic Media*, 34, 313–33.

Potts, R. and Martinez, I. (1994). Television viewing and children's beliefs about scientists. *Journal of Applied Developmental Psychology*, 15, 287–300.

Project Censored. (1996). Project Censored's top ten censored stories of 1995. Press release.

Reep, D. and Dambrot, F. (1989). Effects of frequent television viewing on stereotypes: "drip drip" or "drench"? *Journalism Quarterly*, 66, 542–56.

*Reimer, B. and Rosengren, K. (1990). Cultivated viewers and readers: a life-style perspective. In N. Signorielli and M. Morgan (eds.), *Cultivation analysis: new directions in media effects research* (pp. 181–206). Newbury Park: Sage.

Robinson, J. P. and Godbey, G. (1997). *Time for Life: the surprising ways Americans use their time*. University Park: Pennsylvania University Press.

Rosenberg, M. (1968). *The logic of survey analysis*. New York: Basic Books.

Rosengren, K. (1984). Cultural indicators for the comparative study of culture. In G. Melischek, K. Rosengren and J. Stappers (eds.), *Cultural indicators: an international symposium* (pp. 11–32). Vienna: Verlag der Osterreichischen Akademie der Wissenschaften.

*Rothschild, N. (1984). Small group affiliation as a mediating factor in the cultivation process. In G. Melischek, K. Rosengren and J. Stappers (eds.), *Cultural indicators: an international symposium* (pp. 377–87). Vienna, Austria: Verlag der Osterreichischen Akademie der Wissenschaften.

*Rothschild, N. and Morgan, M. (1987). Cohesion and control: relationships with parents as mediators of television. *Journal of Early Adolescence*, 7, 299–314.

*Rubin, A., Perse, E. and Taylor, D. (1988). A methodological examination of cultivation. *Communication Research*, 15, 107–34.

Ruddock, A. (1997). *Cultural studies: eclecticism and orthodoxy*. Unpublished manuscript.

*Ryan, J., Bales, K., and Hughes, M. (1988). Television and the cultivation of adolescent occupational expectations. *Free Inquiry in Creative Sociology*, 16(1), 103–8.

Sarbin, T. (1986). Prediction and clinical inference: forty years later. *Journal of Personality Assessment*, 50, 362–9.

Schiller, H. (1983). Information for what kind of society? In J. L. Salvaggio (ed.), *Telecomunications: issues and choices for society* (pp. 24–33). New York: Longman.

Schramm, W., Lyle, J. and Parker, E. (1961). *Television in the lives of our children*. Stanford: Stanford University Press.

Secunda, E. (1990). VCRs and viewer control over programming: an historical perspective. In J. Dobrow (ed.), *Social and cultural aspects of VCR use*. Hillsdale, NJ: Erlbaum.

*Shanahan, J. (1993). Television and the cultivation of environmental concern: 1988–1992. In A. Hansen (ed.), *The mass media and environmental issues* (pp. 181–97). Leicester, England: University of Leicester Press.

  *(1995). Television viewing and adolescent authoritarianism. *Journal of Adolescence*, 18, 271–88.

  (1996). Green but unseen: marginalizing the environment on television. In M.

Morgan and S. Leggett (eds.) *Mainstream(s) and margins: cultural politics in the 90s* (pp. 176–93). Greenwood Press, 1996.

Shanahan, J. and Jones, V. (1998). Cultivation and social control. In D. Demers and K. Viswanath (eds.), *Mass media and social control*. Ames: Iowa University Press.

Shanahan, J. and McComas, K. (1997). Television's portrayal of the environment: 1991–1995. *Journalism and Mass Communication Quarterly*, 74(1), 147–59.

(1999). *Nature stories.* Cresskill, NJ: Hampton Press.

Shanahan, J., Morgan, M. and Stenbjerre, M. (1997). Green or brown? Television and the cultivation of environmental concern. *Journal of Broadcasting & Electronic Media*, 41(3), 305–23.

Shapiro, M. (1991). Memory and decision processes in the construction of social reality. *Communication Research*, 18, 3–24.

Shapiro, M. and Lang, A. (1991). Making television reality: unconscious processes in the construction of social reality. *Communication Research*, 18(5), 685–705.

Shortland, M. (1988). Mad scientists and regular guys: images of the expert in Hollywood films of the 1950's. *Proceedings of the Joint Meeting of the British Society for History of Science and the History of Science Society* (pp. 291–8), Manchester, England.

Shrum, L. (1995). Assessing the social influence of television: a social cognition perspective. *Communication Research*, 22(4), 402–29.

(1996). Psychological processes underlying cultivation effects: further tests of construct accessibility. *Human Communication Research*, 22(4), 482–509.

(1997). The role of source confusion in cultivation effects may depend on processing strategy: a comment on Mares (1996). *Human Communication Research*, 24(2), 349–58.

(in press). The effect of television portrayals of crime and violence on viewers' perceptions of reality: a psychological process perspective. *Legal Studies Forum*, 28.

Shrum, L. and Darmanin, V. (1998). Understanding the effects of television consumption on judgments of crime risk: the impact of direct experience and type of judgment. In K. Machleit and M. Campbell (eds.), *Society for consumer psychology 1998 winter conference proceedings*.

Shrum, L. and O'Guinn, T. (1993). Processes and effects in the construction of social reality. *Communication Research*, 20, 436–71.

Shrum, L., O'Guinn, T., Semenik, R. and Faber, R. (1991). Processes and effects in the construction of normative consumer beliefs: the role of television. *Advances in Consumer Research*, 18, 755–63.

Shrum, L., Wyer, R. and O'Guinn, T. (1994). Cognitive processes underlying the effects of television consumption. Unpublished manuscript. Rutgers University.

(in press). The effects of television consumption on social perceptions: the use of priming procedures to investigate psychological processes, *Journal of Consumer Research*, 24(4).

Signorielli, N. (1979). Television's contribution to sex role socialization. Paper presented to the Seventh Annual Telecommunications Policy Research Conference, Skytop, PA.

(1986). Selective television viewing: a limited possibility. *Journal of Communication*, 36(3), 64–75.

*(1989). Television and conceptions about sex roles: maintaining conventionality and the status quo. *Sex Roles*, 21, 341–60.

*(1990). Television's mean and dangerous world: a continuation of the cultural indicators perspective. In N. Signorielli and M. Morgan (eds.), *Cultivation analysis: new directions in media effects research* (pp. 85–106). Newbury Park: Sage.

*(1991). Adolescents and ambivalence towards marriage. *Youth and Society*, 23, 121–49.

*(1993). Television and adolescents' perceptions about work. *Youth and Society*, 24, 314–41.

Signorielli, N. and Gerbner, G. (1978). The image of the elderly in prime-time television drama. *Generations*, 3(2), 10–11.

Signorielli, N., Gross, L. and Morgan, M. (1982). Violence in television programs: ten years later. In D. Pearl, L. Bouthilet and J. Lazar (eds.), *Television and behavior: ten years of scientific progress and implications for the 80's, Vol. II* (pp. 158–73). Rockville, MD: NIMH.

*Signorielli, N. and Lears, M. (1992a). Children, television and conceptions about chores: attitudes and behaviors. *Sex Roles*, 27, 157–70.

*(1992b). Television and children's conceptions of nutrition: unhealthy messages. *Health Communication*, 4, 245–58.

Signorielli, N. and Morgan, M. (eds.) (1990). *Cultivation analysis: new directions in media effects research*. Newbury Park: Sage.

Simpson, C. (1994). *Science of coercion*. New York: Oxford University Press.

*Singer, J., Singer, D. and Rapaczynski, W. (1984). Family patterns and TV viewing as predictors of children's beliefs and aggression. *Journal of Communication*, 34(2), 73–89.

Slack, J. and M. Allor. (1983). The political and epistemological constituents of critical communication research. *Journal of Communication*, 33(3), 208–18.

*Slater, D. and Elliott, R. (1982). Television's influence on social reality. *Quarterly Journal of Speech*, 68(1), 69–79.

Smith, T. (1993). *GSS Social Change Report No. 36*. Chicago: NORC.

Sparks, G., Nelson, C. and Campbell, R. (1997). The relationship between exposure to televised messages about paranormal phenomena and paranormal beliefs. *Journal of Broadcasting & Electronic Media*, 41(3), 345–59.

*Sparks, G. and Ogles, R. (1990). The difference between fear of victimization and the possibility of being victimized. *Journal of Broadcasting & Electronic Media*, 34, 351–8.

Stevens, G. (1980). TV and attitudes of fear and alienation. Unpublished Master's thesis, The Annenberg School of Communications, University of Pennsylvania.

Stevenson, N. (1995). *Understanding media cultures*. London: Sage.

Surgeon General's Scientific Advisory Committee on Television and Social Behavior. (1972). *Television and growing up: the impact of televised violence*. Report to the Surgeon General, United States Public Health Service. Washington: Government Printing Office.

Tamborini, R. and Choi, J. (1990). The role of cultural diversity in cultivation research. In N. Signorielli and M. Morgan (eds.), *Cultivation analysis: new directions in media effects research* (pp. 157–80). Newbury Park: Sage.

*Tan, A. (1979). TV beauty ads and role expectations of adolescent female viewers. *Journalism Quarterly*, 56, 827–31.

Tapper, J. (1995). The ecology of cultivation: a conceptual model for cultivation research. *Communication Theory*, 15, 36–57.

Tierney, J. (1997). Our oldest computer, upgraded. *New York Times Magazine*, 28 September.

Tuchman, G. (1978). The symbolic annihilation of women by the mass media. In G. Tuchman, A. K. Daniels and J. Benet (eds.), *Hearth and home: images of women in the mass media* (pp. 3–38). New York: Oxford.

Turow, J. (1989). *Playing doctor: television, storytelling and medical power.* New York: Oxford University Press.

Tyler, T. and Cook, F. (1984). The mass media and judgments of risk: distinguishing impact on personal and societal level judgments. *Journal of Personality and Social Psychology*, 47, 693–708.

UCLA Center for Communication Policy (1995). *Television violence monitoring project report.* Los Angeles, CA: UCLA.

*Umble, D. (1990). Mennonites and television: applications of cultivation analysis to a religious subculture. In N. Signorielli and M. Morgan (eds.), *Cultivation Analysis: new directions in media effects research* (pp. 141–56). Newbury Park: Sage.

*Volgy, T. and Schwarz, J. (1980). Television entertainment programming and sociopolitical attitudes. *Journalism Quarterly*, 57, 150–5.

Wakshlag, J., Viol, V. and Tamborini, R. (1983). Selecting crime drama and apprehension about crime. *Human Communication Research*, 10, 227–42.

*Weaver, J. and Wakshlag, J. (1986). Perceived vulnerability to crime, criminal victimization experience, and television viewing. *Journal of Broadcasting & Electronic Media*, 30, 141–58.

*Weimann, G. (1984). Images of life in America: the impact of American TV in Israel. *International Journal of Intercultural Relations*, 8, 185–97.

Williams, R. (1975). *Television: technology and cultural form.* New York: Schocken Books.

Williams, T. (1986). *The impact of television: a natural experiment in three communities.* Orlando: Academic Press.

*Wober, M. (1978). Televised violence and paranoid perception: the view from Great Britain. *Public Opinion Quarterly*, 42, 315–21.

*Wober, M. and Gunter, B. (1982). Television and personal threat: fact or artifact? *British Journal of Social Psychology*, 21, 239–47.

(1988). *Television and social control.* New York: St. Martin's Press.

*Zemach, T. and Cohen, A. (1986). Perception of gender equality on TV and in social reality. *Journal of Broadcasting & Electronic Media*, 30, 427–44.

Zillmann, D. and Wakshlag, J. (1985). Fear of victimization and the appeal of crime drama. In D. Zillmann and J. Bryant (eds.), *Selective exposure to communication* (pp. 141–56). Hillsdale, NJ: Lawrence Erlbaum.

# Index